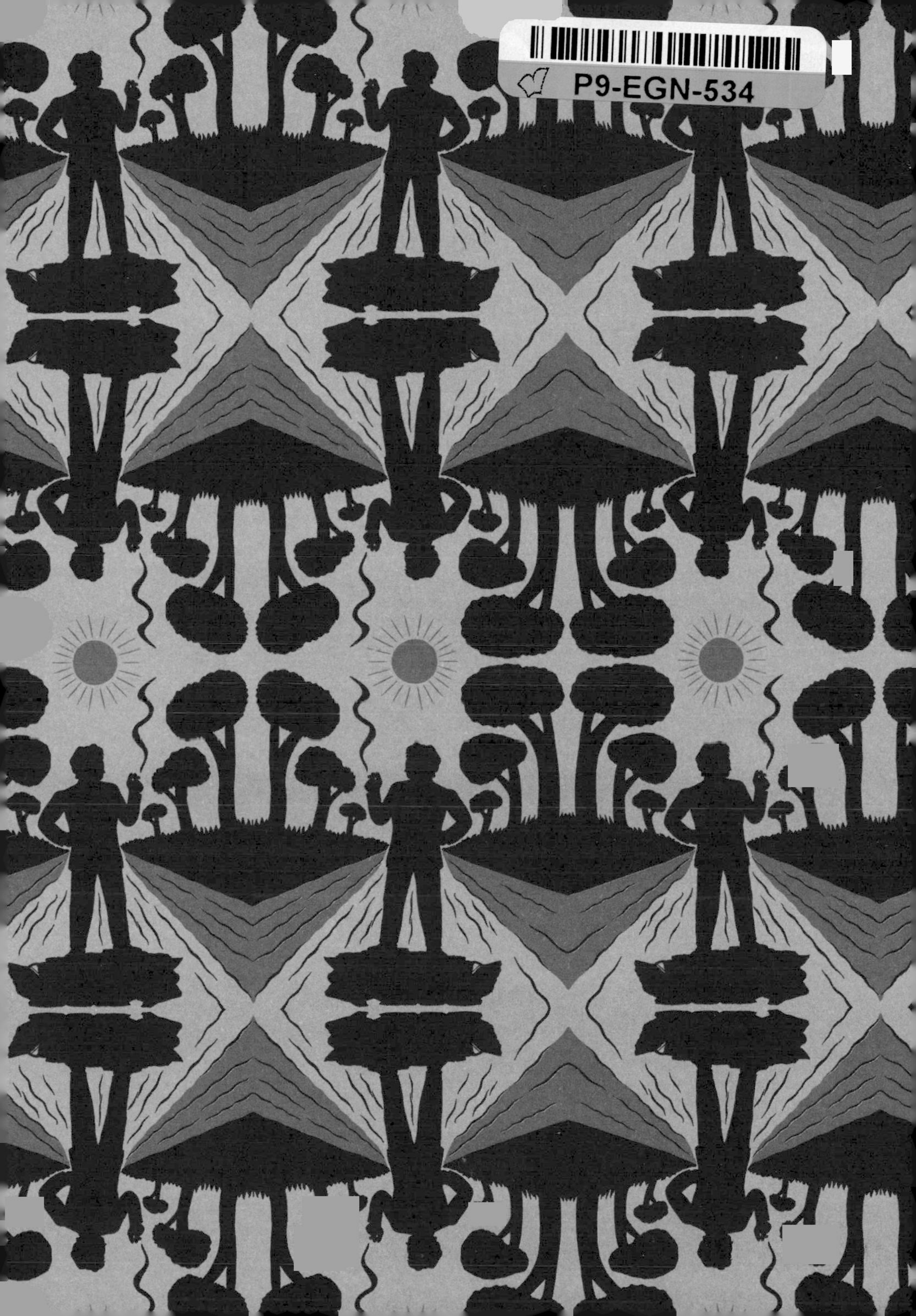

MICHAEL KUPPERMAN

MARK TWAIN'S AUTOBIOGRAPHY 1910 - 2010

MICHAEL KUPPERMAN

MARK TWAIN'S AUTOBIOGRAPHY 1910-2010

Contents

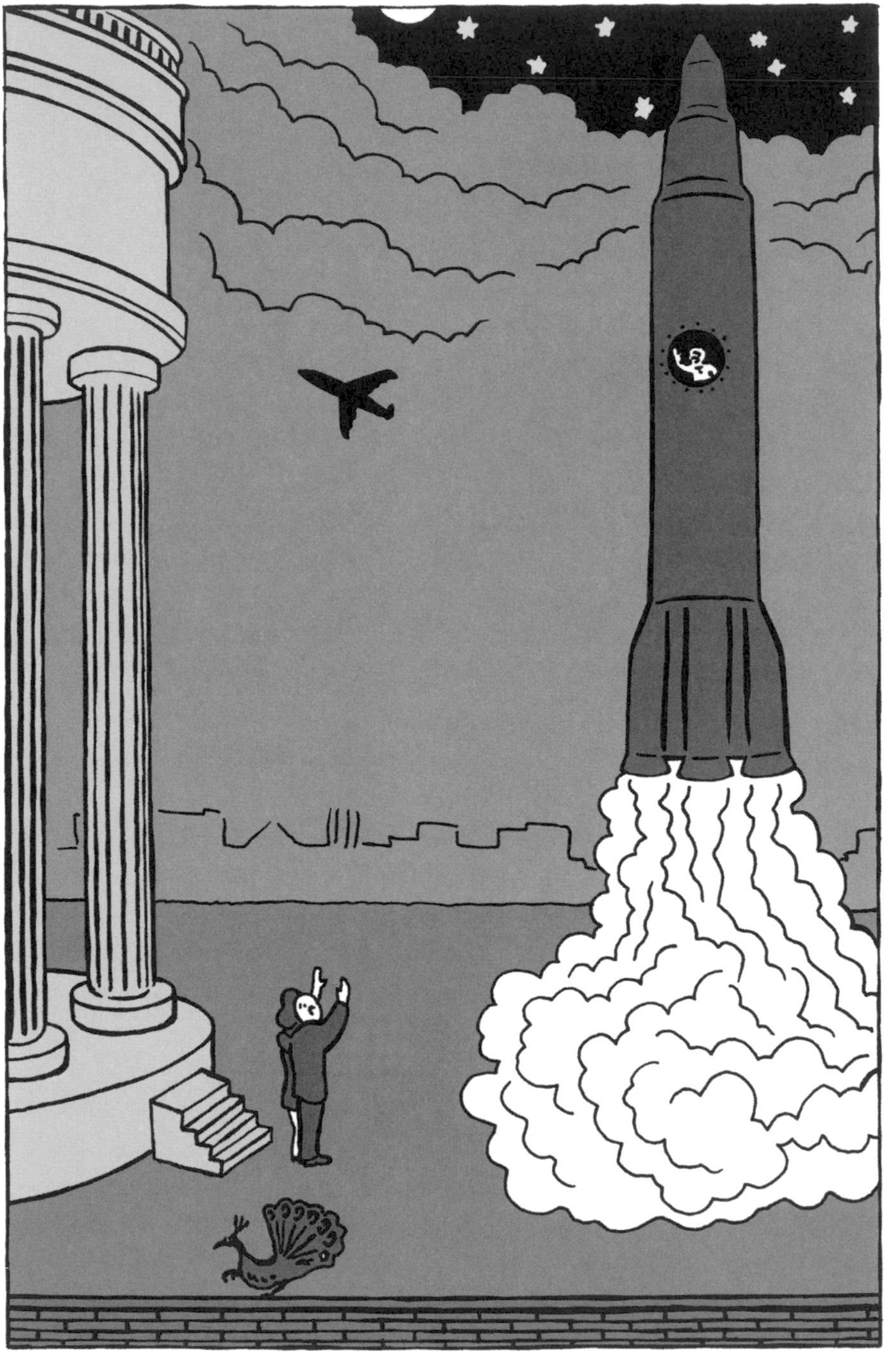

FOREWORD
By Michael Kupperman

This book started with a telegram, which arrived in a FedEx envelope: "Come at once" it commanded, and I followed the return address to a craggy, forbidden isle whose location I am forbidden to divulge. As I plodded through the mist, a figure rose up before me. He was instantly recognizable in his all-white suit, complete with white hair and mustache, that face so familiar from a thousand book covers. He seemed not to have aged at all...

"Here, Mister Kupperman," he said, thrusting a manuscript into my hands. "Publish this, and let the world read of my adventures." "But Mister Twain," I protested, "surely you can get an adequate publishing deal. You are, after all, still quite a respected figure in the world of letters and sentences." "You understand nothing!" twinkled the scribe roguishly; "if you publish it under your name, then people will be free to not believe a word of it! And that's what I want!" He chuckled. "You should decorate it with your silly drawings, to further undermine the credibility. Perhaps a few comical strips as well." And with that he vanished and was gone, as if he had never been. I stumbled forward, and looking behind a bush I discovered him crouching down. "Dammit, I was trying to be mysterious," he grouched. "G'wan, beat it! Get outa here! Gave you the manuscript, what more do you want!" he continued to complain as he stumbled off, holding his back, which apparently he had injured by hiding.

I returned down the slope, only to find the boat gone, and was forced to swim back to shore through the icy water, holding the precious manuscript over my head to keep it dry. I present it to you now, decorated with my silly drawings, and a few comical strips.

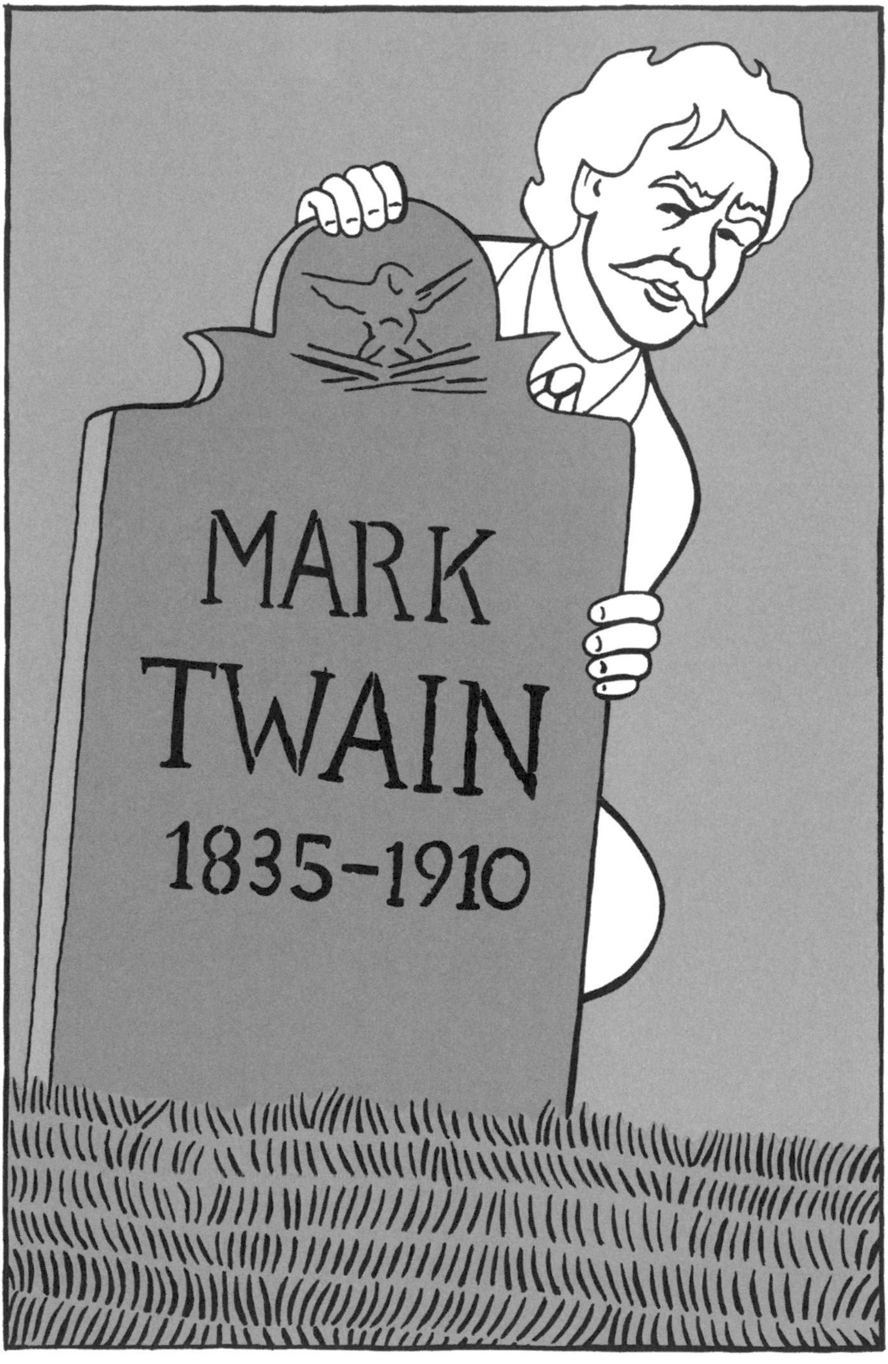
MARK
TWAIN
1835-1910

PREFACE

Greetings, stranger of the future. If you are reading this, it means the written word has survived, that the world of tomorrow still exists, and that for some reason my ramblings are still considered worth reading. My name is Mark Twain, and I write these words to you in the good old days of August 2010.

"What's that," you say? "Didn't you die a hundred years ago, you old coot? I hear your memoirs have just been published, because they had to wait a century after your death," blah blah blah and so on. The truth is I never died, but the same old rumors got exaggerated and then a bunch of other stuff happened, so people forgot I was still alive. And I've kept alive, due to a magic spell cast upon me by a wizard—but I've promised not to tell that tale until 1,000 years more have passed! I suppose by now you all know how I was Jack the Ripper, and why it was in a good cause that I committed those foul murders. Also that I was indirectly responsible for the assassination of President Abraham Lincoln. Hopefully you've forgiven me these indiscretions, and understood the explanations I had to offer in my own defense.

Anyway, I've had a whole new bunch of adventures in the time since. I hope you'll enjoy reading them as much as I enjoyed having them and then writing them down, and then getting paid for it. Especially that last part.

—MT

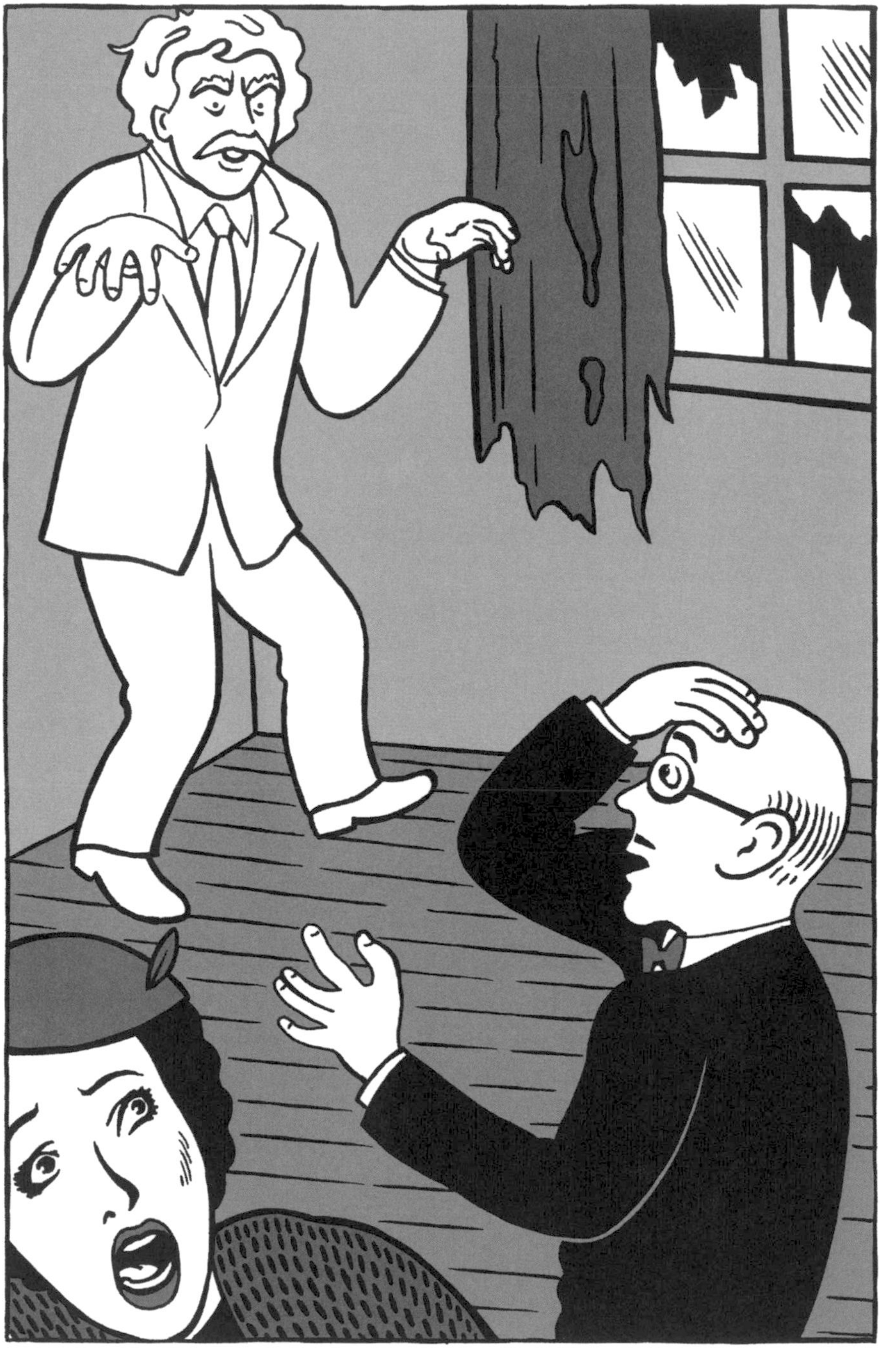

CHAPTER ONE:

A-HAUNTING I MUST GO

In 1910 I became dead, again, and all the world knew it—except it wasn't true. This time my death had been exaggerated out of all proportion, with some newspapers claiming I had been exploded by 10,000 kegs of dynamite while straining stallions tore me in all four directions and a tribe of Indians blew poison darts. Well, none of that had happened. It had all been a misunderstanding involving some rubbing alcohol and a drunken coroner, but I found out that everyone I knew believed me truly and completely dead! When they saw me, they reacted as if I were a ghost, and screamed or fainted, or tried to capture me, perhaps to sell me for display at Professor Wowser's Hauntatorium. Well, I soon got fed up with this type of behavior. I don't know how the real ghosts stand it! The worst part was that nobody would make coffee for me.

After a while, though, I began to enjoy my supposed supernatural status. I was absolved of most of the traditional duties of life, and I delighted in chasing people around the house while moaning "whooooooooooo." When I visited local businesses, they were too petrified to react as I helped myself to armfuls of goods and floated out the door. I took up residence in an abandoned mansion, and lived happily there for a while, terrifying neighborhood teenagers who crept in at night, and sometimes surprising couples as they indulged their carnal desires. Unfortunately my reputation spread, and it wasn't long before the *New York Times* did a feature. Soon the neighborhood was full of louts and gawkers hoping to get a glimpse of Mark Twain's ghost, and it became apparent that it was time for me to move on before someone twigged I was human. When Lady Publicity shines her lovely lamp upon you it's like basking in the pure light of the Sun; but when Johnny Notoriety casts his gaze the effect is mighty noxious. Disguising myself as a nearsighted washerwoman, I slipped out through the crowd one morning and headed for Europe, where I hoped to build a new life.

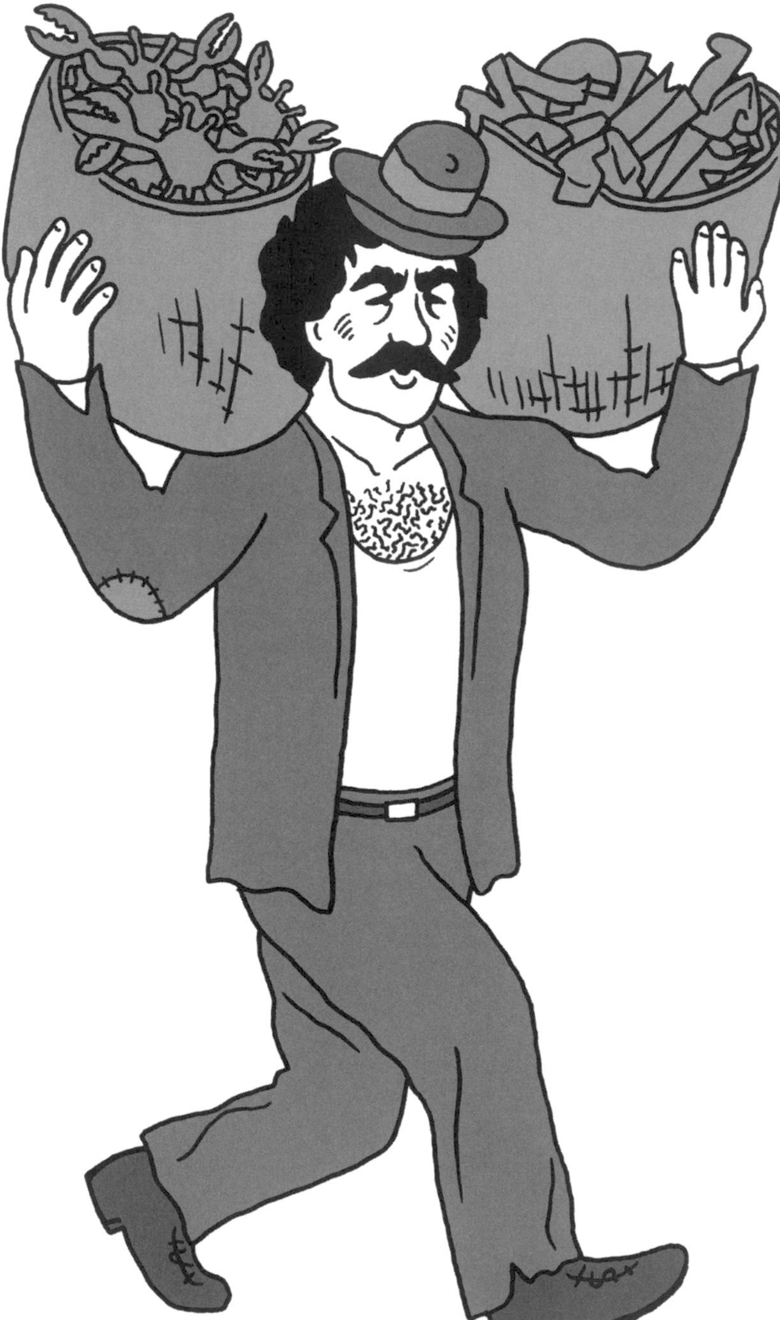

CHAPTER TWO:

MY LATIN PERIOD

When I arrived in Italy I dyed my hair and mustache black and became hot-blooded Michelangelo Buonatestes, the "shoutiest man in Naples." I didn't know a word of the language, but I found that by waving my hands frantically and bellowing random arrangements of vocal noises I could usually get my point across, and soon my small business flourished. I was a crabs-for-scrap man, lugging around loads of crabs and scrap and trading them for each other. I married a lovely woman named Inflammaria, who already had five children from different husbands, and we bought a house together and filled it with monkeys and dogs, all of us shouting and jabbering and gesticulating dramatically in that confined space. I learned a lot of new skills, such as how to gesture with a switchblade while making that "come here and get stabbed" movement with the other hand. Enormous clay jugs were smashed over my head regularly, and every time my eyes would cross and I would stagger around with my arms sticking out before collapsing. For some reason there was a door leading onto the canal right next to the door to the toilet, and every morning I would walk through the wrong door and fall fifteen feet into the canal. I wore a shapeless hat all the time, even in the bath, and I reacted to everything by grimacing wildly and flapping my arms. Honestly, it was the happiest period of my life.

But like all idyllic situations, it came crashing to earth. As with many Italian households, our kitchen was built around a small volcano which provided heat and cooking energy. One day I accidentally sprinkled some pepper in it, which as everyone knows you must never do, and it grew and erupted, destroying the entire house and all our possessions, and forming a lava pool with my hat floating on it. I was feeling restless that day, and when I saw my grieving family crowded around my hat I decided to exaggerate my own death again, and left immediately for London, where I became the cheekiest twenty-three-year-old chimney sweep you ever did see! Unfortunately it was at that exact moment that World War I broke out and I found myself drafted and sent back to Europe, to fight in the trenches.

CHAPTER THREE: WHAT'S SO "GREAT" ABOUT THIS WAR?

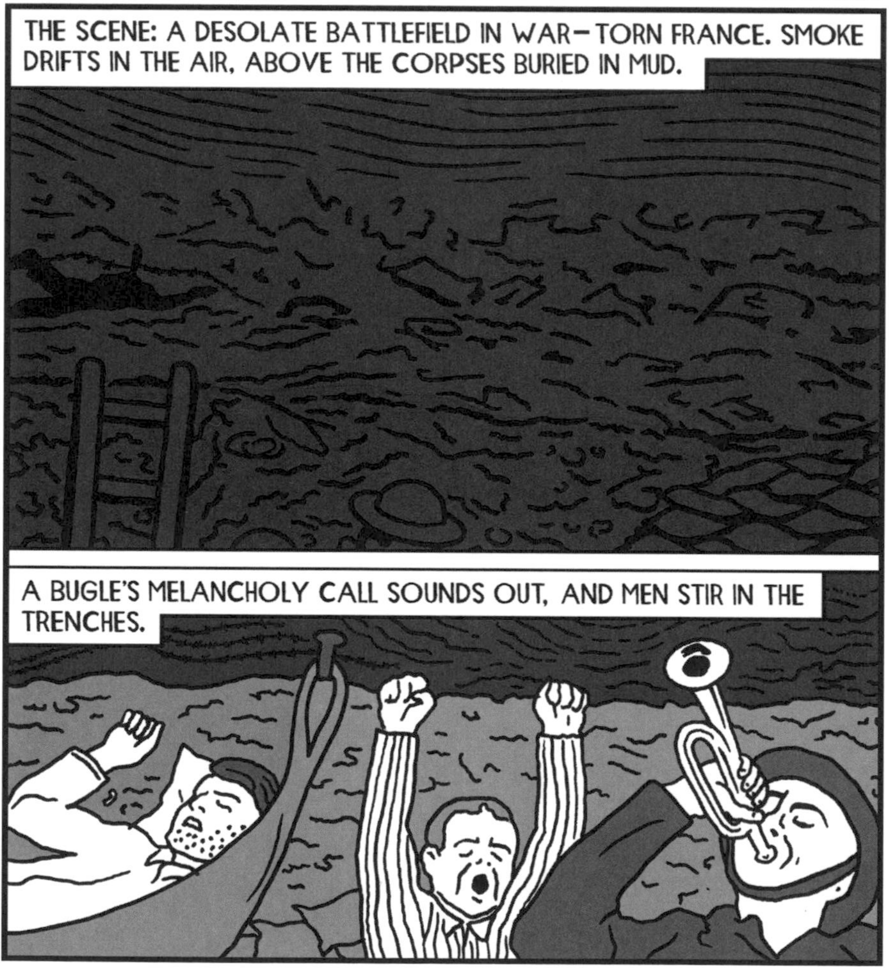

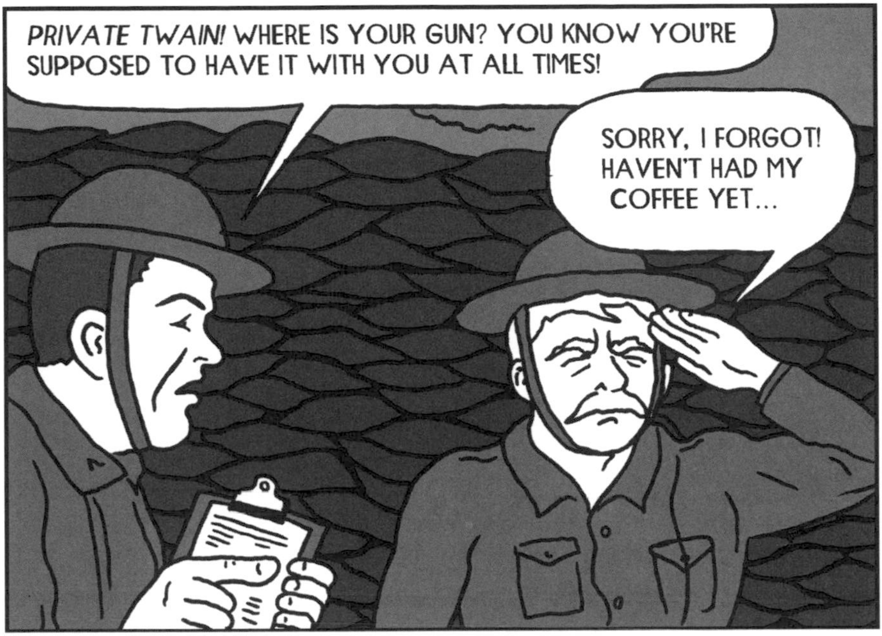
PRIVATE TWAIN! WHERE IS YOUR GUN? YOU KNOW YOU'RE SUPPOSED TO HAVE IT WITH YOU AT ALL TIMES!
SORRY, I FORGOT! HAVEN'T HAD MY COFFEE YET...

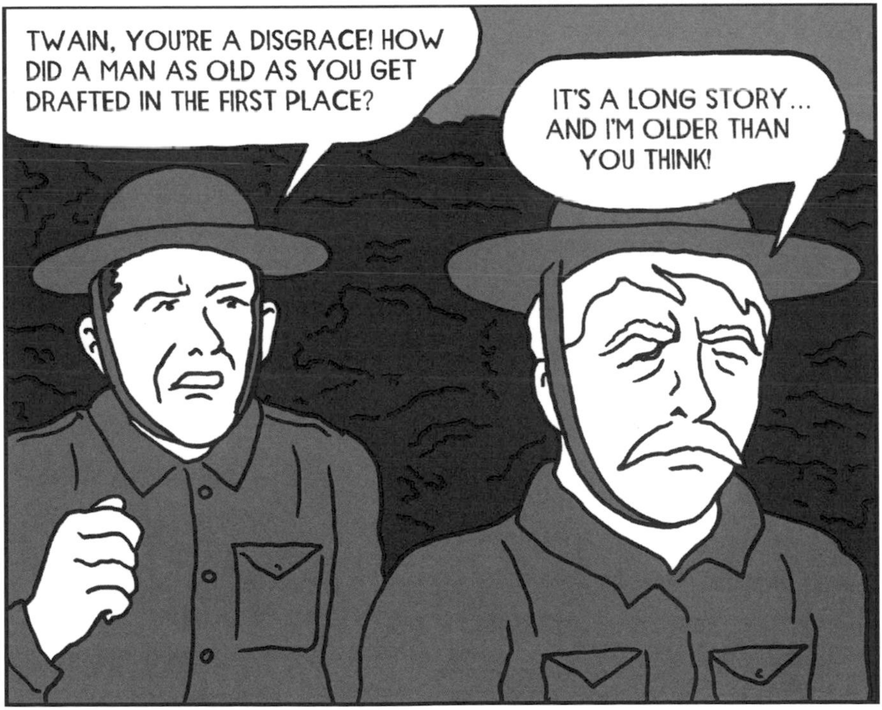
TWAIN, YOU'RE A DISGRACE! HOW DID A MAN AS OLD AS YOU GET DRAFTED IN THE FIRST PLACE?
IT'S A LONG STORY... AND I'M OLDER THAN YOU THINK!

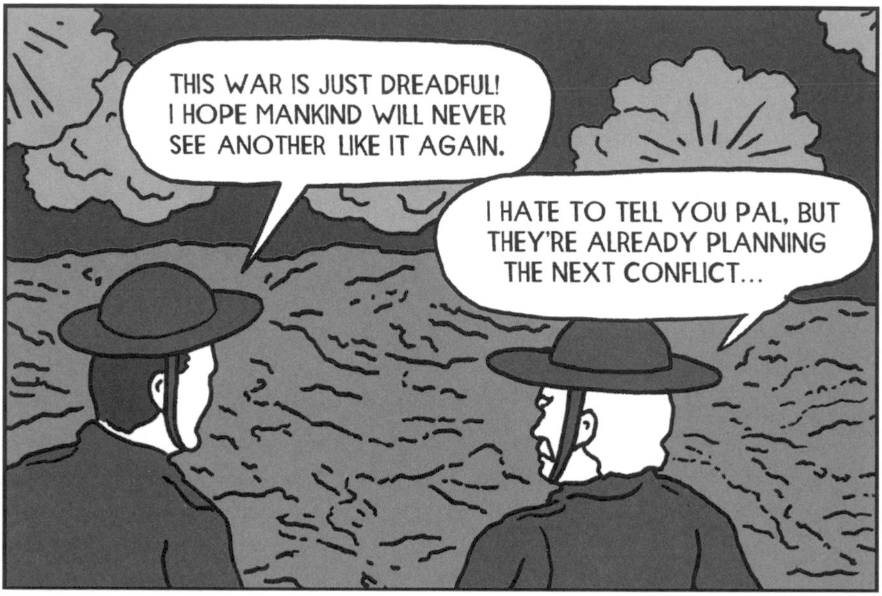
THIS WAR IS JUST DREADFUL! I HOPE MANKIND WILL NEVER SEE ANOTHER LIKE IT AGAIN.
I HATE TO TELL YOU PAL, BUT THEY'RE ALREADY PLANNING THE NEXT CONFLICT...

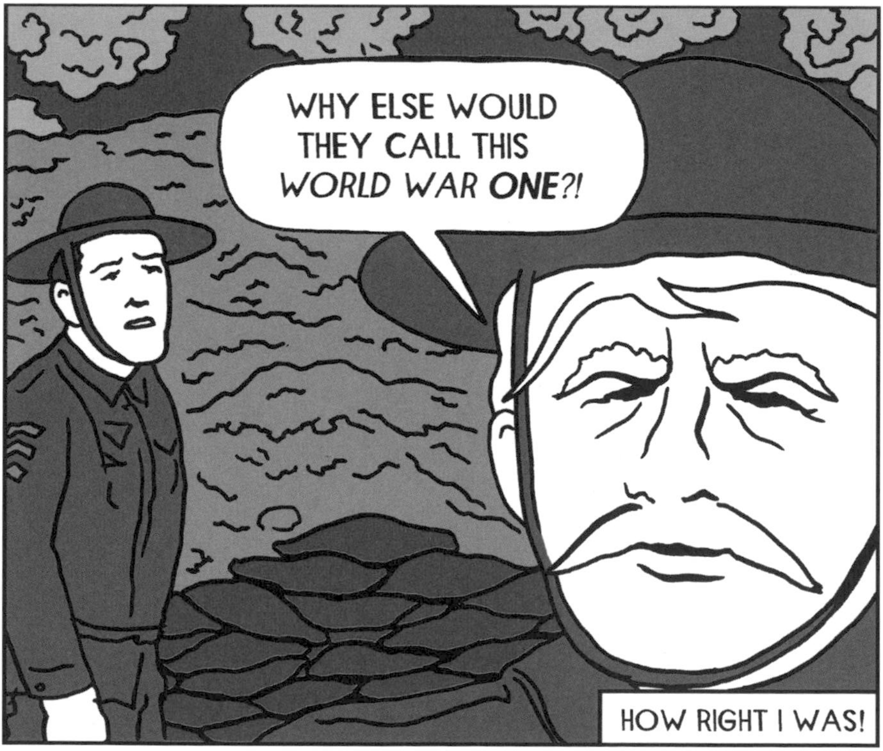
WHY ELSE WOULD THEY CALL THIS *WORLD WAR* **ONE**?!
HOW RIGHT I WAS!

CHAPTER FOUR:

I INSPIRE A FUTURE PARTNER

When the war was over I decided I was tired of anonymity, and started to write and lecture again in my own name. The world was in such a state of confusion that hardly anyone noticed that I had supposedly died, and soon I was as popular as I had always been. In the early 1920s I set out on a tour of European institutions of learning, to show the youths of those countries what a splendid thing thinking actually is when demonstrated properly.

I have always enjoyed inspiring the young, and I do it whenever possible. Thanks to my elevated lifespan, I've even been able on a few occasions to inspire people as kids and then again as old people! It's inspiring for me to inspire others so that they may continue the chain of inspiration onwards. Recently I consulted on an interactive 3D Fantasy Computer fully interactive online video gaming platform that is designed to teach kids how great it is to enjoy a smelly old book.

One day in 1921 I was touring the University of Vienna, inspiring all the bookworms and poindexters (some of them female!) when I noticed a microscope. I sauntered over and, on a whim, twisted the magnification knob further than anyone else had ever turned it. There, revealed in all their glory, were some little dots which had a peculiar energy of their own. Everyone gasped, finally someone around there was showing some initiative and doing something positive. "Hey, look at that, those specks are great! They look very interesting, maybe they're important. You there, you should study them" I said to a timid, heavily mustached nerd who was lurking nearby. He nodded and immediately scurried over, bending over the microscope as I sashayed on, feeling like I had done a very good deed. Little did I know that he would study them very carefully, and that he was Albert Einstein, who would become celebrated in all the Science Halls of Europe; and that he would quickly become an older man like myself, and that we would later team up and have adventures together! At that time I had no idea.

When I met him again, more than twenty years later, he had oldened up to a remarkable degree, and any observer would have taken us as contemporaries. He was now a world-famous physicist, and had directly contributed to America's recent victories. "I see you managed to blow up more of the world," I chided him gently. "I blew up the part that stopped there from being more blowing up," he pointed out. Clearly he had given this a great deal of thought. I studied him—he had become a white-haired, mustache-wearing man much like myself. I knew right then we would have many adventures together.

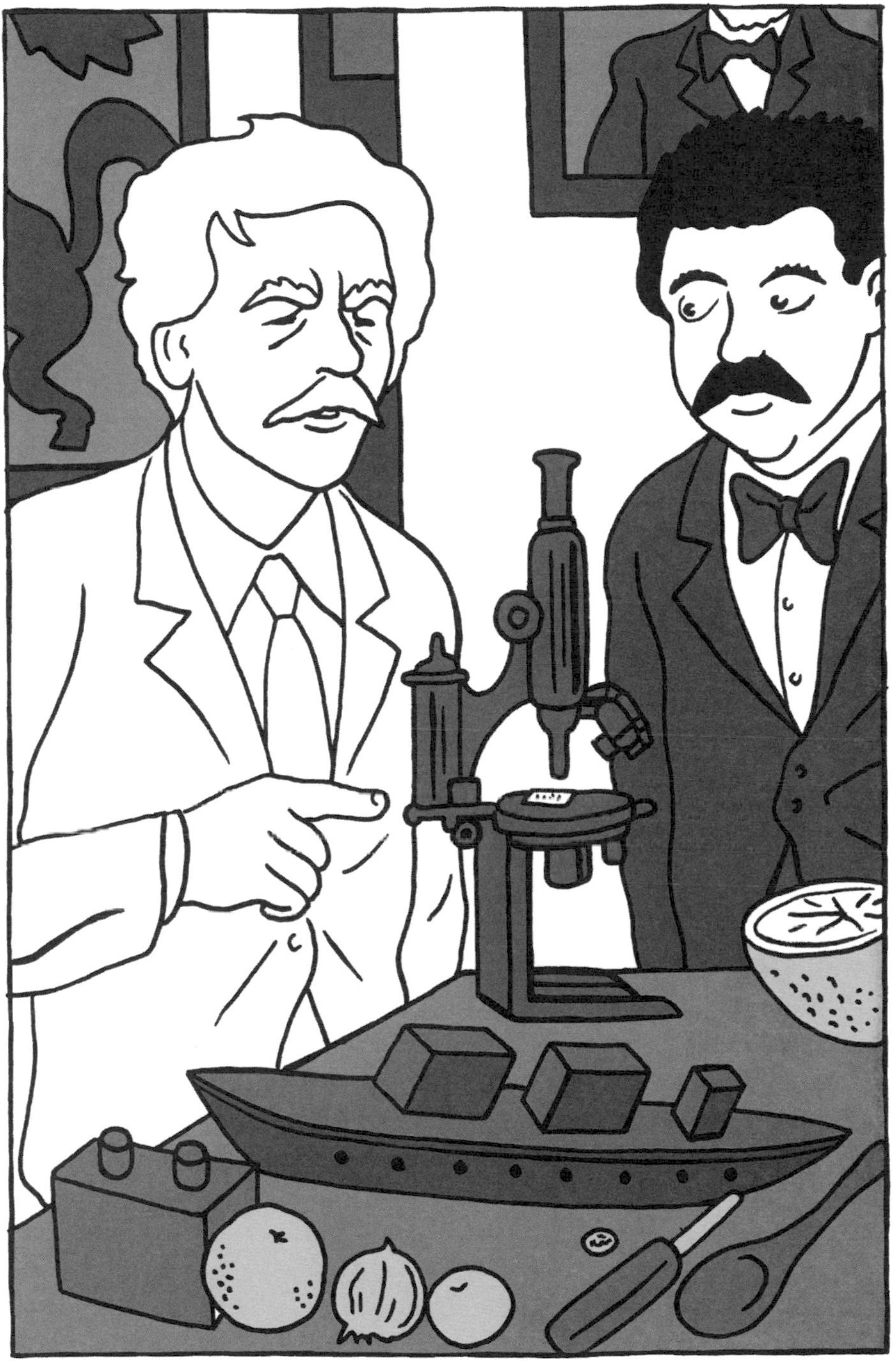

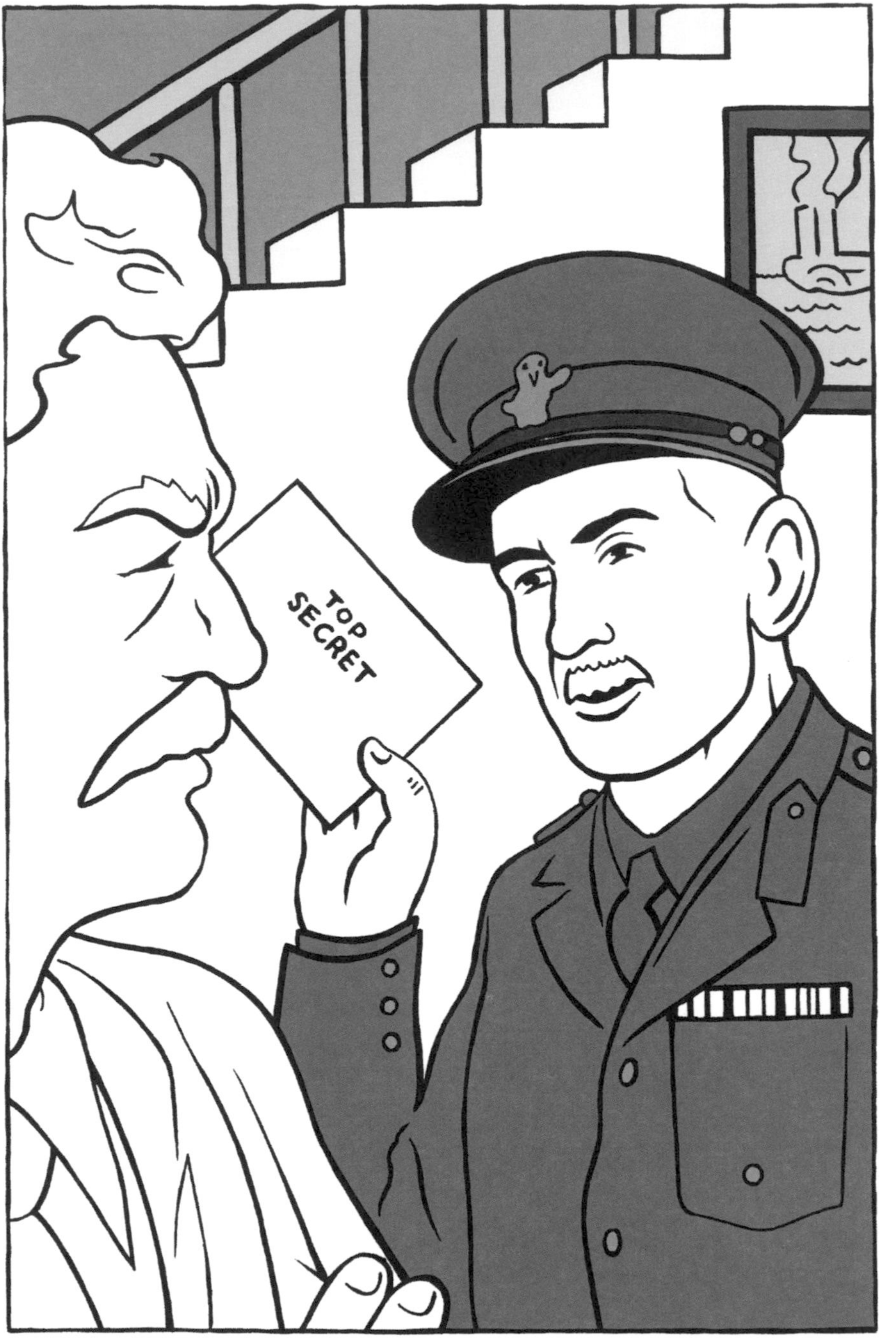
TOP
SECRET

CHAPTER FIVE:

AVOIDING ADVENTURE

Back in my beloved United States, I resumed my career of goofing off and loafing around. That was interrupted one day by a visit from a most unusual man. He introduced himself as "Colonel N" and told me he was "on the side of the angels"; somehow I believed him. He had a devil-may-care twinkle in his eyes and his jawline spoke of derring-do and adventure. "Mister Twain, I have come to you with a most dramatic proposition," he told me. "But to find out what it is I'm talking about you will have to come with me to Asia Minor." "No," I said, "I don't think I'll be doing that." "Well then, accompany me as far as Portsmouth," he countered. "No, I don't think so." "Very well," he said, "I hoped it would all be a nice dramatic surprise, but I guess I have no choice but to tell you, I'm here to recruit you for a new supergroup of extraordinary men and women. You're needed to save the world."

Apparently a madman named Seltzer Ravioli (such a ridiculous name!) had threatened to drain the world's oceans dry unless an enormous ransom was paid. To prove he could actually do it, he had submitted a large oil painting of him doing it to the Royal Academy competition, coming in third; a raft of eminent experts had testified that the painting was plausible. To prevent this catastrophe, Colonel N had developed his amazing plan, which involved forming an ultimate action squad of dynamic characters and sending them down to Asia Minor in a hot air balloon. Besides me there was to be Ahab from *Moby-Dick*, Dorothy from *The Wizard of Oz*, Bomba the Jungle Boy, Ichabod Crane (of *Headless Horseman* fame), Nosferatu, and the Campbell's Soup Twins. "You'll all be disguised as dancing girls, straight from the Sultan's harem," he explained. "How long can you hold your breath? You may have to swim through an overflowing sewer. Also I hope you can erotically satisfy a Japanese businessman."

He stood and faced me. All his cards were on the table and he had nothing more to do than beg. "Please, time is of the essence; I'm sure you see now how vital it is that you accompany me and join my bunch of astonishing adventurers."

"Well, here's the thing," I said. I explained that I couldn't possibly take part in his adventure, which pained me greatly, but really there were important matters I needed to attend to, and I wished him the best of luck. In fact, I had been dabbling in the manufacture of alcoholic lollipops, an experiment which led nowhere but pleased me greatly. (My recipe involved maple syrup, cognac, hardening agents, and some twigs for sticks). "Also," I added, "all those other characters you mentioned are fictional characters, and I am a real person. The threat you are describing, and the perpetrator involved, also sound too ludicrous to be actual," and with that I shut the door in his face. How surprised I was three weeks later to read of the deaths of Ahab from *Moby-Dick*, Dorothy from *The Wizard of Oz*, Bomba the Jungle Boy, Ichabod Crane, Nosferatu, and the Campbell's Soup Twins, all crushed, scalded, or drowned in raw sewage in Asia Minor (although later Nosferatu turned up married to a Japanese businessman). I'll confess I felt quite regretful for a while, especially when all the oceans did in fact dry up completely. Sometimes it can be hard to tell when people are serious.

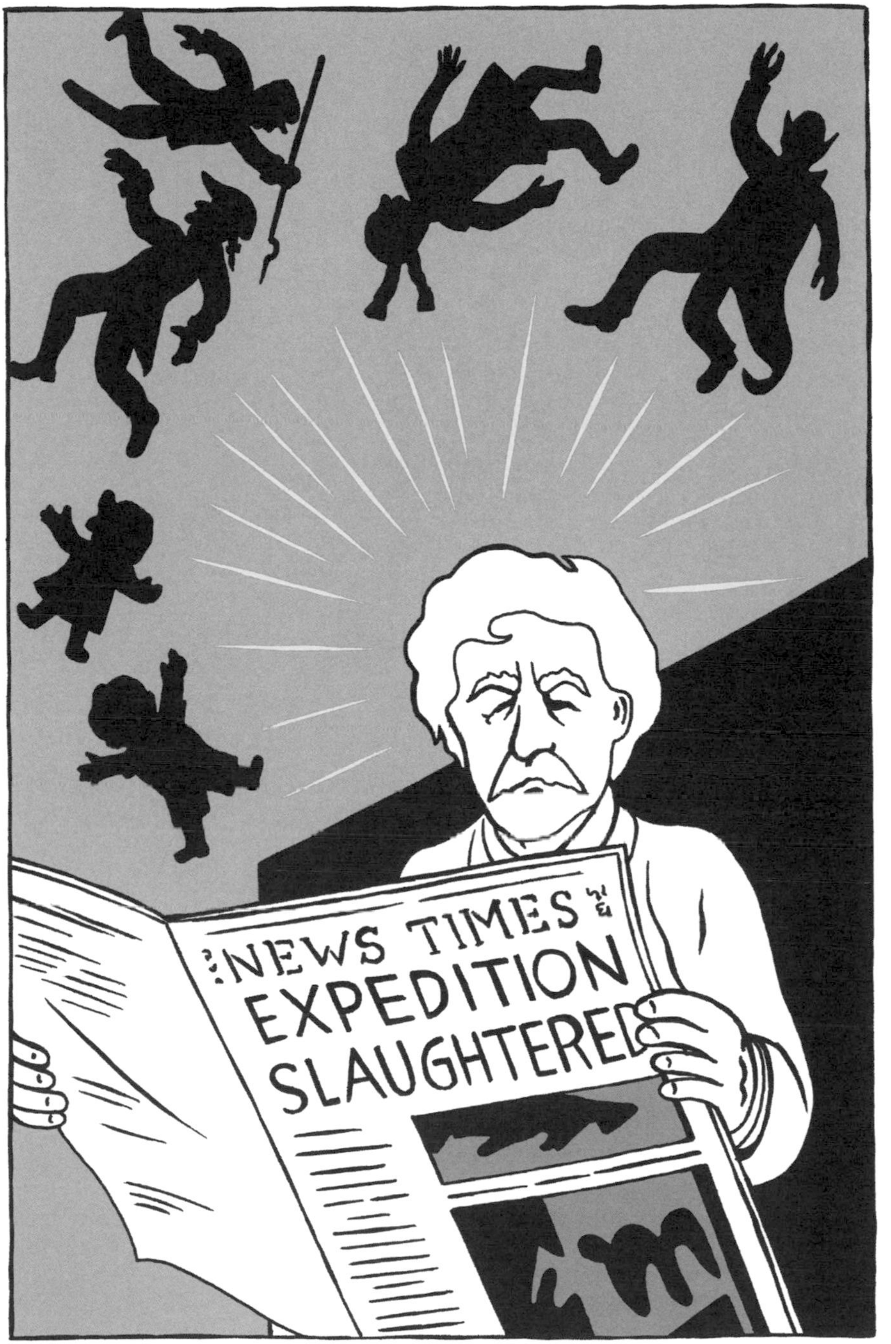
NEWS TIMES
EXPEDITION SLAUGHTERED

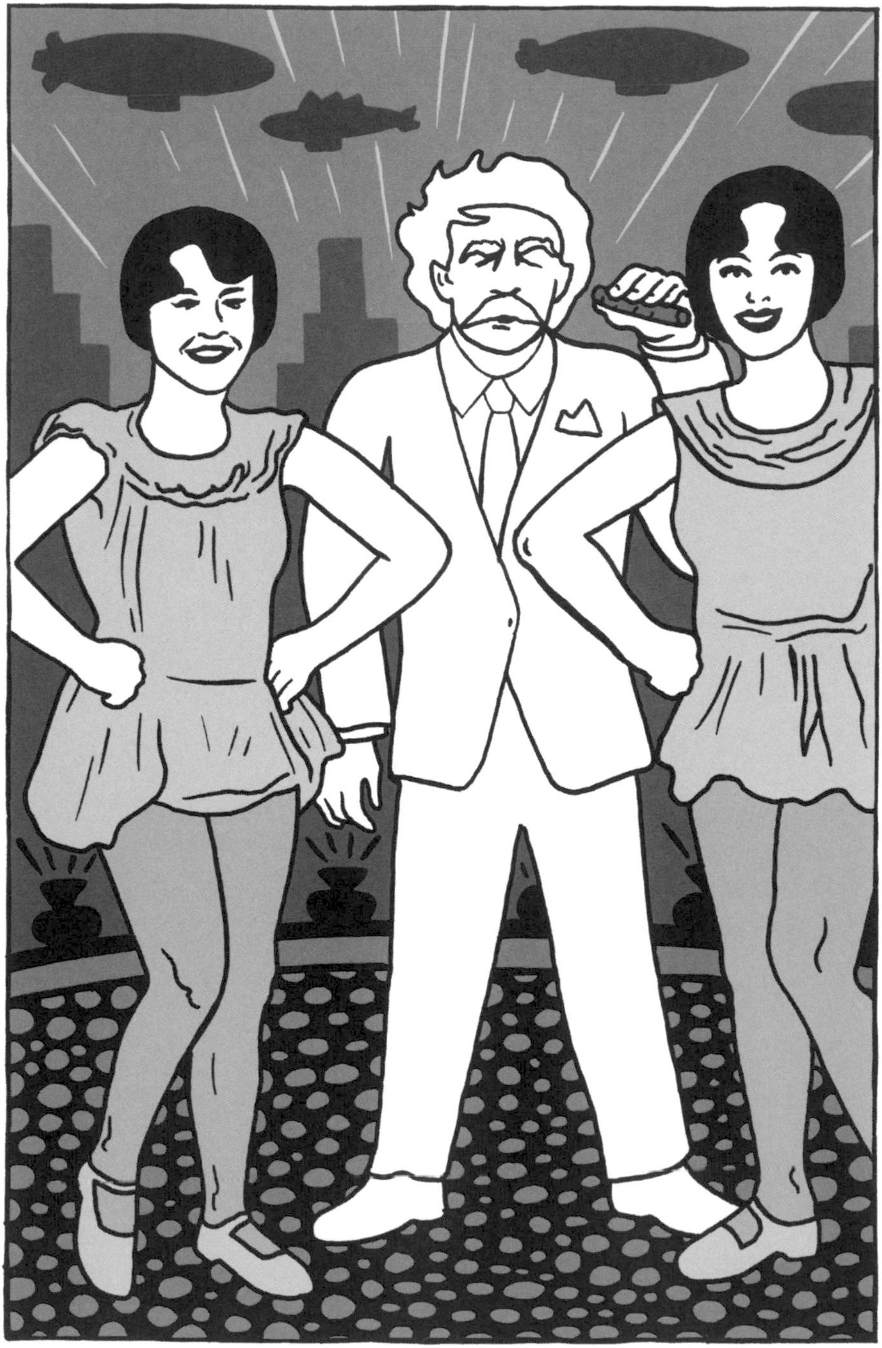

CHAPTER SIX

THE ROAR OF THE TWENTIES

In the 1920s money was free and plentiful, and Prohibition had made bootleg hooch cheap and delicious. People thought the good times would never end, and called the age The Jazz Age, after jazz music, which was the music of the age. I was living the high life myself, writing aphorisms for the local newspaper, and traveling among my seventeen houses in my steam-powered jet car. I had three radio shows on the DLUX Radio Network ("Mark Twain's World," "Twain And Friends," and the situated comedy "Ever The Twain"), and I toured the country making appearances at smokers, stag parties and graduations. It seemed like the good times would never end.

And, for a while, they didn't. An average weekend might see me taking a leisurely dirigible cruise over to California, where I would spend the weekend guesting at Pickfair (Mary Pickford and Douglas Fairbanks' house) or Gishgoo (Lillian Gish and Red Gooding's ranch). Everybody had a private zoo and we'd all be drunk and making out with the animals—not me, of course, I kept my head. (One time, I'll admit, I did try to smooch a bee and I got a quite nasty sting on the lips for my trouble. Serves me right.) There were swimming pools full of champagne and football fields full of foie gras. You would have sworn the fun was going to go on forever.

But nobody would've corrected you, because they would have thought the same thing. Herbert Hoover gave a speech where he said "The age of prosperity currently upon us will almost certainly continue throughout the rest of human history." 1926 saw a moneystorm of incredible proportions, where dollars were literally floating in the air through most of the summer all across the United States. The sewers were backed up with diamonds, and garbage cans were made of solid gold. Gangsters shot at each other with platinum tommy guns full of emerald bullets, and rats were caught in silver traps baited with savings bonds. Wealth was everywhere.

It looked as if the party couldn't possibly stop... but it did!

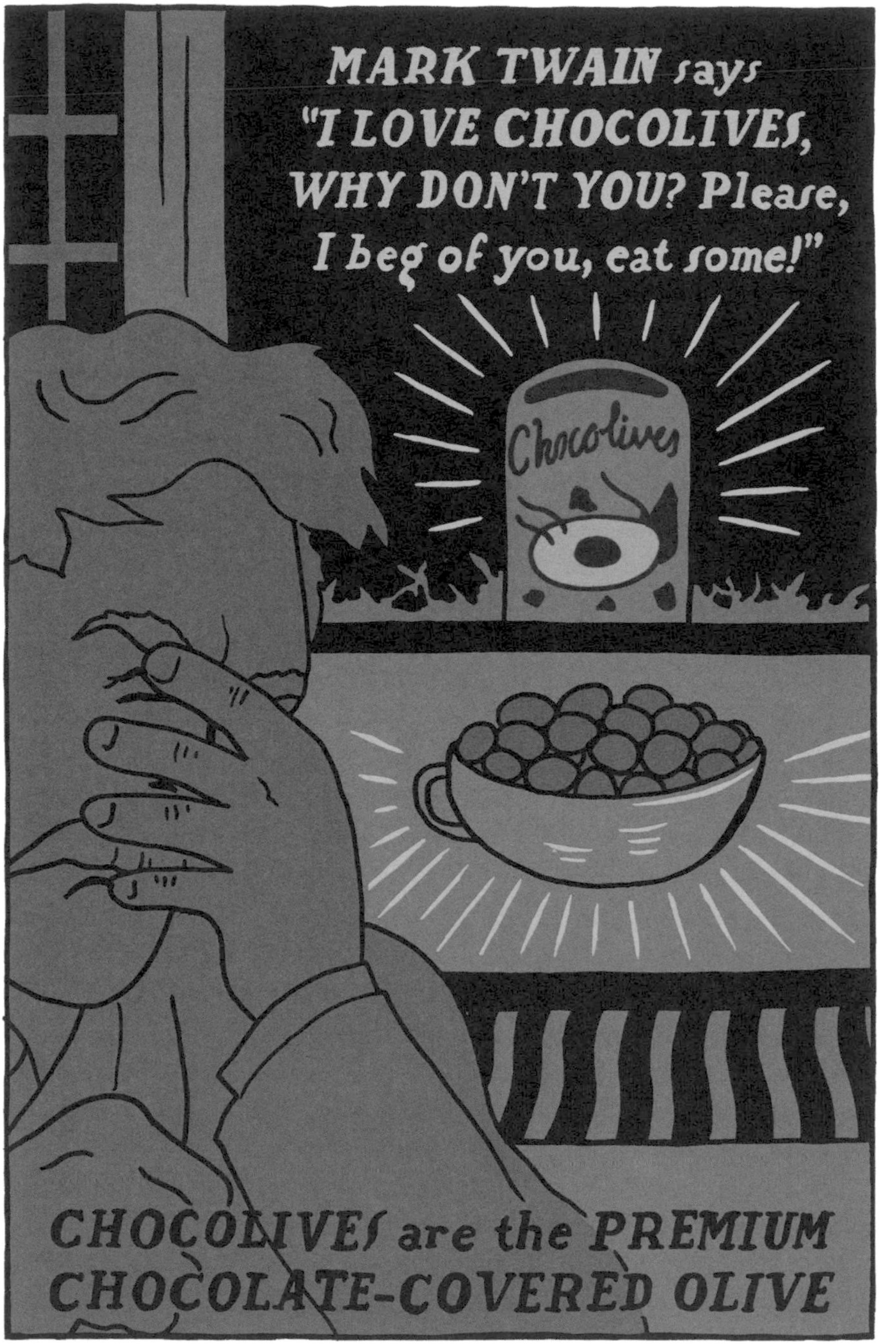
MARK TWAIN says
"I LOVE CHOCOLIVES, WHY DON'T YOU? Please, I beg of you, eat some!"
Chocolives
CHOCOLIVES are the PREMIUM CHOCOLATE-COVERED OLIVE

CHAPTER SEVEN

DRIFTS AND GRIFTS

In 1929 the Great Depression was declared and I lost all my money. Everyone I knew did! One moment it was there, the next it was not. Like everyone else, I had made some disastrous investments, the worst of which was Chocolives. This South American/Greek co-venture seemed like it couldn't fail, but it turned out that nobody likes chocolate-covered olives. I sunk every penny I had into it, and ended up storing 250,000 cans in my house. Luckily I lost my house the following week.

All of my possessions and property were immediately seized by the bank, which then itself went out of business. Suddenly there was no money anywhere, and starvation and misery reigned in the land. There was dirt for lunch and dust for dinner, and only tears left to bathe in.

I didn't mind too much, though, as it gave me an excuse to resume my career of drifting! Drifting is the great American pastime, the ultimate expression of freedom and a lifestyle choice I recommend to anybody. When life gets awkward or unpleasant, when your job or marriage becomes too much to take, why not drift? Simply go to the nearest river, construct a raft using the materials you find on the banks, jump on it and float away to freedom. Wherever your raft lands you have a chance to start your life anew!

The 1930s were the driftiest period in human history. Hundreds of thousands of people, freed from their houses and savings, had taken to roaming, and though many of them used trains instead of rafts, I was delighted to meet so many new enthusiasts. I adapted to this new "hobo" style of traveling, and delighted in technological advancements such as the bindle and the new secret language of signs; but I am a raft man at heart, and many's the time, when my boxcar was passing near to a river or creek, that I threw together the available materials into a raft and leapt with it onto the water. I've been told this practice can be described as "cross-platform drifting."

The handiest way of supporting oneself when drifting is grifting. One routine I used to delight in was "the Penny Grift"; I worked the simplest version of this popular con, and it kept me fed and watered many a day. I would place a penny on the ground near where my mark was going to be walking, then I would wait. When the mark appeared, I would pretend to spot the penny and swoop it up. "Look, a penny!" I would shout. "What a lovely penny! I am so lucky to have found this penny, it is a very charming coin!" I would show the penny to the mark, and hug it and kiss it with a great show of affection. "My new child the penny is very sad. Because he is the only penny here. It is making me sad. How lonely this penny is! If only he had a brother!" I would keep this up until the mark got the hint and drew another penny from his pocket and handed it to me, then I would rejoice: "Hahaha! How happy they are together! Look, penny, the nice man (or woman) gave you a brother! Here, you should kiss each other! That's it, kiss! Mwah mwah mwah!" In this way, I would amass pennies until I had 365 of them, called "a year" in penny-grifting circles; this I could exchange for goods and services.

At times I would feel a touch of oversolitudedness, also known as loneliness, and would seek company amongst my fellow hobos. They were a literary bunch, and we began to hold impromptu readings of our scribblings, which evolved into a more competitive kind of event. In fact I may venture to say that between us we devised the precursor of the modern "poetry slam," with one man reading his verses while the other hobos shouted abuse. We'd yell "Shut up! What is that garbage?! You're an idiot!" until he gave up. Then it was the next fella's turn. I don't think I ever actually heard a poem for all the shouting.

The undisputed king of this game was the feared hobo Robert "Less Taken Road Takin' Bob" Frost, although he faced serious competition from Wallace "Even" Stevens and e.e. "bumming" cummings.

I'll never forget one time Bob and I were tramping along a country road when he said "Whose woods these are I think I know, a guy who'll give us a cup of joe." He was right, we got free coffee and later he fancied up that bit of rhyme and made a lot of money off of it.

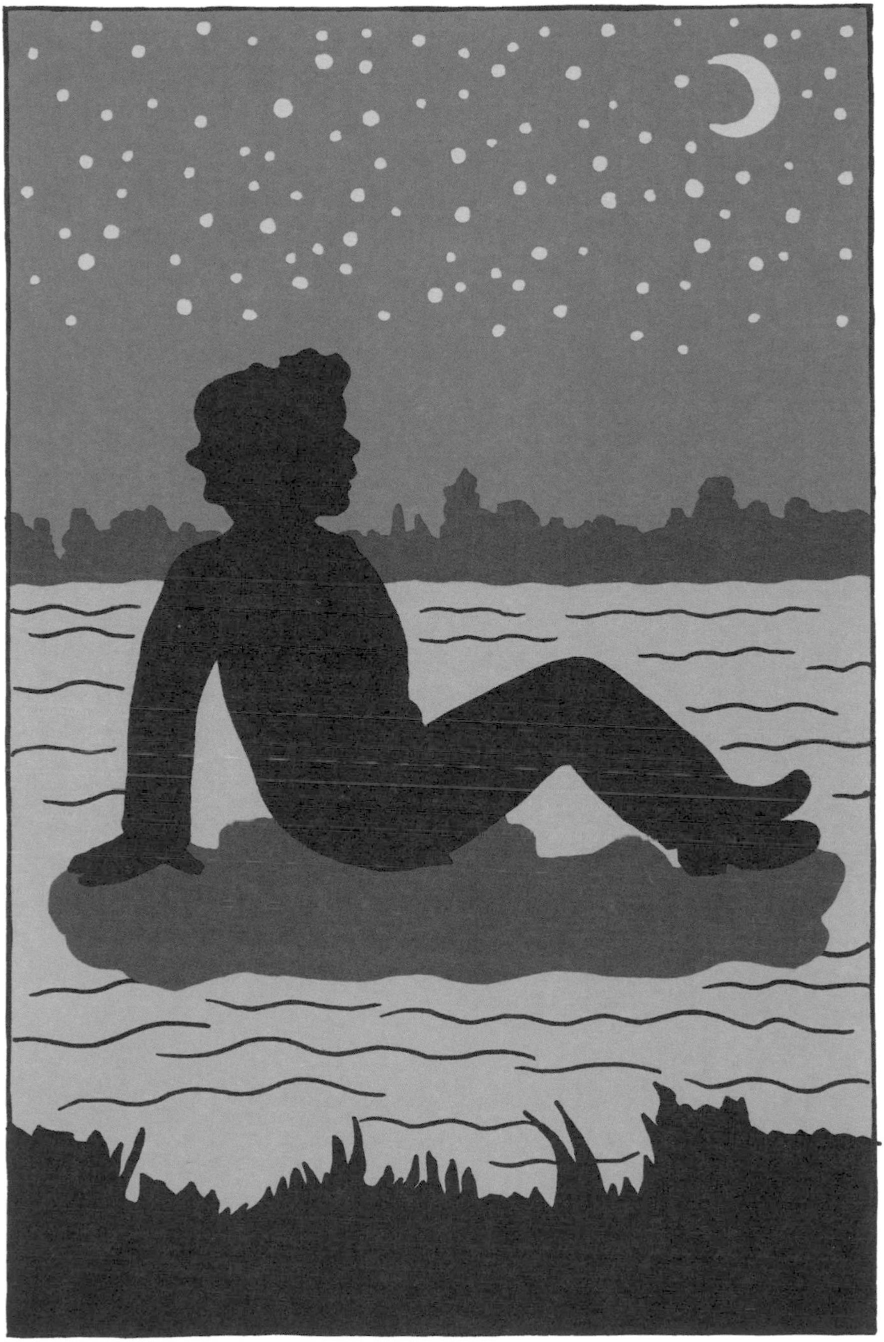

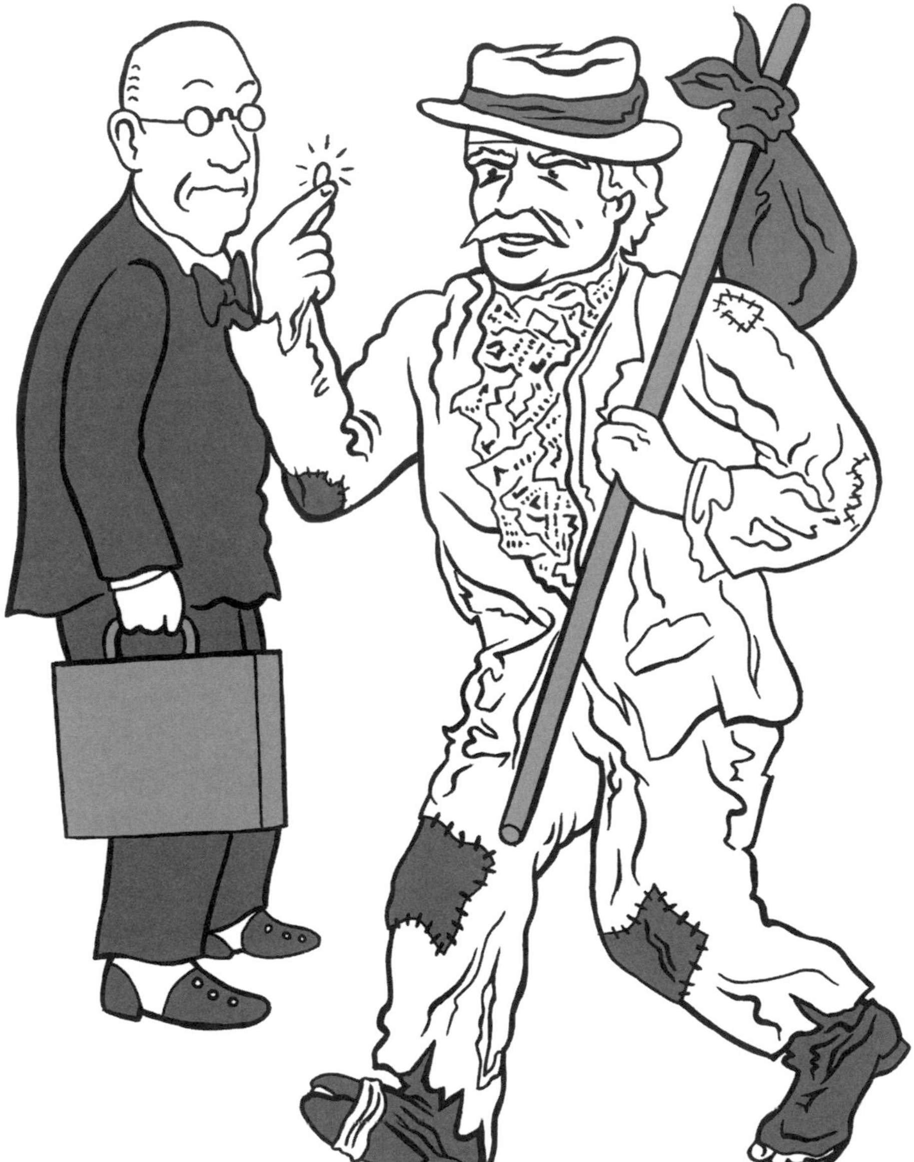

During this time I drifted to and fro across the United States, and enjoyed the freedom a great deal. My clothing was rags stuffed with newspaper, and a stone was my pillow at night (not a great one, either, barely worth the trouble of carrying the damn thing around). I was happy that way, for a while. But I began to get bored with so much freedom, and decided to check my post office box in Hartford, which I had left functioning. I was astonished to find a letter containing an invitation... from the new entertainment capital of the world!

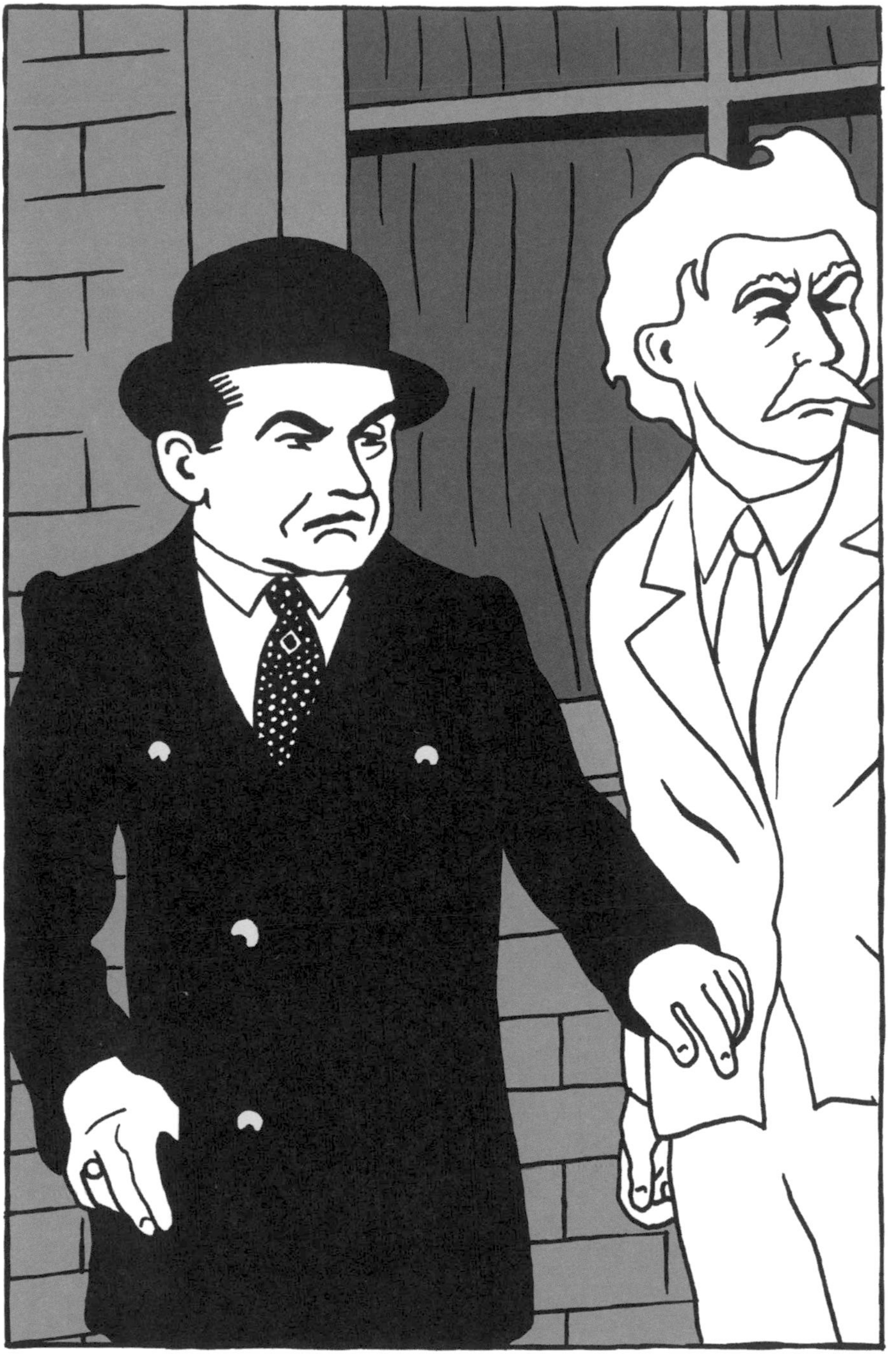

CHAPTER EIGHT:

SHADDUP, YOU RAT!
I SAID SHADDUP

The letter was from Hollywood. "Come and work for us!" it said. My heart was full of conflicting emotions, but my pants were full of lice, scabies, and dirt mites, and so I immediately drifted west, where I headed to the Warner Brothers lot and took a bath. Then, after putting on a new suit, I got down to business, writing. After punching up the dialogue for *Off-Broadway Discount Dancing Dollies of 1934*, I was set to work writing gangster pictures, and quickly produced scripts for such gems of the genre as *Tiny Tyrant*, *Gunfire or Gavels*, *Gats for Spats*, *Shut Up, You Mugs*, *Worms Don't Earn*, *The Amazing Mister Crime Boss*, *Brooklyn Brouhaha*, *Fighting Fugitives*, and my personal favorite, *Murder Me? Nyaah, You Haven't Got The Guts!* starring the great Edward G. Robinson as Mars Atlas. I loved writing for Eddie, he could really make the dialogue sing:

> *Reeko Petroleum: Mars, we gotta rub out that cop's wife. It's business!*
> *Mars: Business, is it? Nyaah! Yah! Why I oughta, nyaah! Nyaahhh...Nyaaah! You lousy punks never understand anything past the sound of your own gats talking! That cop's a friend of mine, and a swell egg, too, see! Anyone who touches his skirt is gonna get a pasting from yours truly! Nyaah! You mugs! Nyah!*

In 1939 I went to see a new movie, never dreaming that it would completely change my attitude towards filmmaking. The movie was *The Wizard of Oz*, and I left the theater marveling at its dazzling portrayal of the wonderland of the imagination. All night long my dreams were full of sizzling witches and dancing dwarves. The next day I went into the office of my boss, John Quincey Warner, and told him I wanted to write pictures set in fairytaleland. "Fartland?" he snorted (he was rather hard of hearing); "Twain, no-one wants to watch a picture set in Fartland. You oughtta be ashamed, that's disgusting." "No, FAIRYTALEland," I retorted. "Where the fairy tale people live, like in *The Wizard of Oz*." "Oh, now I get it," he scowled. "Twain, we make gangster pictures. If you want to write nursery rhyme pictures, you should go and work for someone else."

Undeterred, I began inserting fairytale material into my gangster scripts, bit by bit. The change wasn't too noticeable in films such as *School for Stoolies*, but by the time *Bugs Manion in the Wonderland of Curious Elves* was released, the difference was quite noticeable. My bosses, after yelling at me, gave me one last chance with a story called "The Maltese Falcon," and I made quite a few changes from the original script, turning the falcon into a lovable owl and Sam Spade into an actual spade, albeit a talking one who had adventures, and three musical numbers. Bogart seemed to like it, but the squares who ran Warner Brothers didn't, and I was fired.

Unfortunately I had sizable gambling debts, and my sudden unemployment couldn't have come at a worse time. In order to pay off the loan sharks and escape their violence I was forced to take a job writing scripts for pornographic filmmakers Horny Brothers, with their parallel stable of stars such as Humphrey Blowgart and Beddy Davis. Other great stars included Fonda Peters, Betty Grabass, Erhole Fillin' and Basil Rashbone. I sincerely hope that no copies survive of films such as *Little Sleazer* or *The Maltese F*ckin'*, both of which I wrote under duress. It was a great relief when a message came from my old friend Winston Churchill, asking me to come to London immediately. World War II had just started, and it seemed my help was needed, once again.

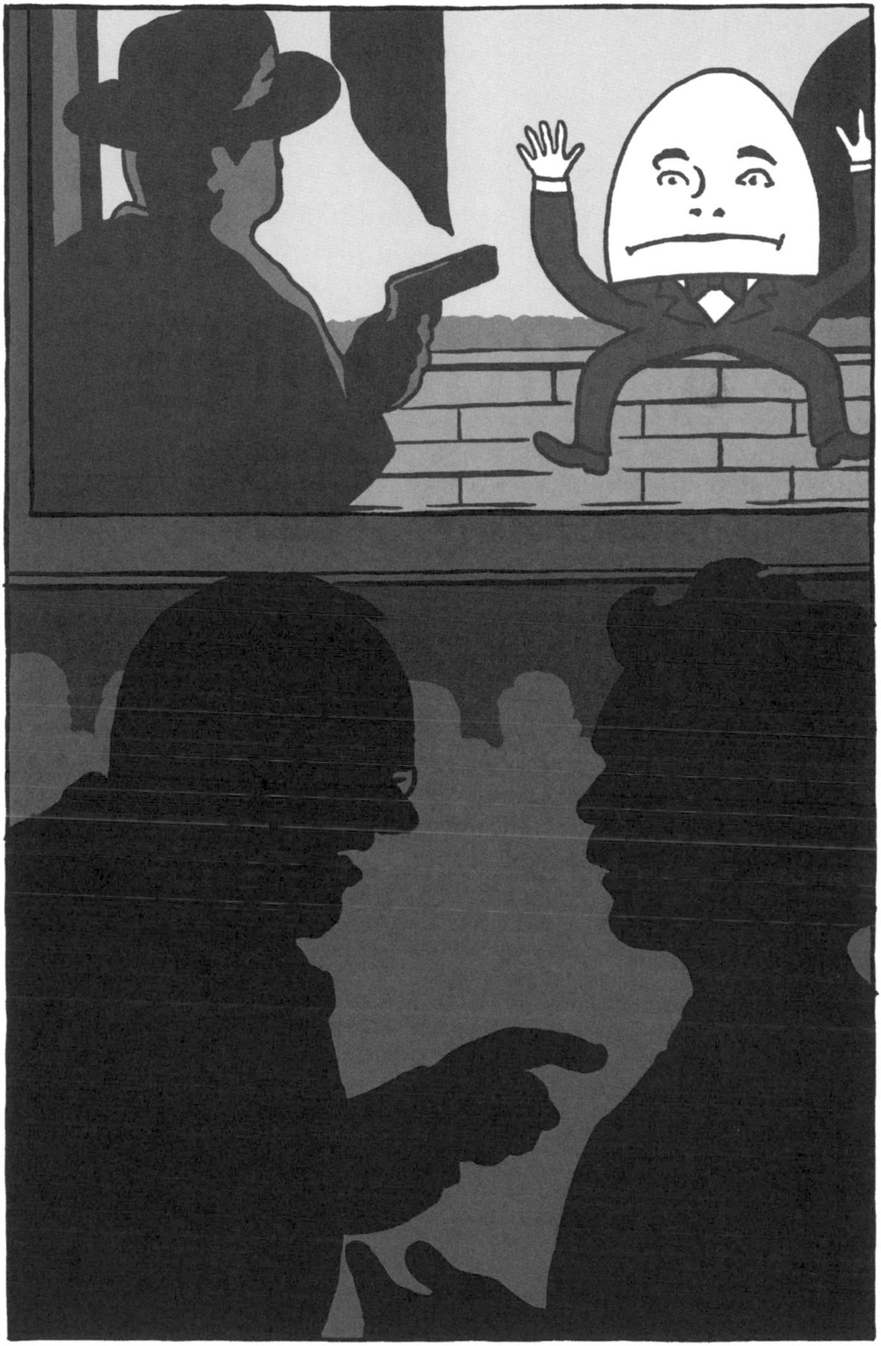

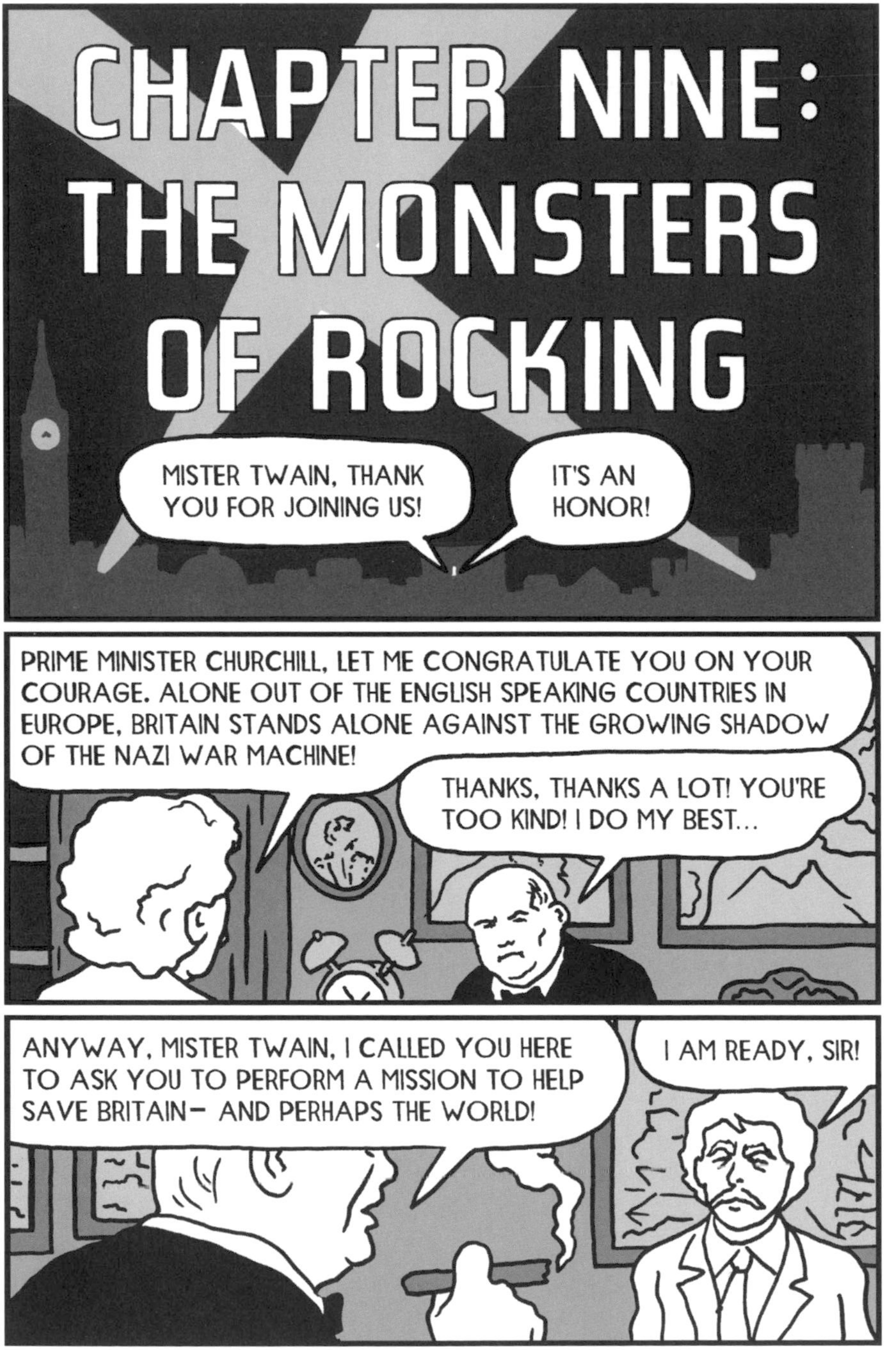
CHAPTER NINE: THE MONSTERS OF ROCKING
MISTER TWAIN, THANK YOU FOR JOINING US!
IT'S AN HONOR!
PRIME MINISTER CHURCHILL, LET ME CONGRATULATE YOU ON YOUR COURAGE. ALONE OUT OF THE ENGLISH SPEAKING COUNTRIES IN EUROPE, BRITAIN STANDS ALONE AGAINST THE GROWING SHADOW OF THE NAZI WAR MACHINE!
THANKS, THANKS A LOT! YOU'RE TOO KIND! I DO MY BEST...
ANYWAY, MISTER TWAIN, I CALLED YOU HERE TO ASK YOU TO PERFORM A MISSION TO HELP SAVE BRITAIN– AND PERHAPS THE WORLD!
I AM READY, SIR!

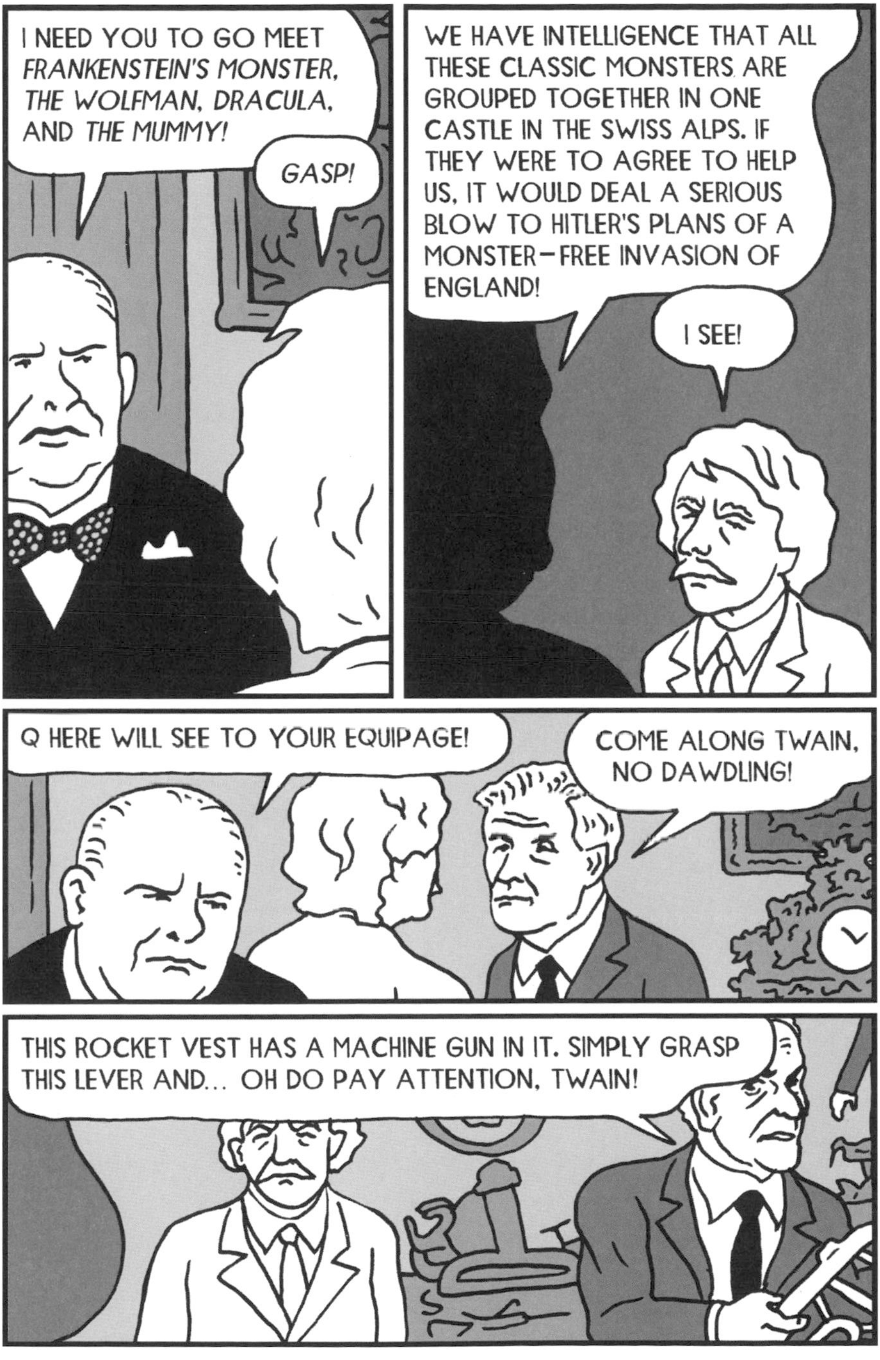
I NEED YOU TO GO MEET *FRANKENSTEIN'S MONSTER, THE WOLFMAN, DRACULA,* AND *THE MUMMY!*
GASP!
WE HAVE INTELLIGENCE THAT ALL THESE CLASSIC MONSTERS ARE GROUPED TOGETHER IN ONE CASTLE IN THE SWISS ALPS. IF THEY WERE TO AGREE TO HELP US, IT WOULD DEAL A SERIOUS BLOW TO HITLER'S PLANS OF A MONSTER-FREE INVASION OF ENGLAND!
I SEE!
Q HERE WILL SEE TO YOUR EQUIPAGE!
COME ALONG TWAIN, NO DAWDLING!
THIS ROCKET VEST HAS A MACHINE GUN IN IT. SIMPLY GRASP THIS LEVER AND... OH DO PAY ATTENTION, TWAIN!

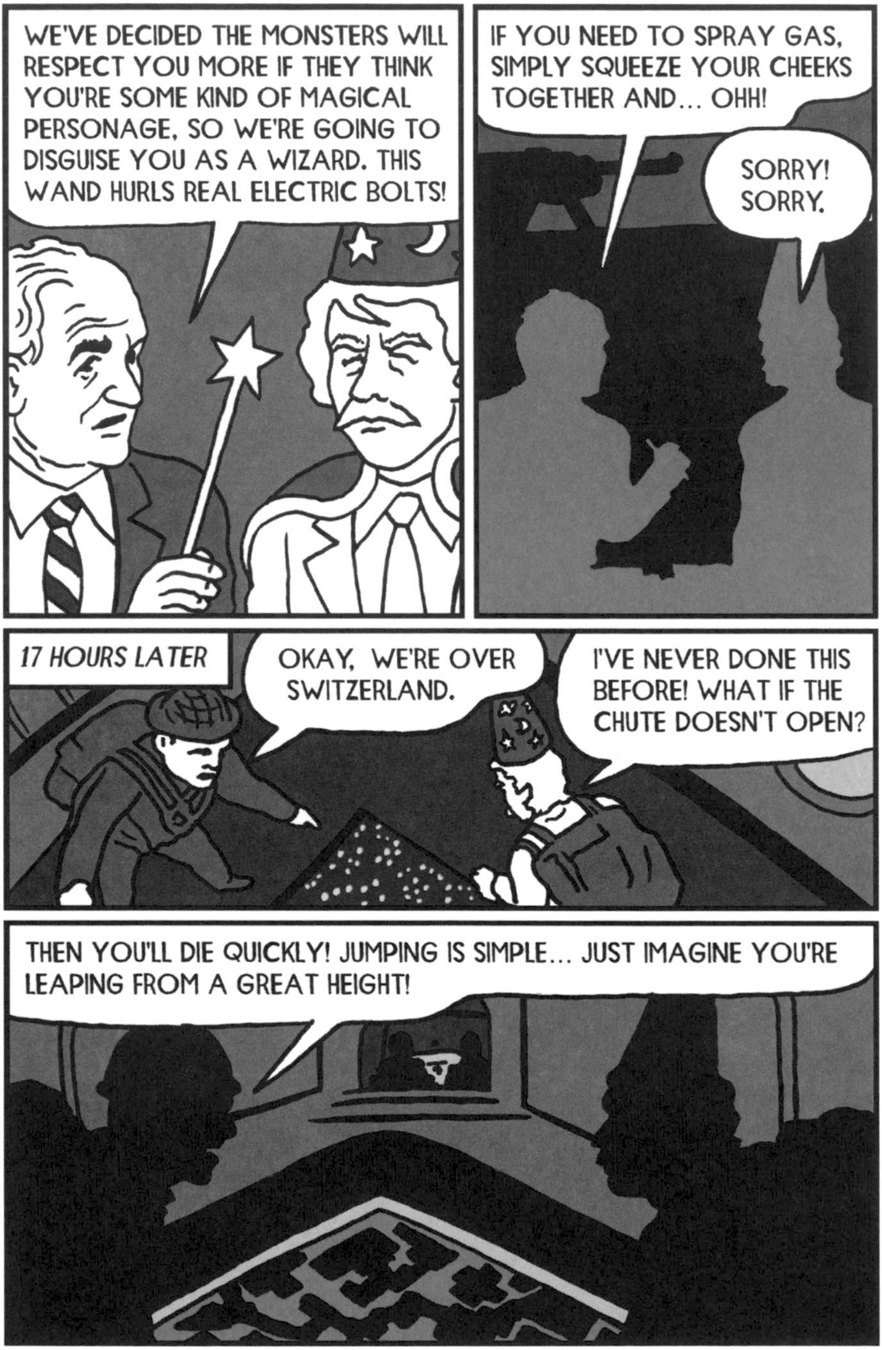
WE'VE DECIDED THE MONSTERS WILL RESPECT YOU MORE IF THEY THINK YOU'RE SOME KIND OF MAGICAL PERSONAGE, SO WE'RE GOING TO DISGUISE YOU AS A WIZARD. THIS WAND HURLS REAL ELECTRIC BOLTS!
IF YOU NEED TO SPRAY GAS, SIMPLY SQUEEZE YOUR CHEEKS TOGETHER AND... OHH!
SORRY! SORRY.
17 HOURS LATER
OKAY, WE'RE OVER SWITZERLAND.
I'VE NEVER DONE THIS BEFORE! WHAT IF THE CHUTE DOESN'T OPEN?
THEN YOU'LL DIE QUICKLY! JUMPING IS SIMPLE... JUST IMAGINE YOU'RE LEAPING FROM A GREAT HEIGHT!

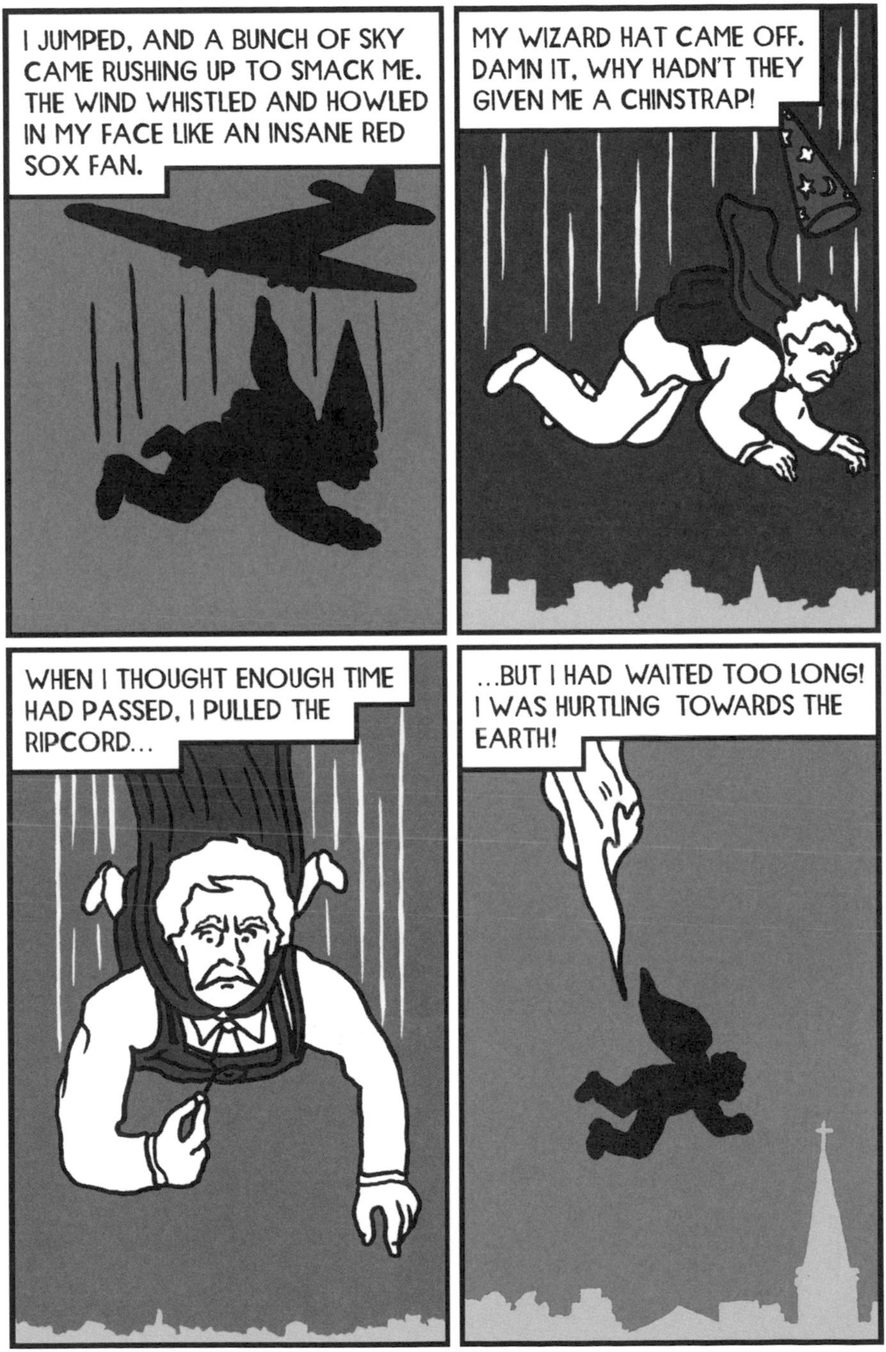
I JUMPED, AND A BUNCH OF SKY CAME RUSHING UP TO SMACK ME. THE WIND WHISTLED AND HOWLED IN MY FACE LIKE AN INSANE RED SOX FAN.
MY WIZARD HAT CAME OFF. DAMN IT, WHY HADN'T THEY GIVEN ME A CHINSTRAP!
WHEN I THOUGHT ENOUGH TIME HAD PASSED, I PULLED THE RIPCORD...
...BUT I HAD WAITED TOO LONG! I WAS HURTLING TOWARDS THE EARTH!

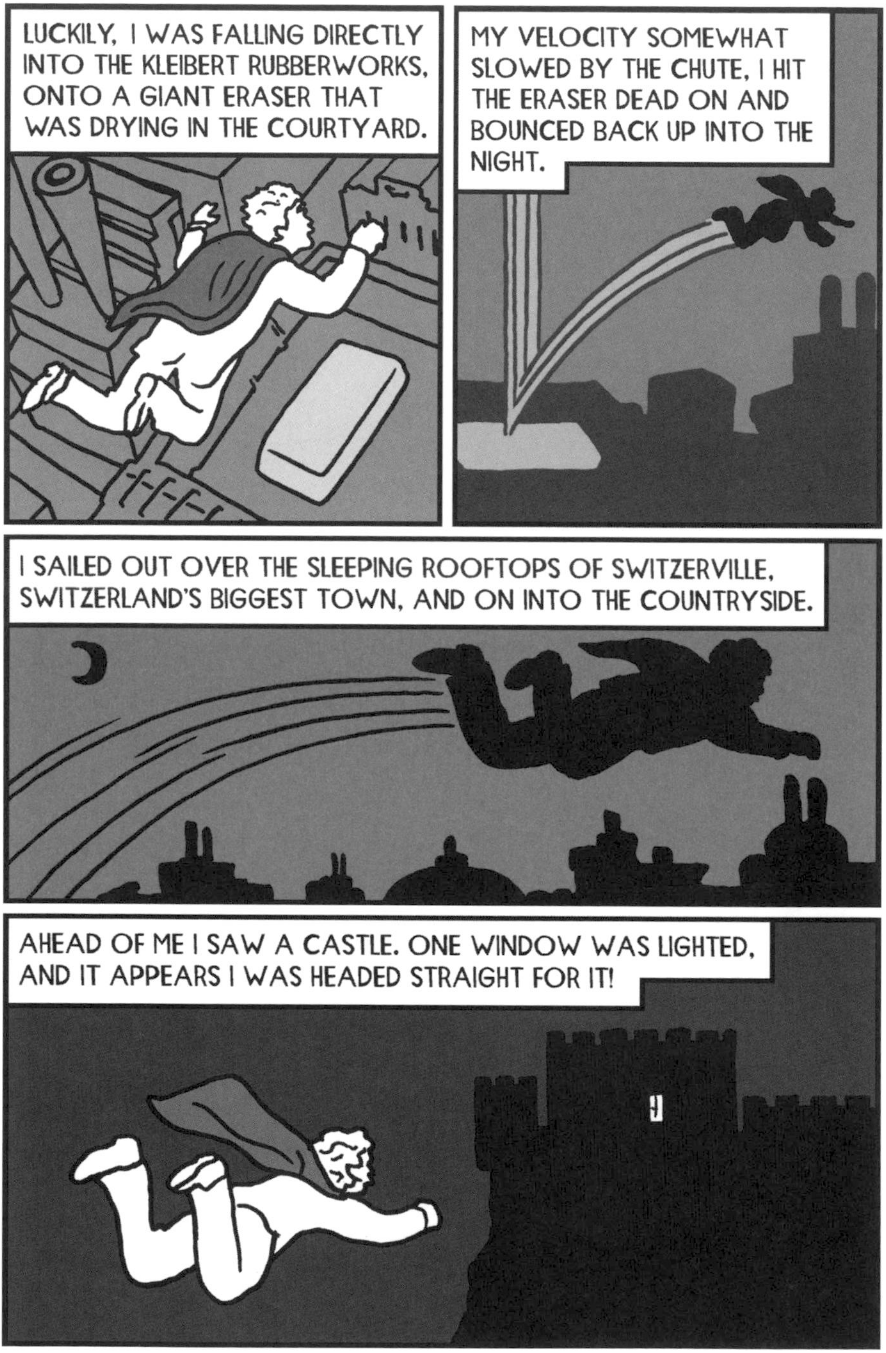
LUCKILY, I WAS FALLING DIRECTLY INTO THE KLEIBERT RUBBERWORKS, ONTO A GIANT ERASER THAT WAS DRYING IN THE COURTYARD.
MY VELOCITY SOMEWHAT SLOWED BY THE CHUTE, I HIT THE ERASER DEAD ON AND BOUNCED BACK UP INTO THE NIGHT.
I SAILED OUT OVER THE SLEEPING ROOFTOPS OF SWITZERVILLE, SWITZERLAND'S BIGGEST TOWN, AND ON INTO THE COUNTRYSIDE.
AHEAD OF ME I SAW A CASTLE. ONE WINDOW WAS LIGHTED, AND IT APPEARS I WAS HEADED STRAIGHT FOR IT!

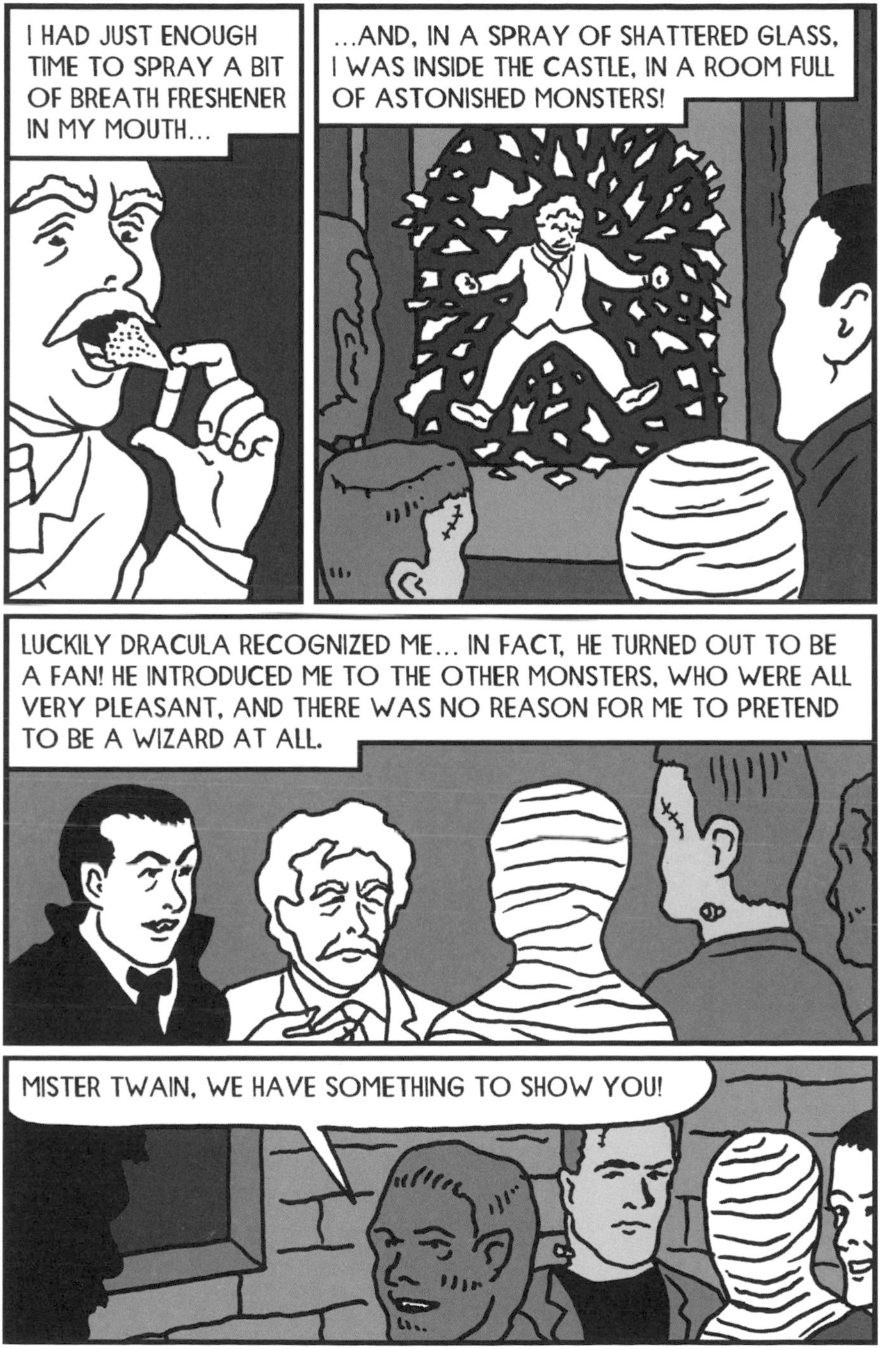
I HAD JUST ENOUGH TIME TO SPRAY A BIT OF BREATH FRESHENER IN MY MOUTH...
...AND, IN A SPRAY OF SHATTERED GLASS, I WAS INSIDE THE CASTLE, IN A ROOM FULL OF ASTONISHED MONSTERS!
LUCKILY DRACULA RECOGNIZED ME... IN FACT, HE TURNED OUT TO BE A FAN! HE INTRODUCED ME TO THE OTHER MONSTERS, WHO WERE ALL VERY PLEASANT, AND THERE WAS NO REASON FOR ME TO PRETEND TO BE A WIZARD AT ALL.
MISTER TWAIN, WE HAVE SOMETHING TO SHOW YOU!

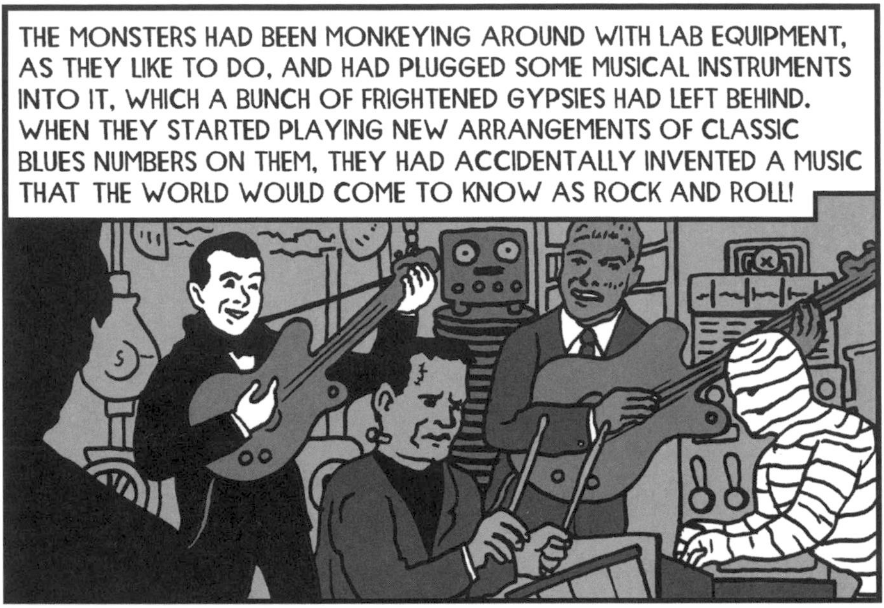
THE MONSTERS HAD BEEN MONKEYING AROUND WITH LAB EQUIPMENT, AS THEY LIKE TO DO, AND HAD PLUGGED SOME MUSICAL INSTRUMENTS INTO IT, WHICH A BUNCH OF FRIGHTENED GYPSIES HAD LEFT BEHIND. WHEN THEY STARTED PLAYING NEW ARRANGEMENTS OF CLASSIC BLUES NUMBERS ON THEM, THEY HAD ACCIDENTALLY INVENTED A MUSIC THAT THE WORLD WOULD COME TO KNOW AS ROCK AND ROLL!

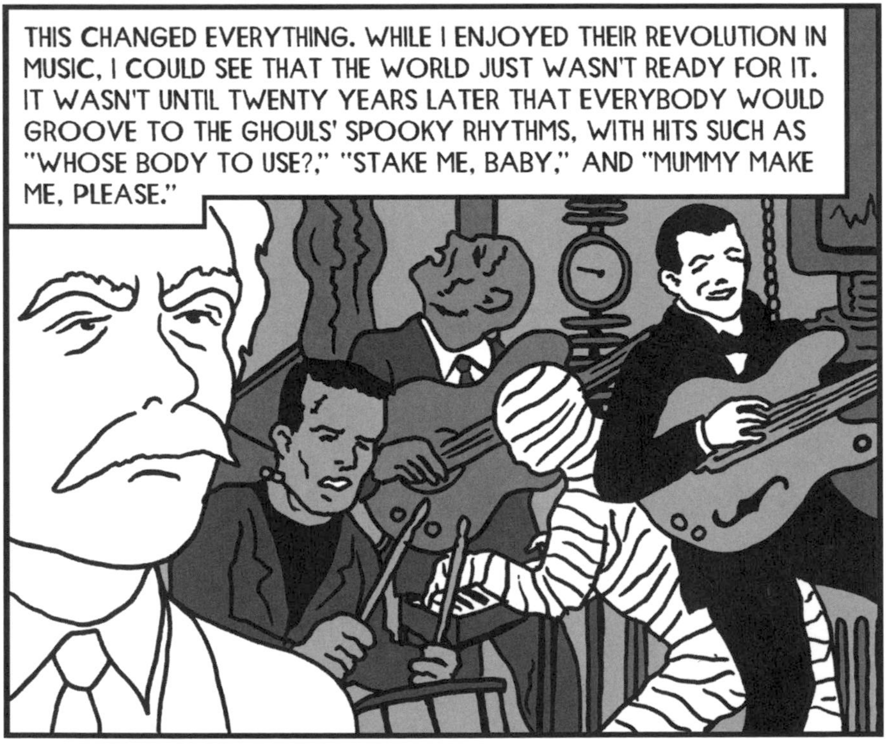
THIS CHANGED EVERYTHING. WHILE I ENJOYED THEIR REVOLUTION IN MUSIC, I COULD SEE THAT THE WORLD JUST WASN'T READY FOR IT. IT WASN'T UNTIL TWENTY YEARS LATER THAT EVERYBODY WOULD GROOVE TO THE GHOULS' SPOOKY RHYTHMS, WITH HITS SUCH AS "WHOSE BODY TO USE?," "STAKE ME, BABY," AND "MUMMY MAKE ME, PLEASE."

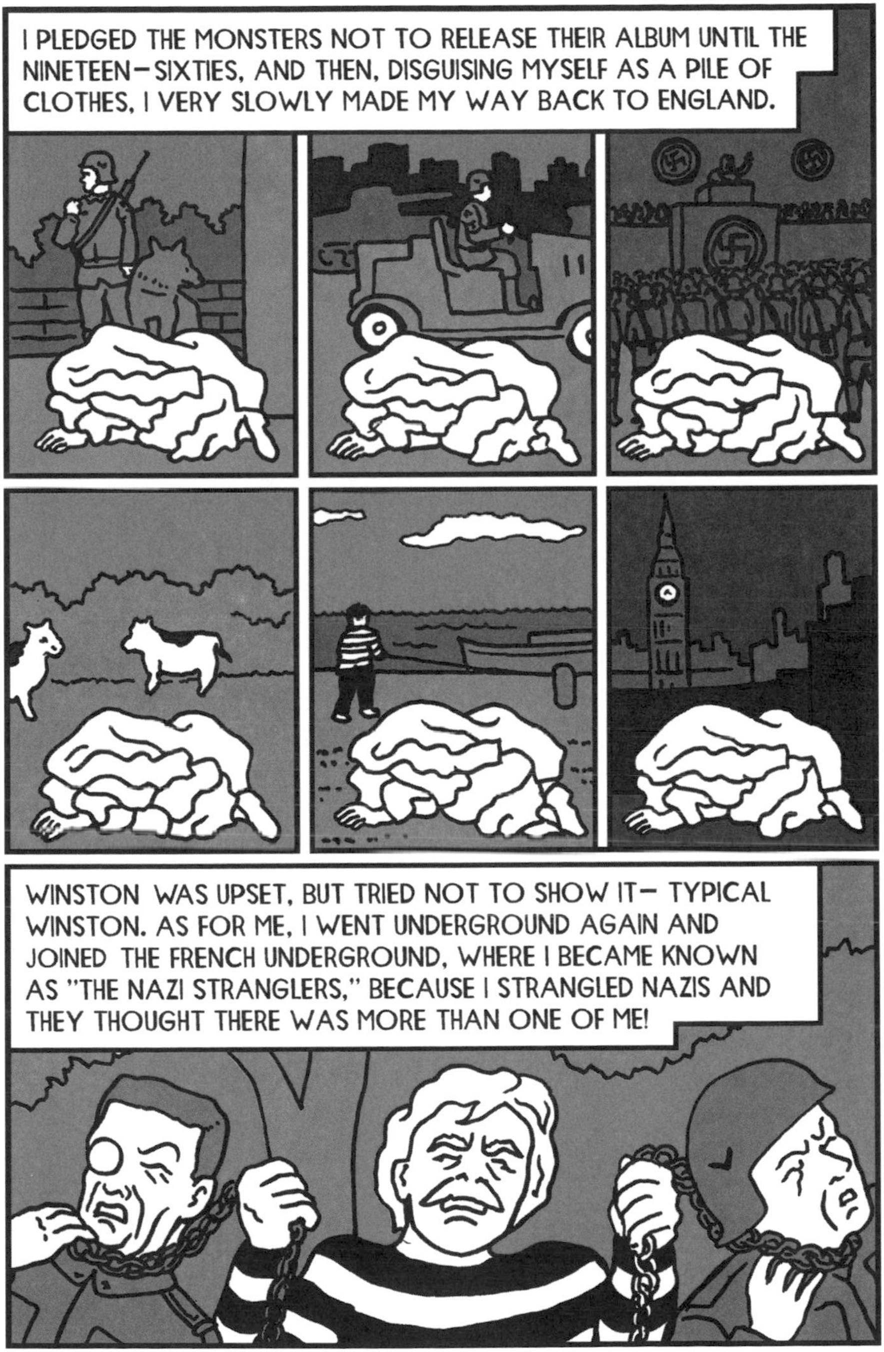
I PLEDGED THE MONSTERS NOT TO RELEASE THEIR ALBUM UNTIL THE NINETEEN-SIXTIES, AND THEN, DISGUISING MYSELF AS A PILE OF CLOTHES, I VERY SLOWLY MADE MY WAY BACK TO ENGLAND.
WINSTON WAS UPSET, BUT TRIED NOT TO SHOW IT— TYPICAL WINSTON. AS FOR ME, I WENT UNDERGROUND AGAIN AND JOINED THE FRENCH UNDERGROUND, WHERE I BECAME KNOWN AS "THE NAZI STRANGLERS," BECAUSE I STRANGLED NAZIS AND THEY THOUGHT THERE WAS MORE THAN ONE OF ME!

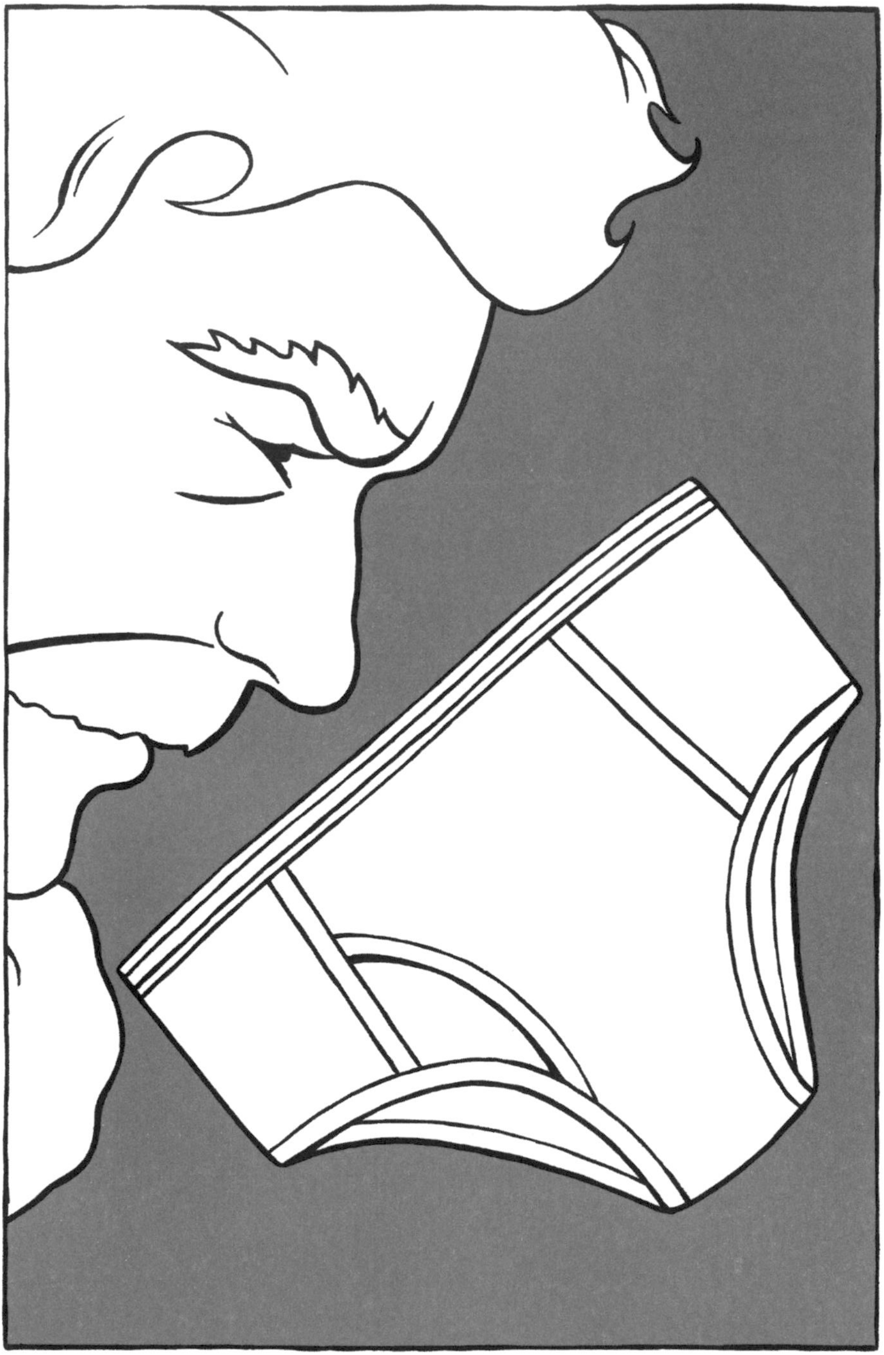

CHAPTER TEN

FROM HUCK FINN TO HUCKSTER

After the war I drifted home with a chestful of medals, some of which I had actually won. Everyone supposed I had died once again, and so I was free to be anonymous. I took up a career as a Mark Twain impersonator, touring schools and hospitals while spouting my famous aphorisms. I even attended a Mark Twain imitator's convention, and came in third in the Mark Twain costume contest. It was all very pleasant, but I was getting bored with it all, and I found I needed a change.

As I thought about our modern age, it seemed to me that the propaganda industry, now called the advertising industry, was where the action was. With my skill and charm it wasn't hard for me to get a job writing copy for one of the major agencies, Driscoll and Webber. I was given a little cubicle right next to the bear toilets (there was a zoo in the building). I certainly had plenty of incentive to try to improve my position!

My first assignment was to write an ad for Swankeroo Underwear. I sat and stared at a pair of their thin cotton briefs, and wondered what I could possibly say to encourage their purchase. I thought about human nature, and the contradictory impulses that govern our actions. And suddenly I knew what to write. My ad went like this:

> *You worm. You stinking, dirty little grub, you aren't worthy to be called a human being. You disgusting pail of vomit, you don't even deserve to exist! Scum! Worthless scum! If there weren't laws against it I'd— what's that? You're wearing Swankeroo Underwear? My apologies, SIR!*

It was a huge hit, and sales of Swankeroo boxers and briefs rose considerably. My technique of abusing the consumer, with the only means of escaping that abuse the purchase of the item represented, was instantly embraced by the entire advertising industry. I was given a swanky corner office, and my days were full of three-martini lunches and sexy affairs with an array of glamorous secretaries. I was living the dream!

My next advertising assignment was for GI Drink, the World War II beverage that had been developed for our troops from a failed version of penicillin, mixed with vanilla and clam juice. Most consumers agreed that it was awful, and the returning soldiers all had stopped drinking it as soon as other beverage options became available. I tried another variation on my abuse theme:

> *You jerk, you make me sick. Spitting on the flag. Spitting on the corpses of those brave men who fought and died for your country! You're a traitor, that's what you are! I wish I had a mob handy, I'd—wait, is that GI Drink in your hand? Let me shake your hand,* American!

Sales of GI Drink shot up, although the company folded anyway; they only had a limited supply of the stuff, thank god. My next assignment, and my true masterpiece, was an ad for the Pepper Board. Sales of pepper had been decreasing steadily for years, and they were desperate. Hardly anyone was touching the stuff! I tried a reversal of my previous strategy:

> *Johnson, you're a young man with your whole future ahead of you, and I'm going to give you a promotion and a raise! You'll have a corner office of your own, and you'll be able to afford a fancy new house for you and your wife to start a family in! Congrat— Wait, are you not using any pepper? You don't like it? Well I never! You're fired, ya scum! Human garbage like you makes me sick! Your wife told me you're useless in every department! You're probably crawling with disease, too—get out of here, ya filth! Officer, arrest this man!!!*

Since that campaign, I am proud to say that pepper has been placed next to salt at every meal served since then, and it was all my doing.

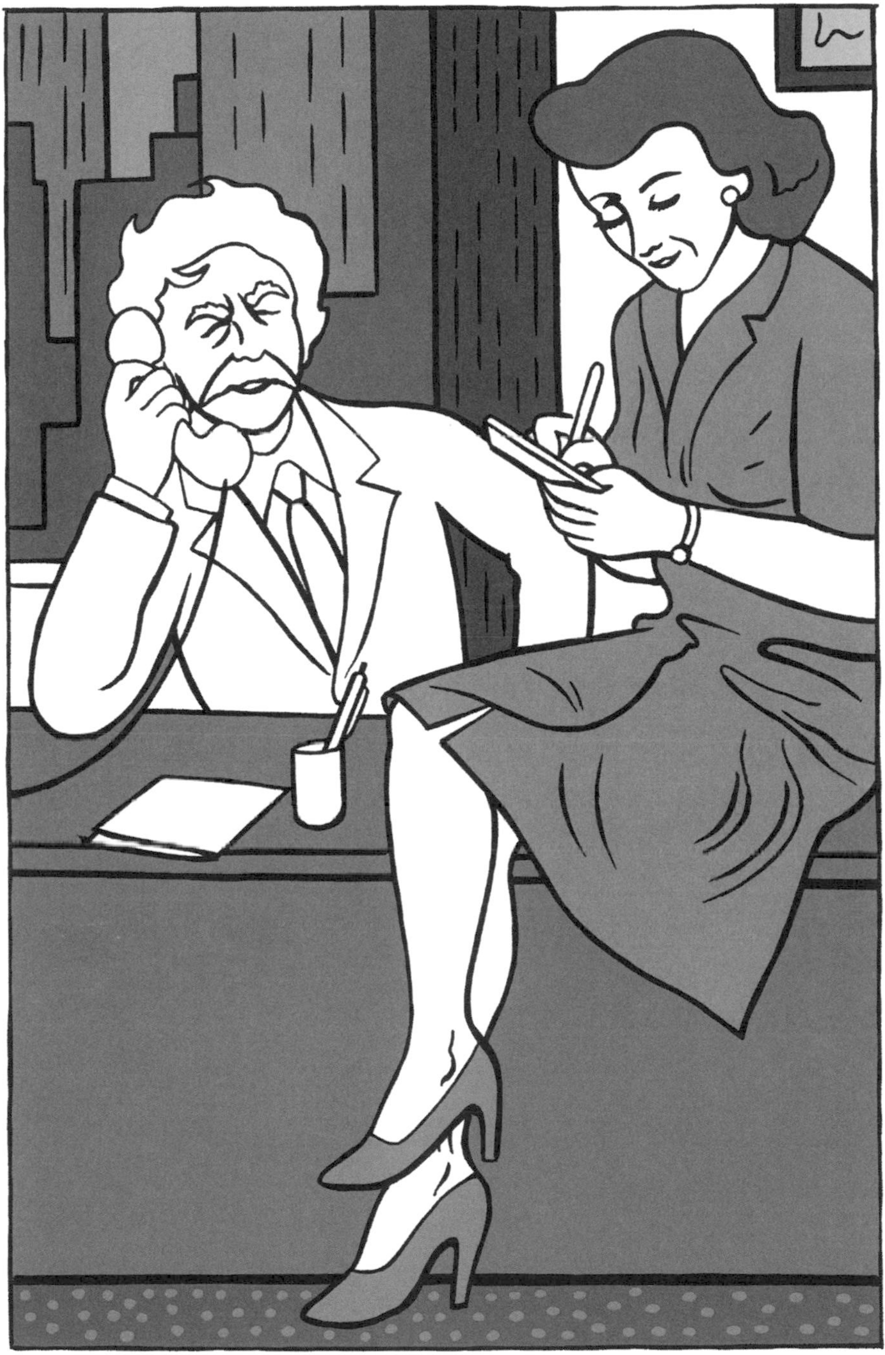

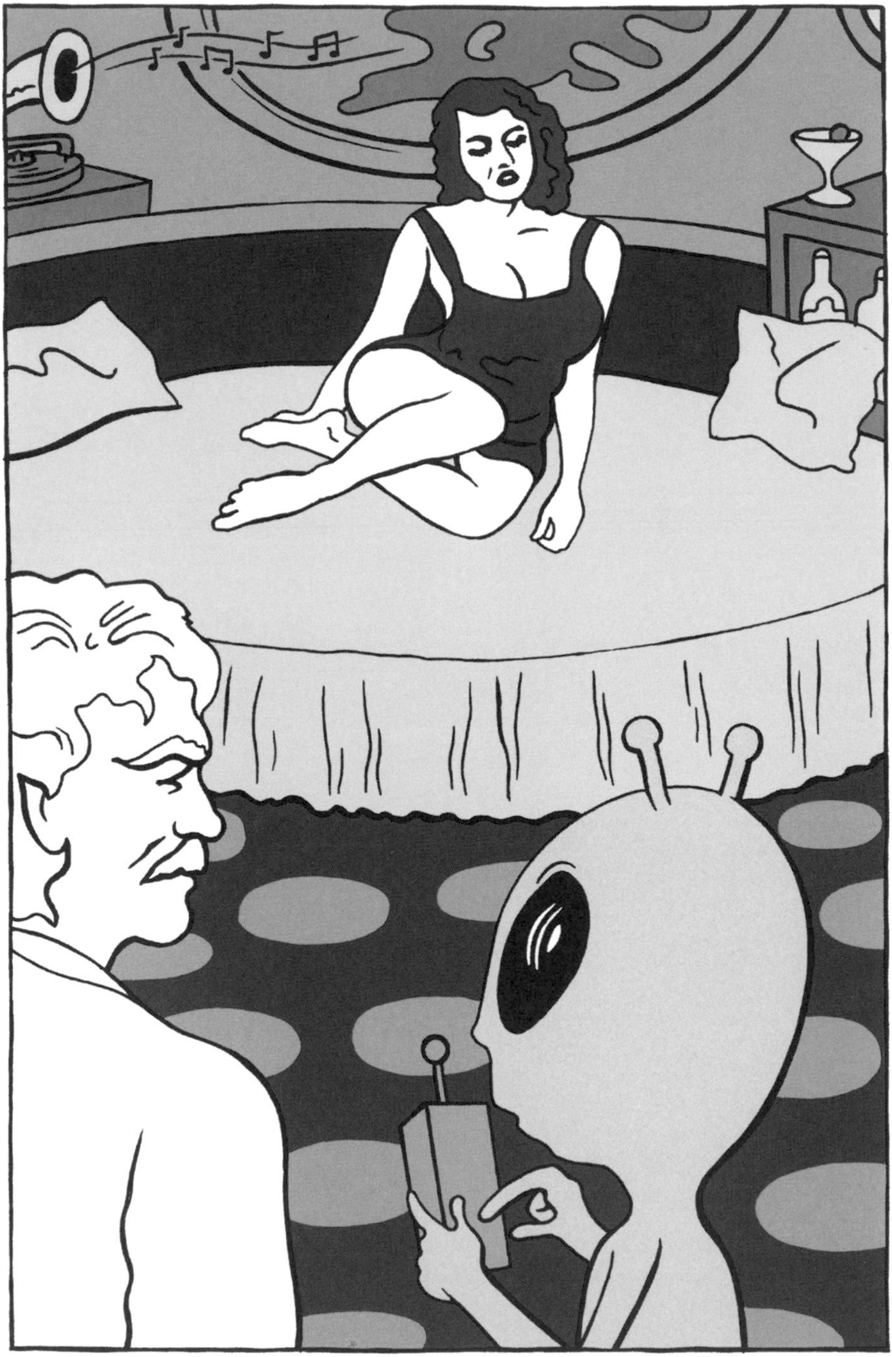

CHAPTER ELEVEN

WE ARE NOT ALONE

In 1947 I took a vacation in New Mexico. Almost immediately a UFO appeared overhead and beamed me out of my car. I was pissed, but not for long. The aliens had also kidnapped Sophia Loren, and wanted me to have sex with her while they watched and compiled their alien data. "How about it, Sophia?" I said. She gave me such a murderous look, I realized that I'd totally blown it with her. "Nothing doing, aliens," I shouted, trying to act defiant. They finally gave up after plying us for hours with their alien liqueurs and oysters. When I saw Sophia again, years later, she pretended we had never met before, but I could tell she hadn't forgiven me.

Another time Al Einstein and I were driving around in rural Pennsylvania when a large silver flying saucer appeared floating next to us. An alien stuck his head out of the hatch. "Pull over! We want to examine your rectums!" "Nothing doing!" I shouted, and put pressure on the gas pedal. The saucer sped up, trying to get in front of us and force us off the road. Only my skillful driving kept us moving forward, the sides of our car scraping against alien metal. I went on two wheels around a perilous mountain curve, then used a collapsed shack as a ramp to jump over a rushing creek, yet still the saucer stayed with us. It shot laser beams at our tires and squirted grease on the road ahead of us, but somehow I managed to keep us out of their clutches. Finally the sun came up and the aliens, disgusted, veered off into space. "Thank goodness," said Al. "If they had gained access to the information contained in our anuses the consequences could have been serious."

I encountered aliens several other times that year; obviously an article about Earth had just appeared in the alien equivalent of the *New York Times* travel section. My least favorite was a bunch of brains in jars that brought me to an alien world to fight in their gladiator zoo. Those jar-heads at first wagered against me, but I used my training in the gentlemanly art to great effect, and boxed many a futuristic combatant's chin, so that soon the brains were placing bets on me as high as seven or eight "quatloos" in each match. Among my fellow zoo-fighters was an alien female who I taught about kissing, that simple pleasure which enlivens the human spirit and a nice way to say 'thank you.' Later I described this experience to an aspiring television producer named Gene Roddenberry, and he incorporated it into his fanciful series 'Star Trek,' although he made my kissing partner a giant-bosomed comely wench, instead of the pleasantly non-humanoid mauve blob she had actually been.

But there were some positive encounters, too; while strolling along the Atlantic City boardwalk one August evening I met an extraordinary little fellow named "Bleepio, the Space Robot." He didn't say much, but responded to nearly everything with a series of beeps and boops and whirs and clicks that somehow let you know exactly what he was thinking. Eventually he returned to his home planet, but I will always treasure the memory of his humorously wise-sounding noises.

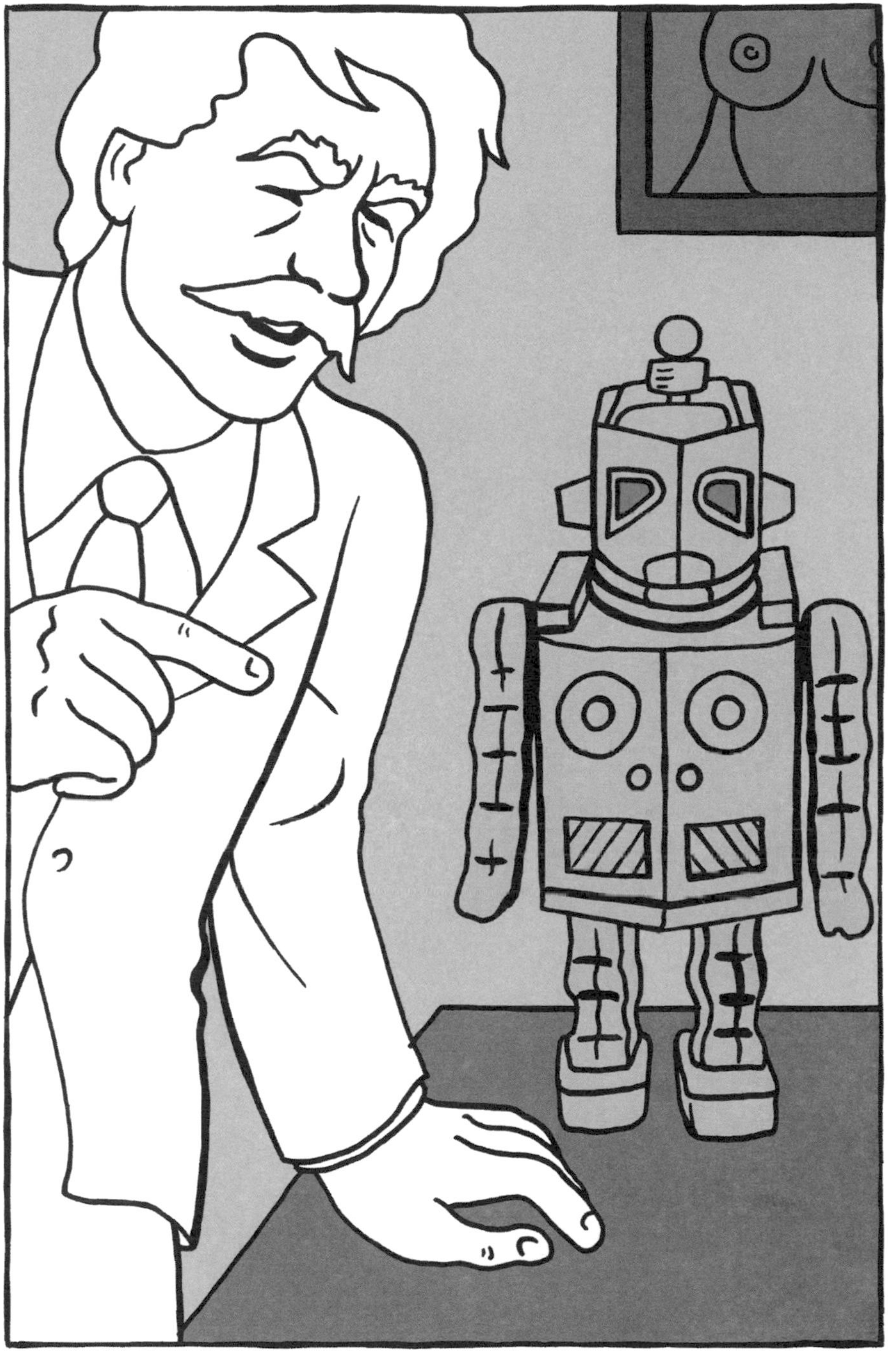

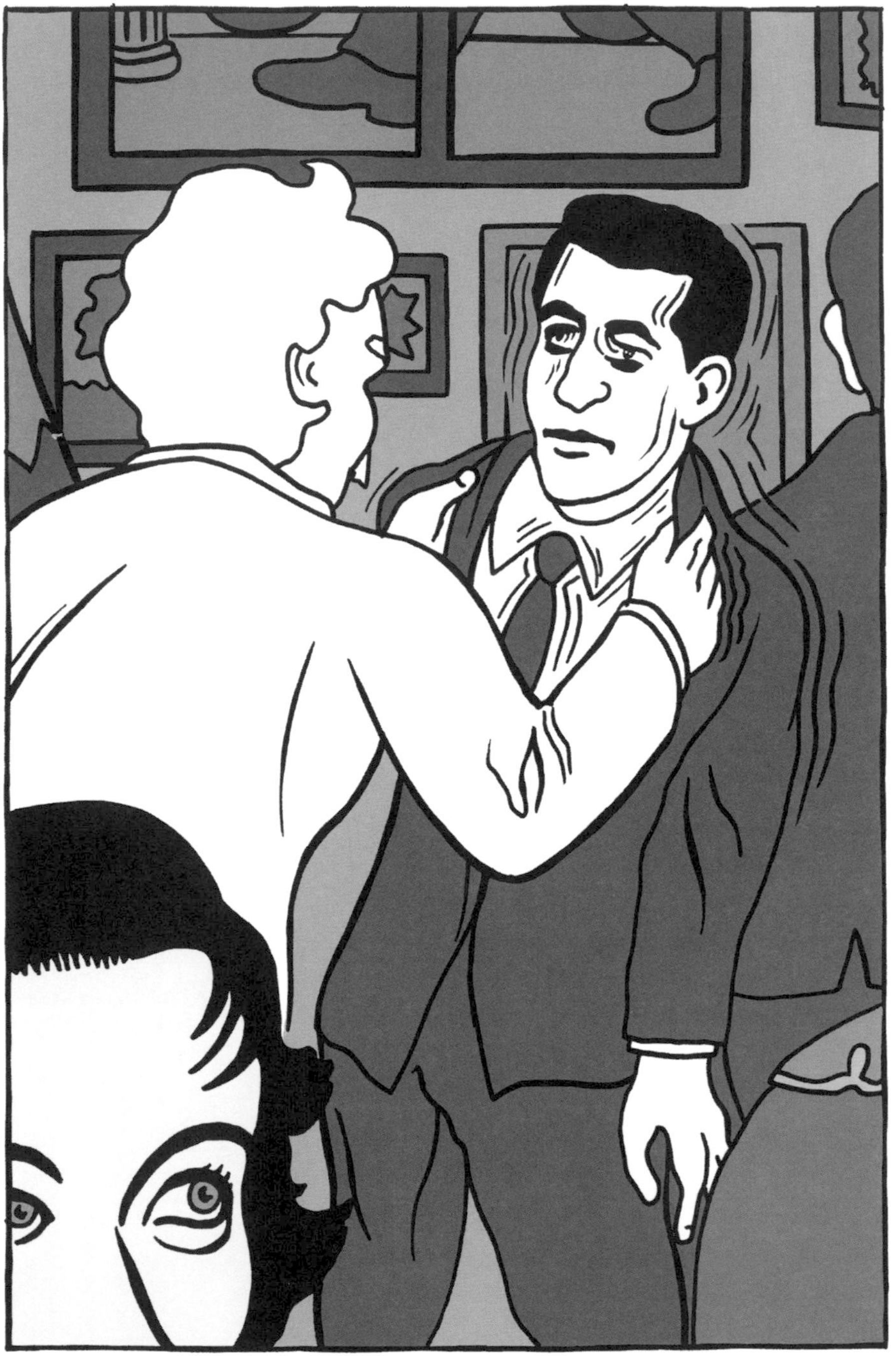

CHAPTER TWELVE

GENIUSES CAN BE DIFFICULT

After the war many writers were bursting to share their creative juices with the world. Many of these young writers I met and encouraged, the young J. D. Salinger being one of them. I met him at a party given by my friend Elsa Lanchester, who was for years the reigning hostess of the Greenwich Village literary party scene. They could be quite noisy, which is probably why I misunderstood Elsa when she introduced him; I thought she was telling me that he was a juvenile delinquent, "J.D." of course being the initials denoting that class of youth thug. I had been reading and writing a great deal of editorials at that time on the "J.D. menace," all prophesying the death of civilization at the hands of these baby-faced menaces who lacked all self-control. So I saw in this encounter a chance to confront the problem head-on, face to face.

"How do you feel society has failed you?" I shouted at the startled author of *Catcher in the Rye*. "Why are you so angry?" I grabbed him by the front of his jacket as he seemed on the verge of escaping. "Do us adults seem weak to you?" I shouted. "I'm not so weak!" and I got his head under my arm. "Apologize to society's victims!" I berated him, but he slipped from my grasp and ran from the party to the street, where he managed to jump in a cab just before I would have snagged him again. Apparently after this he became very reclusive and rarely came out in public, I wonder why.

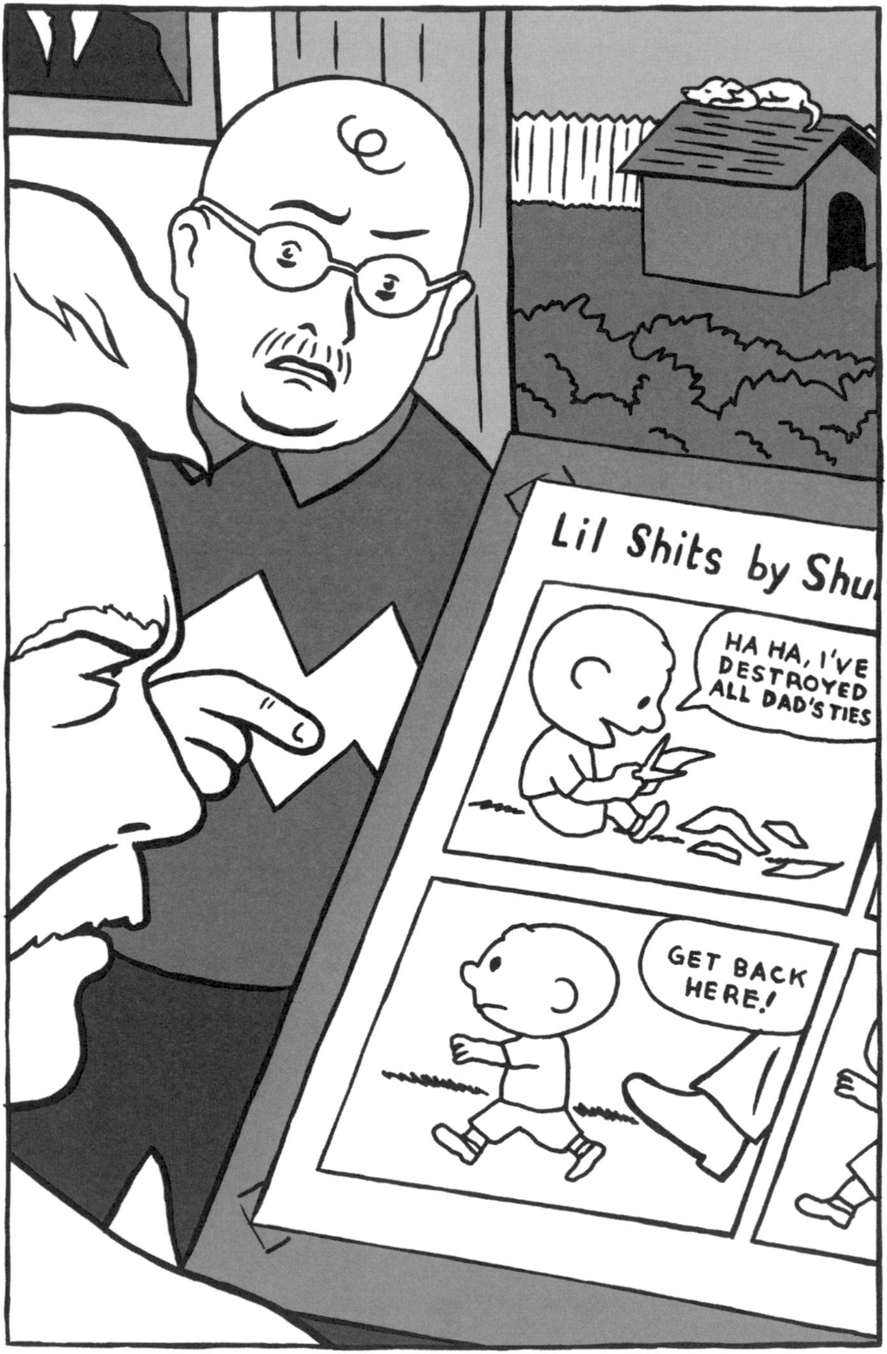
Lil Shits by Shu
HA HA, I'VE DESTROYED ALL DAD'S TIES
GET BACK HERE!

CHAPTER THIRTEEN

I CONTINUE TO INSPIRE

During this period I was invited to a dinner party where I met a young cartoonist by the name of Charles Schulz. He had been struggling, he said, because he hadn't been able to get the syndicate to buy his comic strip, and he was going to have to become a barber if he couldn't get it sold right away (his wife's father was a powerful rancher who had gotten into his head that he should cut hair). "Well, show it to me," I said. "Maybe I can help you with some suggestions."

The next day I visited his trailer and he showed me his strip. It was called *Li'l Shits* and showed a bunch of kids misbehaving and being generally unbearable. They were complete monsters who did nothing but annoy their parents, who were large wind instruments. "It doesn't look like you like children very much," I pointed out. "Also, all this swearing. This is the Fifties after all. Why don't you try to do something from the kids point of view?" "Hmmm," he said, and it was clear that my words had inspired him.

Of course the resulting strip, *Goobers* or whatever it's called, has garnered worldwide praise all over the place, and made Schulz a gazillionaire in the process. But he seemed to conveniently forget my part in the process, and in interviews would tell a story about how he got the idea for the strip from watching Lola Falana dance. But Lola Falana didn't start her performing career until 1964, when Sammy Davis Jr. cast her in his musical *Golden Boy*. Need I say more?

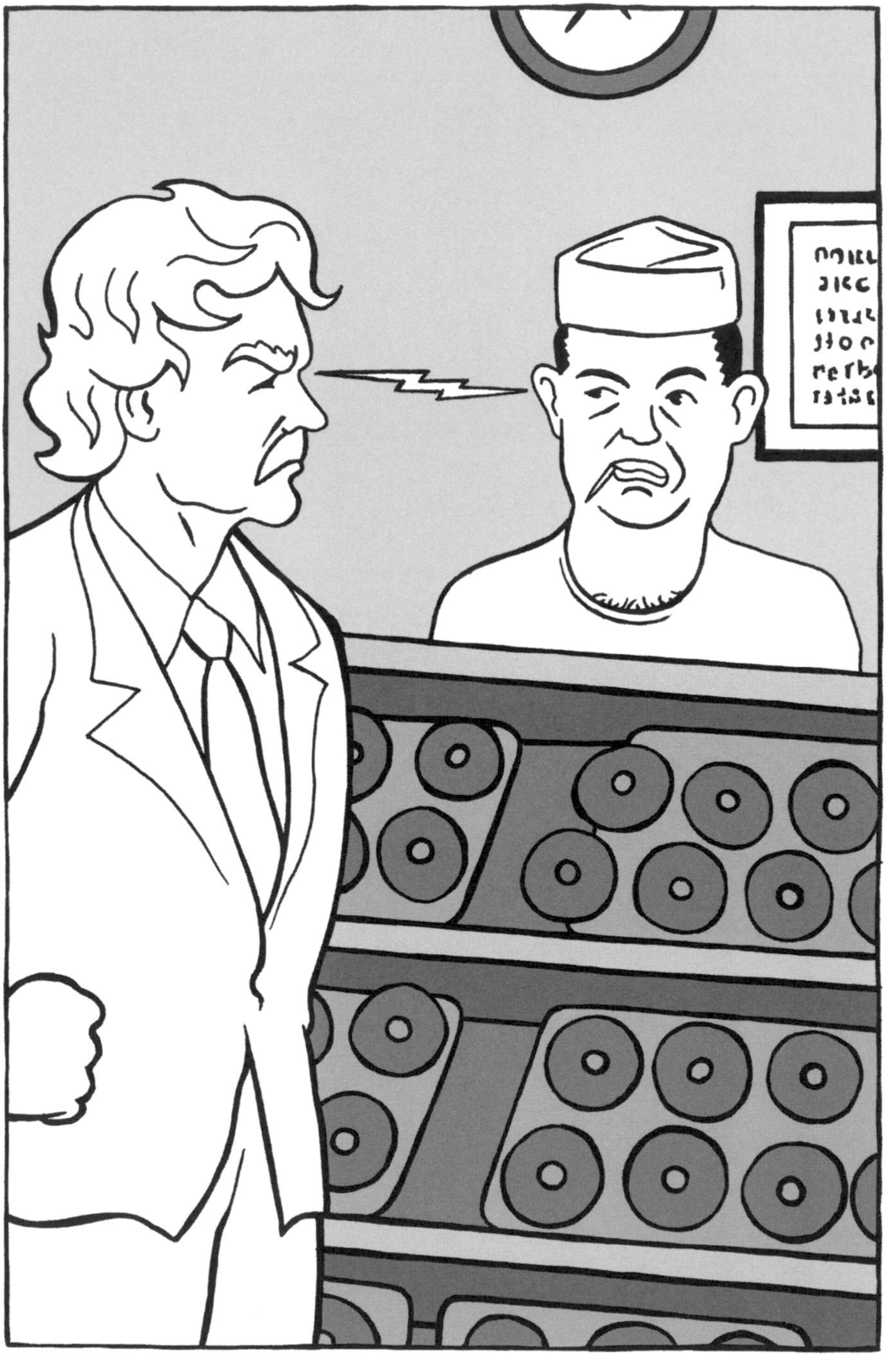

CHAPTER FOURTEEN:

I CONTROL THE CONTROLLING GAZE

In 1953 the movie *You Are Getting Sleepy* came out and was an instant hit. Hypnotism, for years limited to nightclub acts and carnival kidnappings, was now a popular fad, practiced at cocktail parties and battleship launchings. Assigned to write an article on the subject by *Hey You!* magazine, I underwent hypnosis administered to me by the famous Abscuroculist Heinrich von Werscherscherscherch. The results were incredible—I found greater mental clarity and also experienced what it was like to be a chicken, in excruciating detail. Chickens have hard lives.

Intrigued as I was at this point, I received training in hypnosis until I qualified as a Master Hypnotist and a member of the Royal Association of Hypnotists in seven kingdoms. I could warp reality in the perception of others and reveal the truth behind any lie; I could convince the strongest-minded human that they were trapped inside an egg or a giant face on Mount Rushmore. I decided to use my newfound powers to try to get myself some free donuts.

The man behind the counter at the donut store had been somewhat less than courteous ever since I had prematurely tried to hypnotize him during my first month of practice. Now as I re-entered the donut store he fixed me with a chilly glare. I sauntered up to the counter, then I threw upon him my hypnotizingest glare. "You are getting sleepy," I told him. "No, you are getting sleepy," he retorted, his hypnotic eyes boring into mine. The son-of-a-bitch had been studying hypnotism too! "You are young George Washington, and you've been caught chopping down the cherry tree," I asserted, and he became the boy President. "I cannot tell a lie," he piped in a childish voice. But it didn't last, and he shook my control free. "You are Anne Boleyn," he said, and it was true! "Don't cut off my head!" I begged my enormous, kingly husband, as powerful hands dragged me to the executioner's block, but then a voice in my mind shouted NO!, and it was my voice, and I was back in the donut shop. "You don't know what donuts are!" I ordered him, and he looked about him, confused because he no longer recognized his stock in trade. He was quick to recover, though, and hit me with the killing blow: "You have no idea how to hypnotize, and from now on it will give you a headache!"

He had won. I had completely lost my hypnotic abilities, and any attempt to regain them made my brain throb. I was forced to pay him for his donuts, but it was a privilege I felt he had earned. He had given me the ultimate lesson in hypnosis.

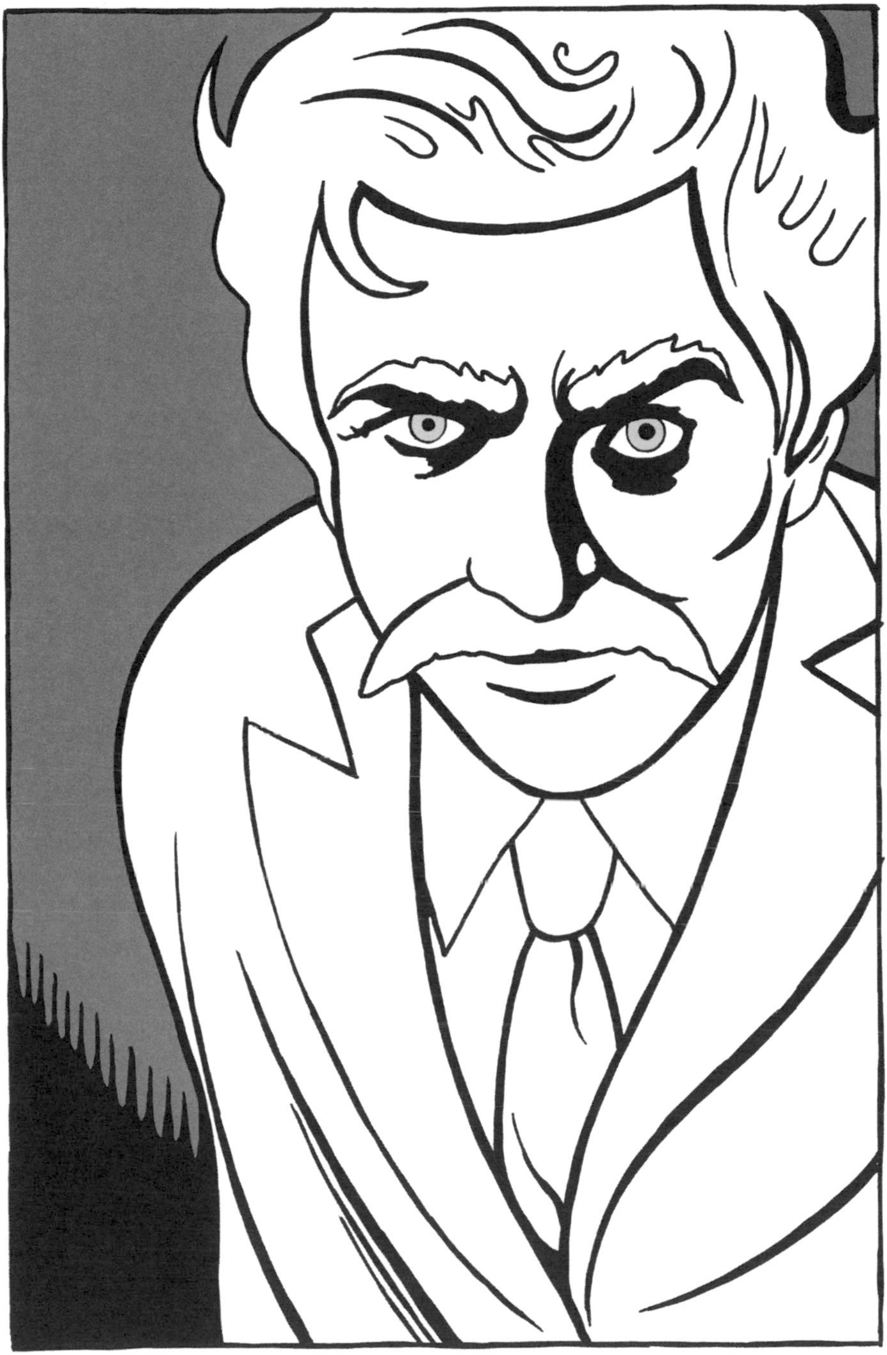

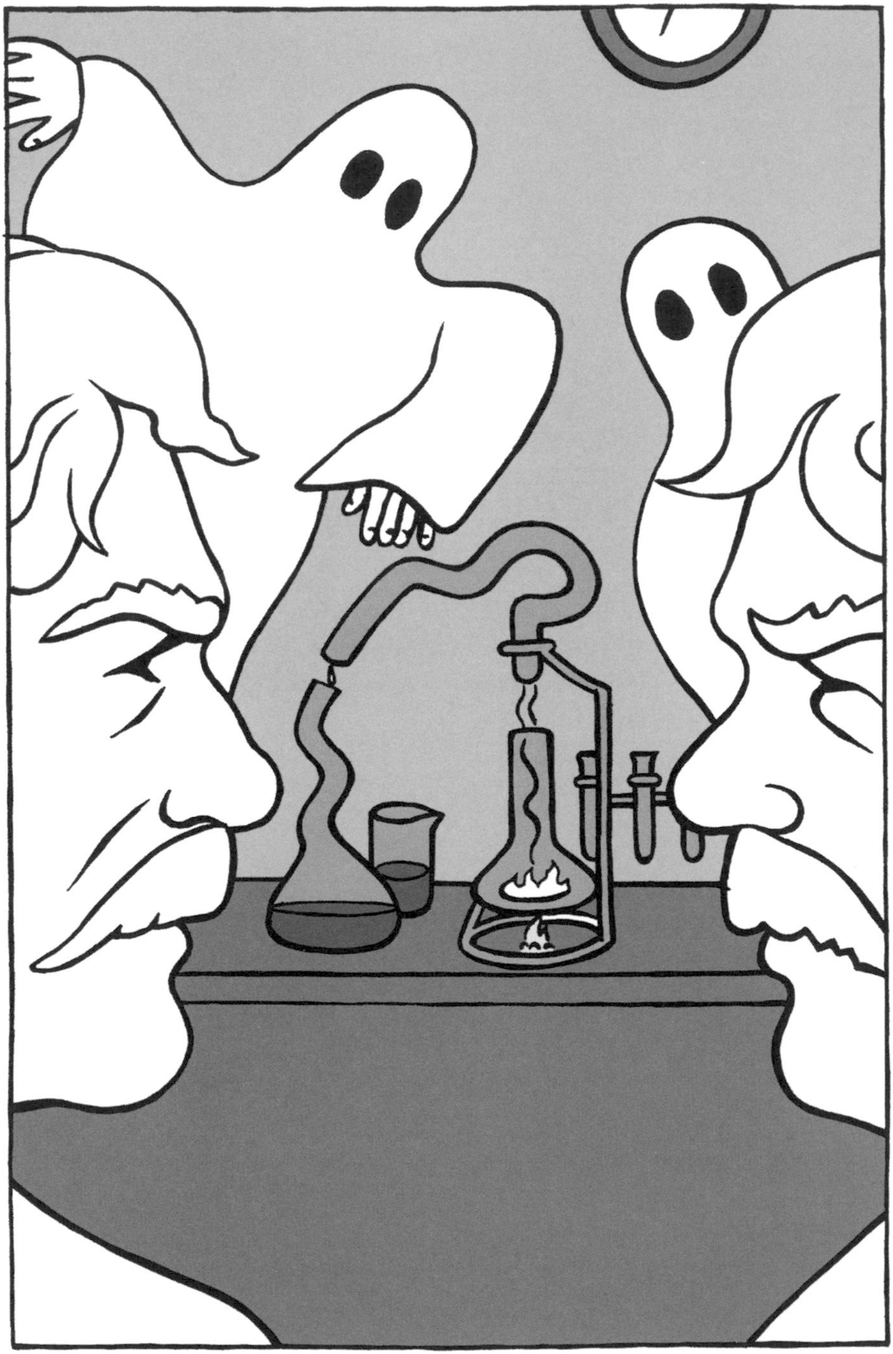

CHAPTER FIFTEEN

A RETURN TO ADVENTURE

It was a pleasant enough existence, but I became restless again and thirsted for adventure. So when a telegram came from my old friend Albert Einstein, asking me to come out to Princeton immediately, I raced out there, hoping there was adventure waiting and ready.

Albert was in the newly opened Nuclear Studies laboratory that the University had just constructed. Everywhere you looked there was fissionable material and sparking electric coils. Al himself seemed agitated. His hair was sticking out at odd angles, more than normal, and his eyes seemed to pop out of his face, about the same as they always did. He greeted me effusively: "Thank God you've come!"

"Thank him later," I replied. "What's the hubbub?" But as I spoke I could see diaphanous shapes rising from behind equipment amid dry ice steam, and the problem was obvious: the lab was haunted! "You have experience in these matters, help me please," begged Al. The situation was serious. If those spooks had gotten their hands on certain implements in that lab they could've blown up half of New Jersey, and not the half that needs it. C'mon, I'm kidding.

"Was this lab built over a graveyard?" I asked Al, who shrugged. I observed the ghosts—there were two of them—as they crept and swayed closer, their unearthly moans chilling my ear. They didn't look Native American, which was a relief (they are very hard to get rid of). But then I noticed something: a tag on one of the ghosts that said MADE IN CHINA. I snatched at it and pulled, and found I was holding a sheet! Revealed underneath, still swaying and moaning because he didn't realize the sheet had been pulled, was none other than singer/actor/comedian Dean Martin. I knew then that the other sheet must conceal his partner Jerry Lewis. They were sheepish now that they had been discovered, in what turned out to be a promotional stunt for their latest film. "We're sorry," pleaded Jerry. "You could've blown up the entire world!" raged Al, exaggerating a little. "Save the clowning for the movies, boys," I advised them. "Don't do it in any more nuclear labs, it isn't safe." They slunk off, suitably chastised, and returned to Hollywood.

"Well, Al, since I'm here and the crisis is over, shall we have an adventure?" I asked. He agreed, although he was still a little PO'd at Martin and Lewis. "Okay, but what shall we do?" "Let's travel through time," I suggested. "Do you have any cudgels?"

As I discovered back in the 19th Century, the human head is the ultimate time machine, when struck in exactly the right way. A blow to the skull, administered properly, will send the skull's owner spiraling backwards through the centuries; he will return automatically when the bashing has worn off. Al recruited the lab chimp, Professor McSmelly, to give us the necessary bonk on the heads with a pair of mallets, which he would wield simultaneously, being ambidextrous as most chimps are. We gathered together some necessary items (I brought a flashlight in case we ended up in the Dark Ages), and as we did it discussed where we might like to go. "I would like to visit Copernicus," said Al. "Well, I want to meet Cleopatra," I said. Of course, this discussion was pointless, as we had little-to-no control over where we went; the best we could hope for was that the chimp would strike both of our heads precisely at the same millisecond, and therefore send us both to the same time zone.

We sat with our backs turned to the lab table on which Professor McSmelly squatted, holding his hammers. "Ready?" Al asked. "Okay! One... two... three!" and the mallets came down. There was a flash of intense pain in my noggin, and then I was falling, falling... falling... and I blacked out.

Consciousness returned slowly, and I opened my woozy eyes. "Ugh!" I heard from close by, and looked over to see Al, tangled in a mulberry bush. Well, the landing might have been a bit rough, but that chimp had done his work like a true professional, and we had landed together. I pulled him out of the bush, and we dusted ourselves off and tried to figure out where we were.

We heard voices nearby, and crawled closer that we might scope out the situation before we revealed ourselves. What we saw amazed us: we were apparently in the seventeenth century, because a young man in

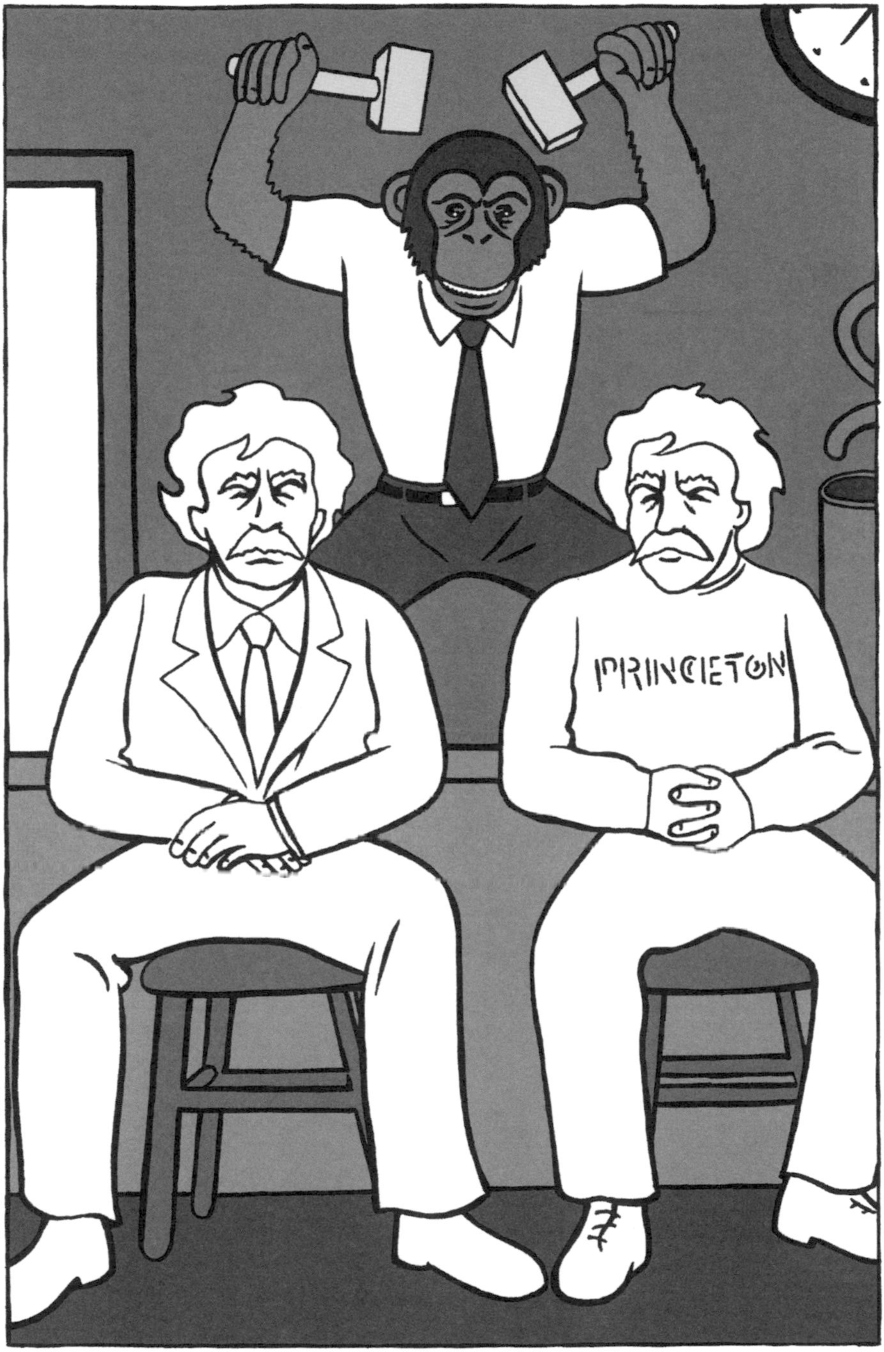
PRINCETON

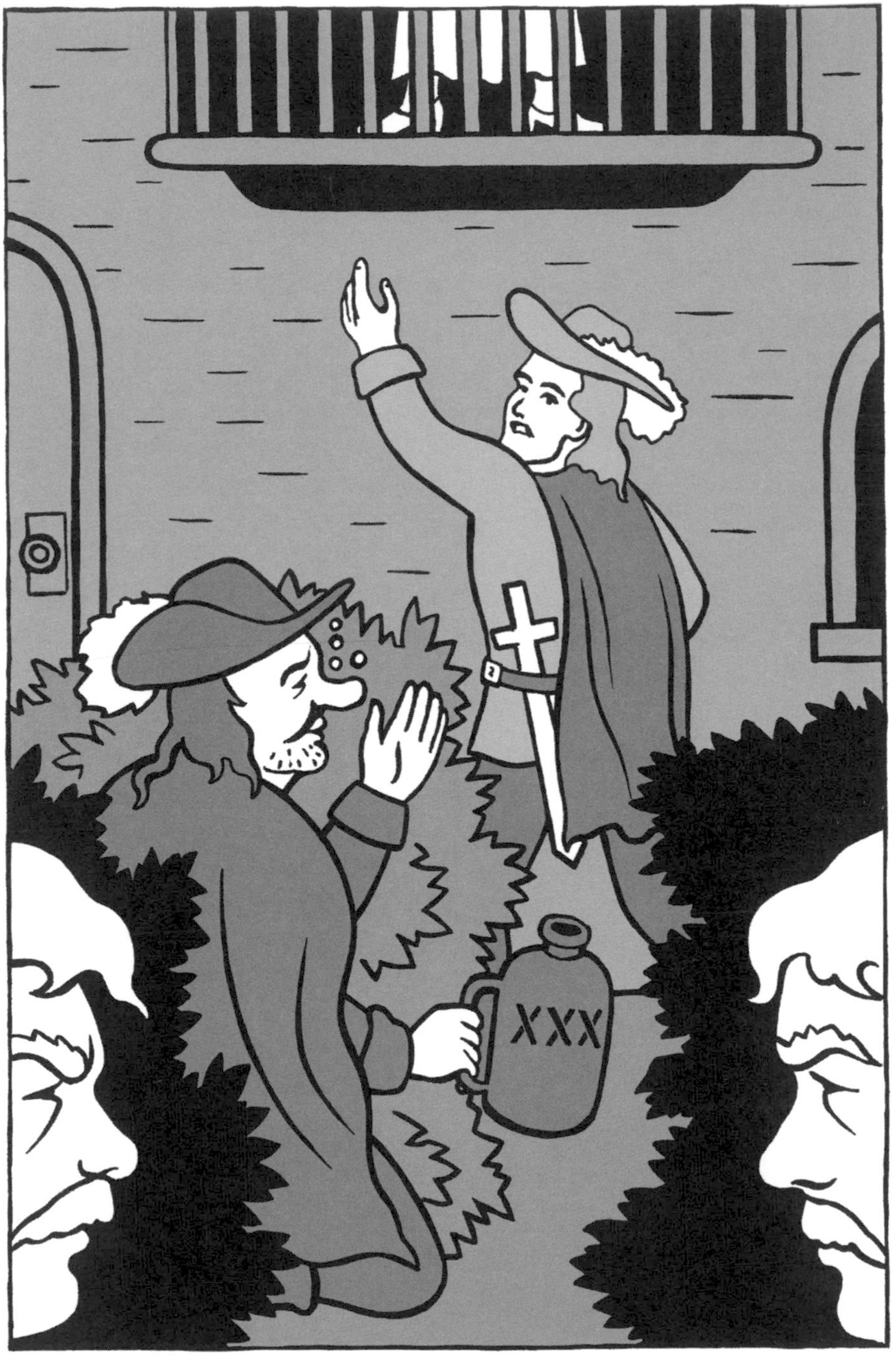
XXX

French musketeer-style getup was shouting up at a fancy balcony. Close to us, an older but similarly dressed man with an enormous nose was crouching behind a bush, his attention on the other man. As a woman appeared at the balcony, both men stiffened with tension. "Say hello to her!" hissed the man behind the bush. "Hello!" shouted the other man. We realized then that we were watching Cyrano De Bergerac coach his friend as he wooed a lady, a scene which has been immortalized in countless plays and movies. What an opportunity!

"Tell her she's got a swell butt!" slurred Cyrano, and we realized he was drunk. "This is terrible!" I hissed to Al. "This is supposed to be an immortal love scene, and he's crocked! He's messing it up!" And it wasn't going well. "Tell her you like her legs and her nose, and most of the bits in between, you like 'em lots," offered Cyrano. "We've got to do something," muttered Al.

I decided to make my move. Crawling stealthily over to Cyrano, I got behind him and put him to sleep by pinching his nose with my hand over his mouth. He started snoring and I took his place. I'm not the most romantic of writers but still I knew I could do better than him. "My sweet love, your lithesome form sends me trembling with delight," I whispered, and the other guy never noticed the substitution, but repeated it all, and she liked it too, I could tell. "More like that!" he hissed at me, and I did my best to oblige. "My sweet love, how I long to sing of thee in a flower of rainbows, and let our love decorate the stars in a multitude of honeyed embraces," etc.

I succeeded in my mission, and the lucky guy scrambled up the vines to get his reward. I watched the lights go out and turned to Al. "It's good to be able to help, but what now?" he asked. "Let's travel further backwards in time," I suggested, producing two mallets. "We'll do each other," but just then there was a sound of fearsome moans, and we saw a couple of people burst into view who were walking and definitely dead. Zombies!

"Cyrano and zombies, eh?" remarked Al. "Interesting." "Think as a scientist, Al," I begged. "What makes zombies? What could have caused this?" He furrowed his brow in thought. "An asteroid, or an alien beam… Since this is the past, maybe a wizard did this."

We watched, helpless, as the zombies shuffled closer. "Looks like we're finally both going to get eaten…" I said as calmly as I could. "Any famous last words?" "You're the writer—help me out with a pithy epitaph!" muttered Al piteously. And then we heard a voice shout out: "CUT!"

"Al, we're in a movie!" I pointed out. Now that we realized that, we were able to notice the lights, boom mikes, reflective screens, camera crane, and other movie paraphernalia we had somehow not noticed. The director was peering at a script. "Wait—was any of that the way it was supposed to be? I didn't know Twain and Einstein were in this film!"

It turned out that Professor McSmelly had not hit us hard enough to send us backwards through time, only enough to render us unconscious. Panicking, he had transported us in Al's station wagon to the nearby Filmatic Studios lot, where he had dumped us behind some scenery. We were examined by the studio doctor who insisted on x-raying our heads and advised us to lay off the time travel for a while.

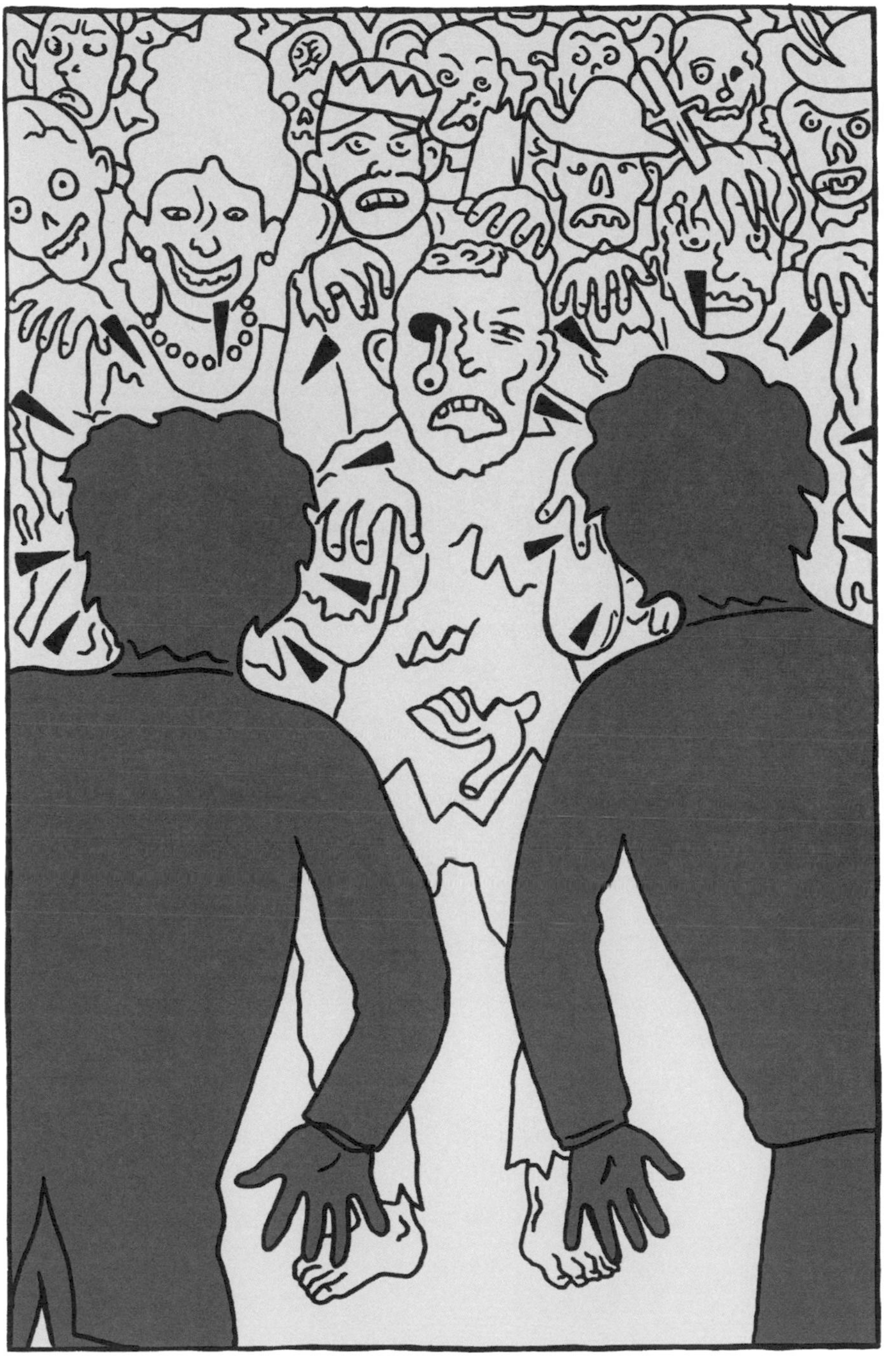

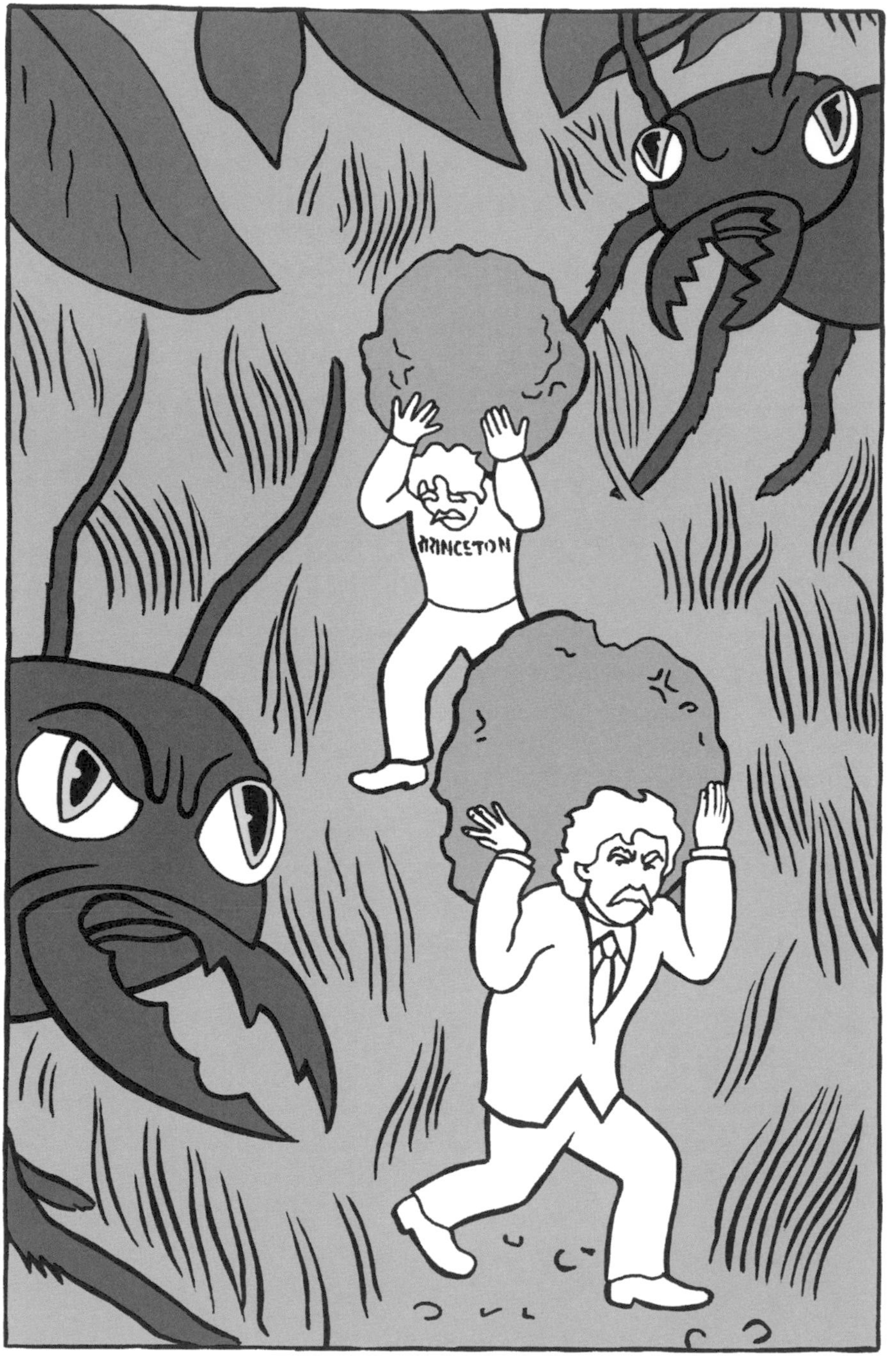

PRINCETON

CHAPTER SIXTEEN

ANT I AM TELLING YOU

Another time Al mixed a potion that was supposed to make us more energetic, so we could impress some girls that taught aerobics at the local community center. We drank down the so-called "supergoo," and suddenly we found ourselves shrinking downwards in size! When we started the ants in the grass were as insignificant to us as ants, but soon we were tiny enough so that those ants looked quite menacing! We quickly agreed to do their bidding, and spent the next few hours struggling under the weight of the crumbs they had ordered us to carry hither and thither. "The way that these ants are directing us to carry these crumbs is giving me some new theories," said Al. "If atoms travelled in the way these crumbs do, the resulting affect could be to make atomic structures tighter." As usual, he won a Nobel prize for this when we unshrunk. But first there was a lot more we had to go through.

When our day's work carrying crumbs around had ended we were led to a row of huts where the shrunken human workers were kept. "You are the first, soon maybe more will join us," chittered the headman in his ant tongue. I pointed out that what had happened with us was a pretty unlikely accident, and that we would probably be going back to our usual giant (to him) sizes, and he had better keep that in mind, lest he tempt our enormous, stampy feet. He blustered and threatened to whip me, but I could tell I had him cowed.

Later, after dinner, one of the native ant girls snuck into my hut. I was prepared to make love to her but then it turned out she had an agenda. "Take me with you," she entreated me. Make me your human-size ant wife." I told her I'd think about it, but I couldn't see being married to an enormous ant as something that would work out—society's just not ready.

The next morning we ate a big ant breakfast—two flea eggs, midge sausage, ant-sized toast, ant coffee—and then it was back to work. Al and I milked the centipedes, slopped out the termites, and swept the ant barn till it was spotless. But as lunchtime approached we could tell our regrowth was imminent. All the ants came to say goodbye. "Remember to… always remember," whispered the King Ant. It wasn't very eloquent but c'mon, he's an ant.

The experience deepened my understanding of what ants go through, and gave me a lasting appreciation of ant culture. It made me quite sympathetic with the ant cause, and whenever I see a crumb I move it around in a way that I think is what they might want.

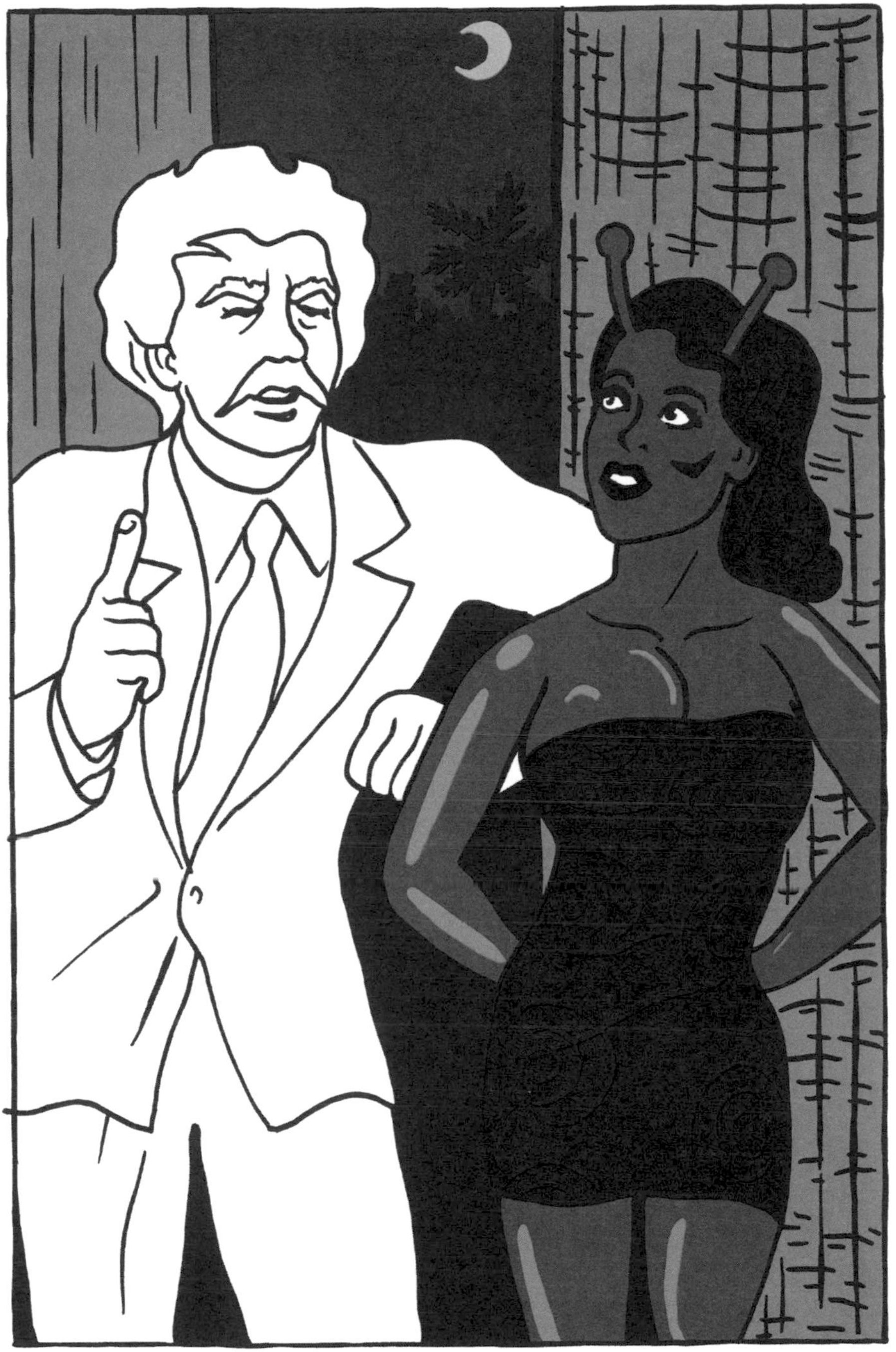

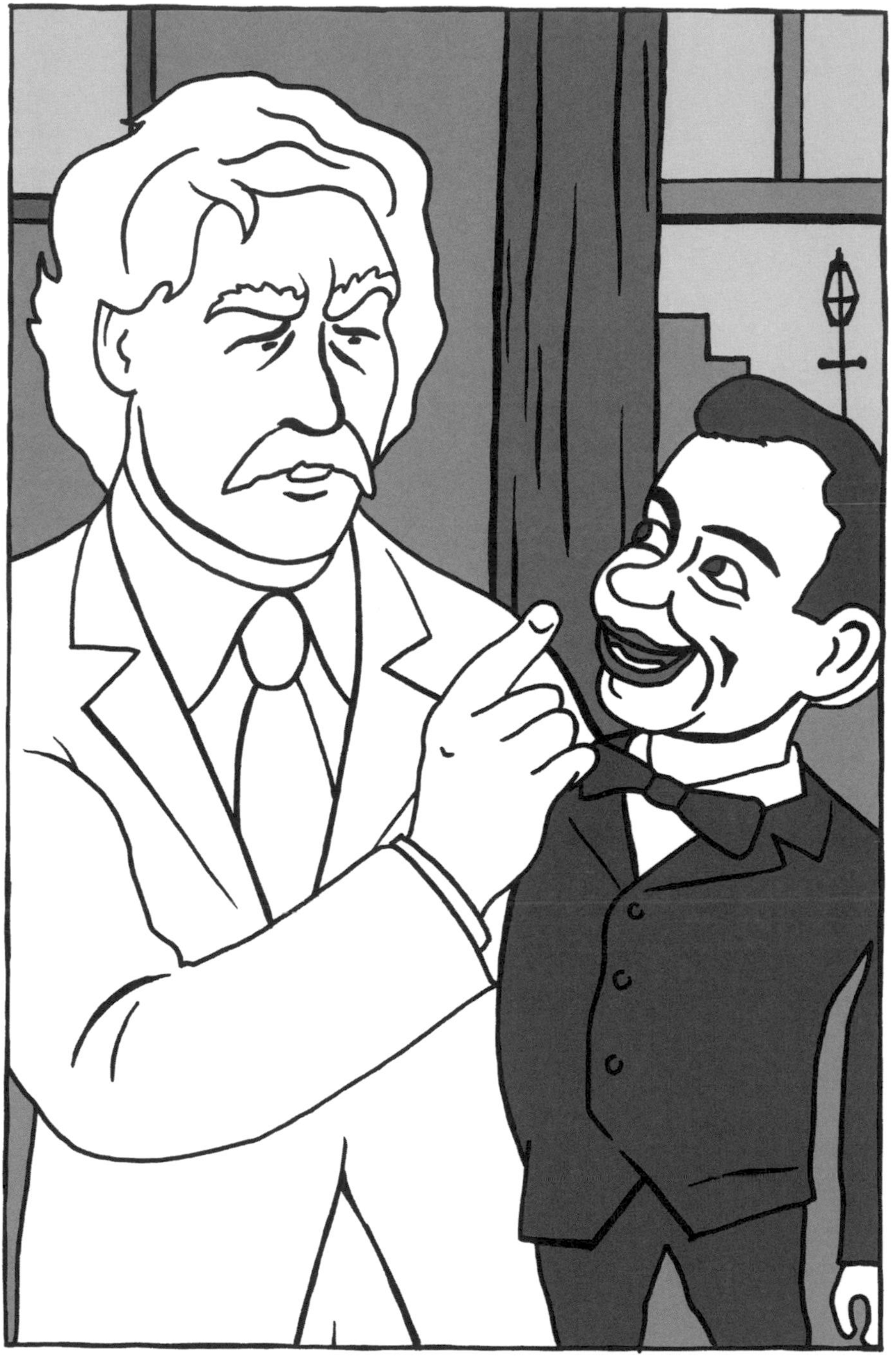

CHAPTER SEVENTEEN:

DUMMYWOOD GAGYLON

1952 saw me considering a change of career, once again. The newspaper had a big ad, VENTRILOQUISTS WANTED, so I went down to the address listed and inquired after employment. "You have no experience? Here, take this" said the man behind the desk, handing me a box. "Come back here in a week and show me how good you've gotten." "I will," I said, and I ran home to open the box. Inside was a ventriloquist's dummy, its mouth frozen in an eternal wooden grimace. I immediately closed the box and went out to a bar for seven hours.

When I came back the box hadn't moved. I wasn't too steady on my feet at this point but I lurched over and pulled the dummy out of the box. "I'm not frightened of you!" I shouted. "You don't scare me a bit!" But I knew it knew I was lying. Throwing it to the floor, I ran to the bathroom where I locked myself in and slept in the tub.

When I awoke the dummy was still where I had thrown it. Cleaning myself up, I resolved to be more mature and approach this problem with fortitude. I snuck up on the dummy and tied it up with baling twine. "You work for me now, there'll be no murderous shenanigans," I said through gritted teeth. Still he made no response. I pulled him over to a chair and sat with him on my lap. It was time to rehearse.

"Ladies and Gentlemen, meet my little friend Woody," I pronounced. "Say hello to the folks, Woody." I swear, as God is my witness, he said nothing and made no movement. Nothing! "You say hello now!" I screamed, helpless with fury, and tried to beat him up, only to realize I was beating up my own hand. The true horror dawned on me: I would have to make the mannequin appear to talk, by moving my hand within it and simulating a voice to answer my own, because it refused to do so itself! I did relax some when I realized how lazy the puppet was. Surely it was too phlegmatic to attack me.

A week later I was back at the ventriloquist employee agency carry-ing Woody proudly on my arm. "Come in," said the man behind the desk, but I was already inside, and I launched into my act with no preamble. The man behind the desk seemed impressed, but took off points for the excessive sexual vulgarity with which I'd decorated the dummy's responses. "Don't swear so much and you should be okay" he said. He then sent me to do my act down a coal mine shaft in Western Pennsylvania.

Doing ventriloquism at the bottom of a mine shaft was exhausting, filthy work. Bent almost double at times, running after miners shouting punchlines in two haggard voices as they rolled around in their little carts. I never found out why coal miners had requested a ventriloquist, but it was at least a way for me to hone my craft. Next I was transferred to a lighthouse, where I rotated in twelve-hour shifts with another vent. When a ship approached too close we were required to get on the radio and do our act, while at the same time warning them of imminent crashiness. Performing ventriloquism over squawky, scratchy radios while men shout angrily at you as they are tossed about by waves, those are tough performance conditions.

Having caused no accidents at my first two postings, I was promoted upwards, landing an actual nightclub gig for the first time. I performed five times a night at the Swollen Orangutang in Miasma, New Jersey, in between a jazz singer, a knife sharpener, and a ballet dancer. Less things were thrown at the stage during my act than during the others, so I continued to move up the ventriloquism booking ladder, getting three half-hours a night at Sloppy's in Bridgeport, Connecticut.

I was so popular at Sloppy's that I became their most successful act ever. By now I had such skill with the dummy—which had still never moved nor spoke—that many in the audience believed me to be a wizard who had enslaved an intelligent piece of wood. Leaving before this madness went too far, I was then told by the agency to proceed to Eastern Europe, Prague to be exact, where I would take residence at the Hotel Suicidé and wait for further instructions. All necessary visas and clearances had been arranged.

At that time Eastern Europe was groaning under the weight of being oppressed by being part of the Soviet Union, which was the worst union that has ever existed. Everything was grim and gray, and no-one smiled and everyone called you "comrade." My passport was examined cautiously

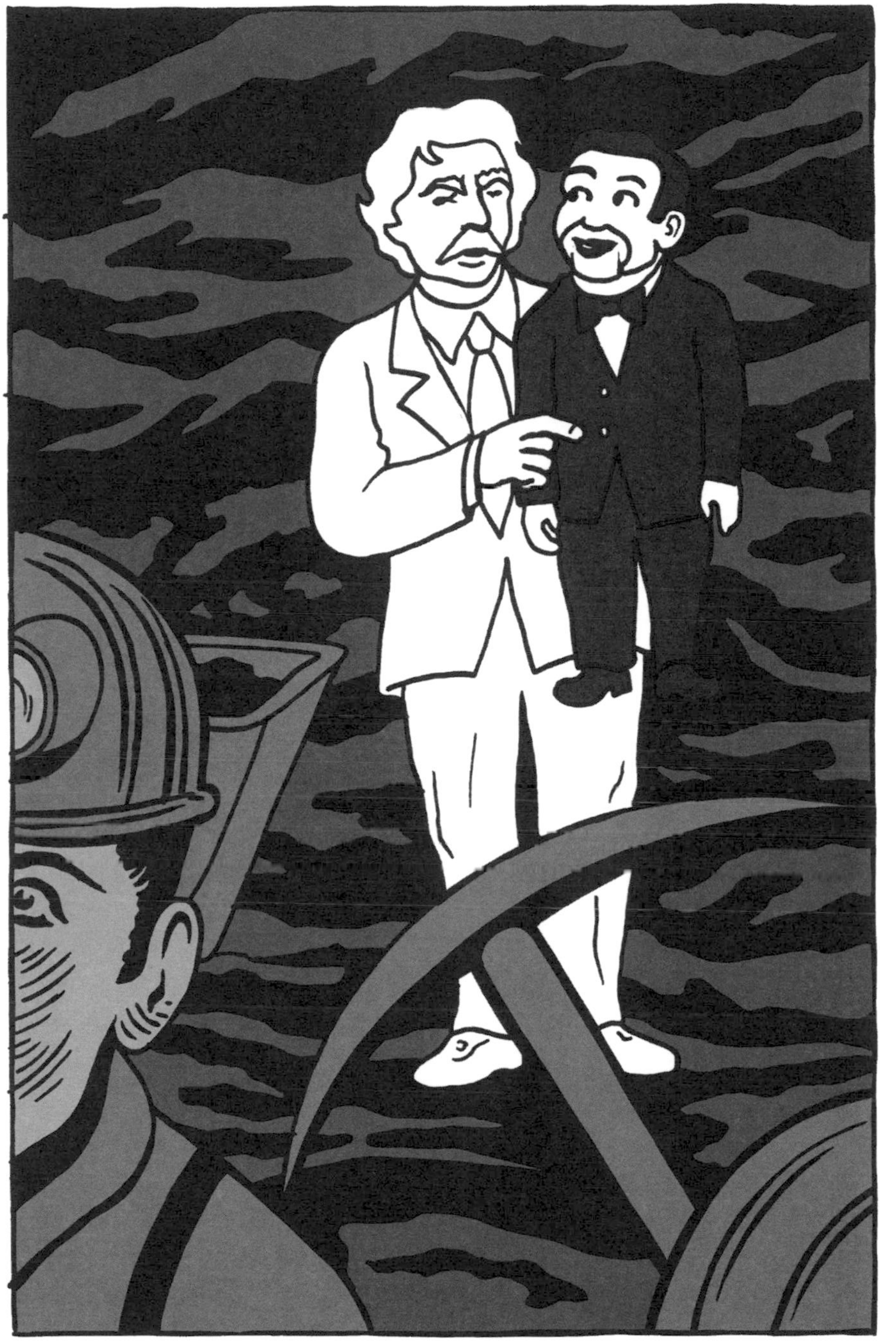

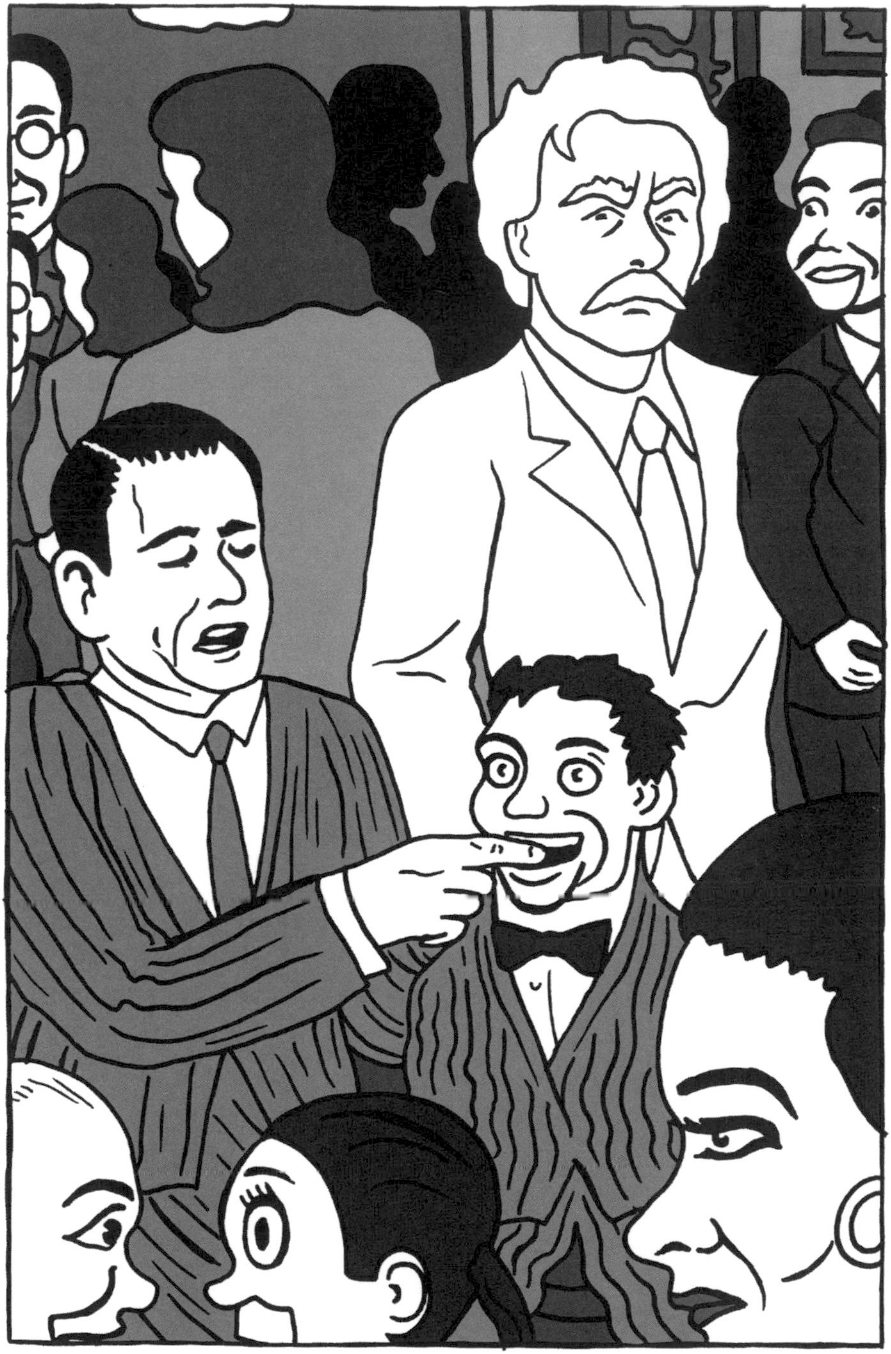

at the border, and then they opened my dummy case. I did about twenty minutes of my act for them before they begged me to be on my way.

My cab led me down side streets, away from the sunlit expanse of central Prague into a darker, more shadowy area. I had none of the local currency with me and was forced to give him an entire bag of pistachios in payment. It was quite a large bag, as I had been hoping to use pistachios as tips and bribes. Nevertheless, I had reached my destination. I entered and was astonished by what I saw. Everyone in the place, from the bellboys to the desk captain to the guests, every single one of them—everyone was a ventriloquist. There wasn't a person in the place who wasn't toting their own dummy. It was a hotel run by ventriloquists, catering exclusively to those of us in the trade!

At first I was delighted, and sought to strike up acquaintances in the hotel bar. But the other vents were chilly, refusing to engage their dummies in conversation with mine. I remained genial, though I did allow Woody to lose his temper once or twice. Still, I was about to depart upstairs to my room when I felt a hand on my shoulder. I turned to face the grayest man I have ever seen, holding the grayest dummy I have ever seen on his elbow. "The dove flies south on weekends to roost with the duck, or so they say," he said. I realized that this was the code password that identified the man as my new employer, and that I was supposed to reply with a phrase of my own. Unfortunately I had swallowed the code before properly memorizing it, and thus struggled to recall what it was. "Something about a pig that… has to go its own way," I finished lamely. My new friend was displeased. "That is not the phrase!' he hissed. "I don't believe you are who you say you are!" I was offended. "Well, if you disbelieve in my existence, I shall disbelieve in yours," I retorted, and we retired to separate corners of the bar, where we glared at each other over steaming mugs of brandy. Finally he came over again several hours later. "I shuppose I have no choish but to ackshept that you are who you say you are," he conceded. He was pretty drunk at that point, but so was I. "Thatsh the shpirit," I replied.

We both had coffee and sobered up. He told me that I was now under the management of the famous Doubletalk Agency, which handled bookings for ventriloquists all over the world. "No longer, Mister Twain, will you work in coal mines. Only the finest nightclubs for you." There was one requirement: I had to attend a ventriloquist "finishing course" at a school outside of Blostivostok.

The next morning a bus took myself and seven other ventriloquists from the hotel to a brick building out in the woods somewhere, where we joined fourteen others. For the next two days we were tested on our abilities and nightclub abilities, and at night we relaxed and watched ventriloquist movies like *The Magnificent Fourteen* or *Twenty-Four Angry Men*. On the third day, the instruction centered on athletic ability and combat training; we learned how to kill a man in secret ventriloquist ways, and how to throw our voices in new and dramatic fashions. That night, we were all treated to a spinning wheel and a voice telling us to "submit and obey." Then a sinister man in a monocle came out and told us that during our acts, we had to recite code that he would plant in our subconsciouses. "This will help us to sink America's foolish submarines!" he exulted, and my fellow vents cheered, because they were all hypnotized. I excused myself to urinate, trying to look as if I was hypnotized also. "There is Man's Room right there!" he pointed out, pointing to the toilet door. "Whenever possible, I take the opportunity to urinate on Nature!" I insisted. He seemed satisfied with this argument, and I slipped out into the night. As I approached some nearby trees, a figure stepped out from behind them... it was none other than the head of the FBI, J. Edgar Hoover. "Hello, Mister Twain," he said.

"It's just like we thought, Mister Hoover—they're spies." I had been undercover for the FBI all along! His eyes glinted over his enormous cigar. "Time to round them up." He whistled and a half-dozen FBI men appeared from the bushes and scurried over. "Arrest everyone in the house—they're all Commies!" The agents prepared to do his bidding but I stopped them all by clearing my throat. "Excuse me, Mister Hoover, but isn't this a Communist country, and not America at all? We're probably in danger of being arrested ourselves." Sure enough, a voice suddenly sounded through a loudhailer: "American freedom scum, you are all under arrest!" We all ran, Hoover and me and the other agents, and we made it over the border just ahead of the communist guards and their barking dogs. Once we were on the other side of that dotted line, we felt free and thumbed our noses at the furious and impotent Eastern Bloc thugs.

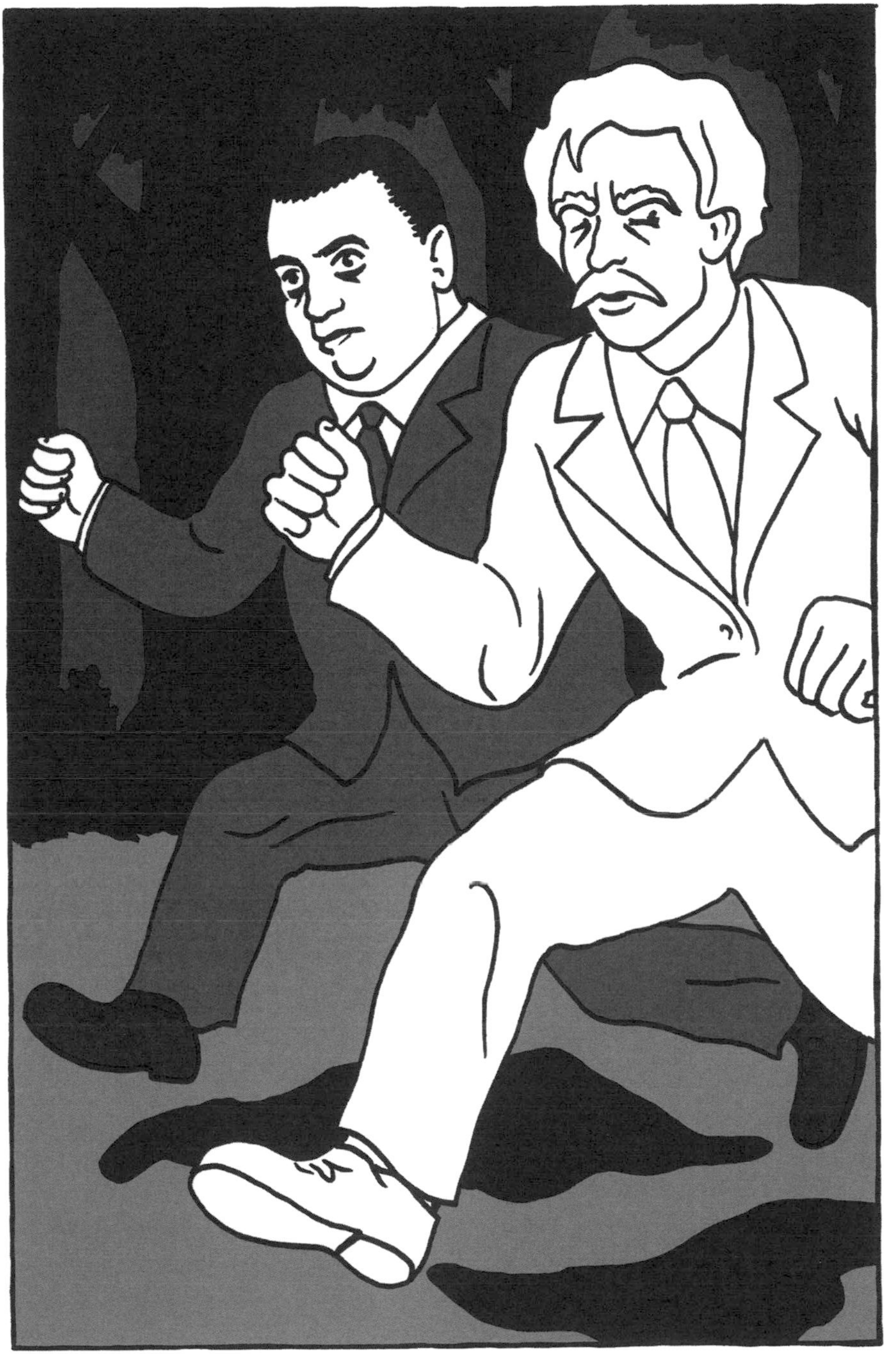

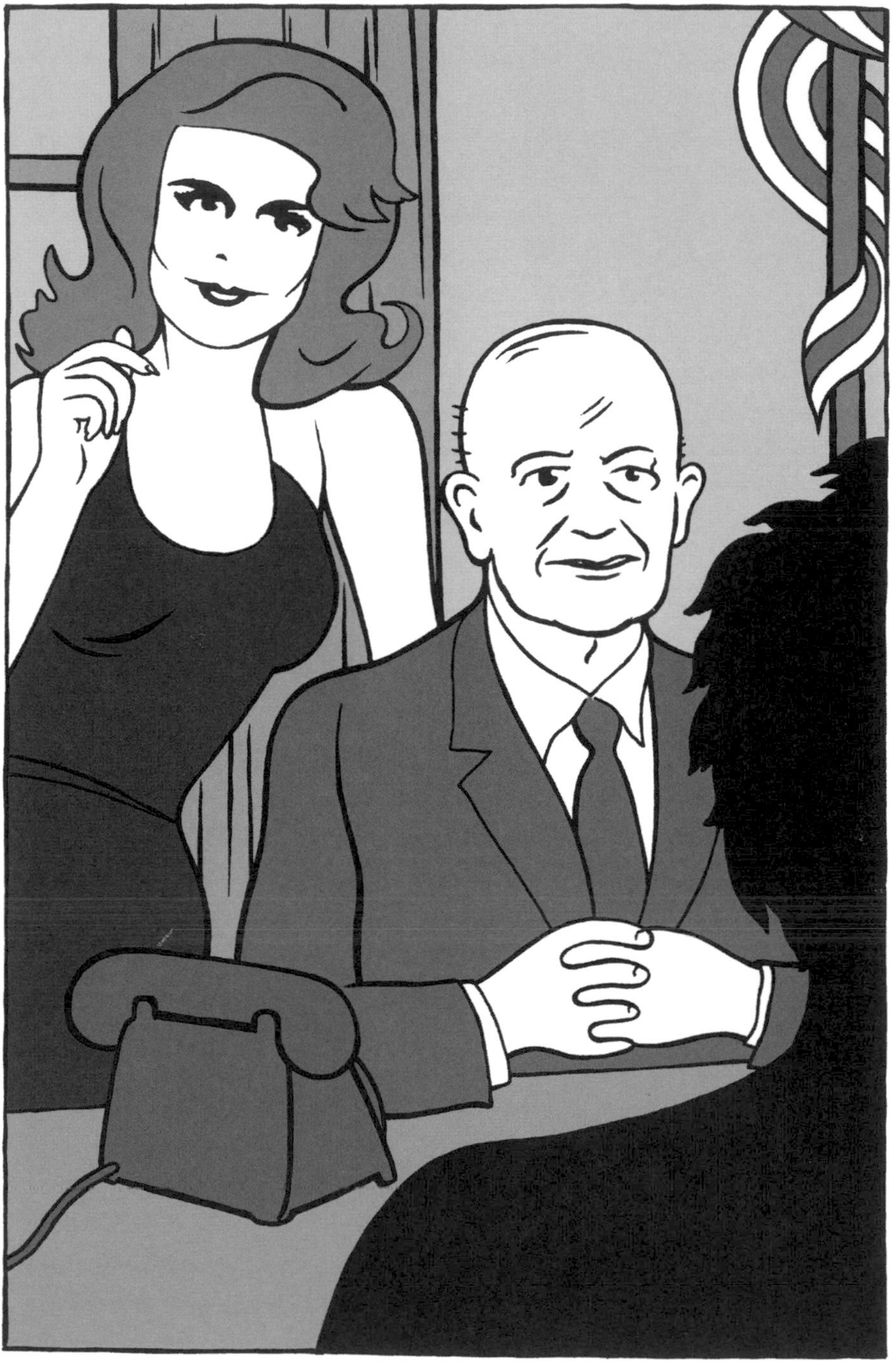

CHAPTER EIGHTEEN

THE FRONTIEST FRONTIER

Back in America, we quickly arrested the whole ventriloquist espionage ring. I continued my spy-busting efforts for the FBI, and I was involved with the rounding-up of many other novelty entertainment acts. And then, in 1958, I was summoned to the White House, at the special request of reigning President Isaac "Ike" Eisenhower. I found him seated in the Oval Office, and, following the pleasantries, he got to the point. "Mister Twain— Mark— I don't know if you heard, but we're in something called The Satellite Age. All kinds of satellites are going up in orbit, not just military or scientific government ones, but businesses and corporations are starting to set up operations up there too. It's a new wild west, right above our heads in the aether! Any kind of funny business might be going on. I need an independent operator—someone with real sharp eyes, and a sharp brain to match—to go up there and check things out. Will you do this for me. Mister Twain?"

"Of course I will, Mister President. You may count on my discretion," I said, and then the office door opened and the most gorgeous woman I have ever seen walked in.

Ike greeted her familiarly, and I realized she was his wife, Mame. Boy oh boy, this lady was one hot dish. "C'mere, baby," said the President, and I jealously seethed in my breast as she sat in his lap and they made out for a bit. Then Ike turned back to me. "Excuse me, Mister Twain, where are my manners? I was hoping you would be our guest here tonight before heading into orbit tomorrow." As he was speaking, Mame and I made eye contact, and it was as if an electric shock had passed through my body. I could tell she was feeling the same way. All through dinner we played footsie while Ike droned on about grain subsidies and National Guard deployments, oblivious to the erotic energy that was building up under the table. Later she tiptoed into my room while here husband lay sleeping and we consummated our lusting attraction. I loved helping my country but now I helped myself to great big hot helpings of wonderful Mame.

The next morning, exhausted from all the sex, I prepared to blast into space. It was hard behaving normally at breakfast, though somehow I managed, and then I walked into the rocket that was waiting on the White House lawn. It had been designed for monkeys, and the controls were very simple, although the only food to eat was bananas, and you had to press a button twenty times to get one. As I shot into space my mind was full of Mame, and I wrote poetry about her in my brain. So many words rhymed with her name: name, of course, and blame, game, frame, maim, tame, came, same... The list goes on... claim, flame, lame, dame, and more. Also reclaim, and reframe. I longed for my return to Earth and a return to Mame's wonderful charms.

Once I was up in Space, I put the parking brake on the rocket and went out in my space suit to look around. There were quite a few satellites scattered around and I went round to check them out. The first one I knocked at and nobody answered; but there was smoke coming from a chimney, and I could spot a still behind the ramshackle space hutch. It seemed that space-age moonshiners had figured out a new way to outwit the revenuers! The next satellite had some dogs in it, and the next after that some monkeys; I made a note to call the space branch of the SPCA. Then there was a swanky one that had been set up by some senators to house their mistresses, away from prying eyes; I joined the ladies for lunch and we made pleasant conversation, until I regretfully took their leave and stepped back into space. But the final satellite was a surprise; the door swung open easily, and inside there was a modest garden store, with potted plants, spades, and gnomes all on display. A young woman was working behind the counter, and as I approached she seemed nervous. "May I help you, sir?" she quavered.

I quizzed her as to why there was a garden store up in orbit, and she explained that it had been set up to cater to all the satellite gardens which were going to be springing up in the next few years. "We're a little early, I guess," she murmured, and then she made an almost imperceptible nod towards the curtain at the back of the room. I drew my pistol and moved towards it. "Well, that's very interesting," I said, keeping my voice steady. "A garden up here will get plenty of sunlight..." I reached

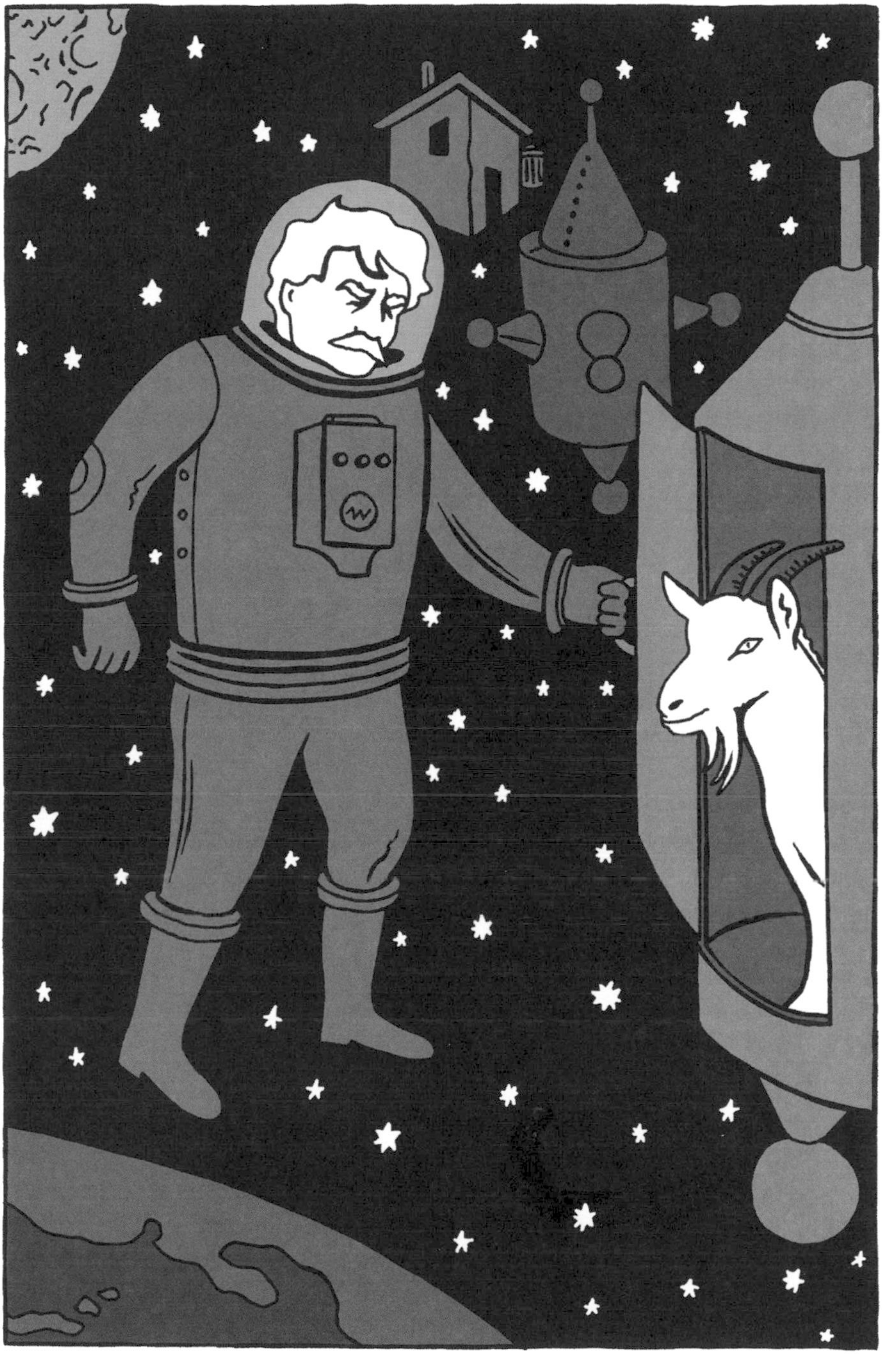

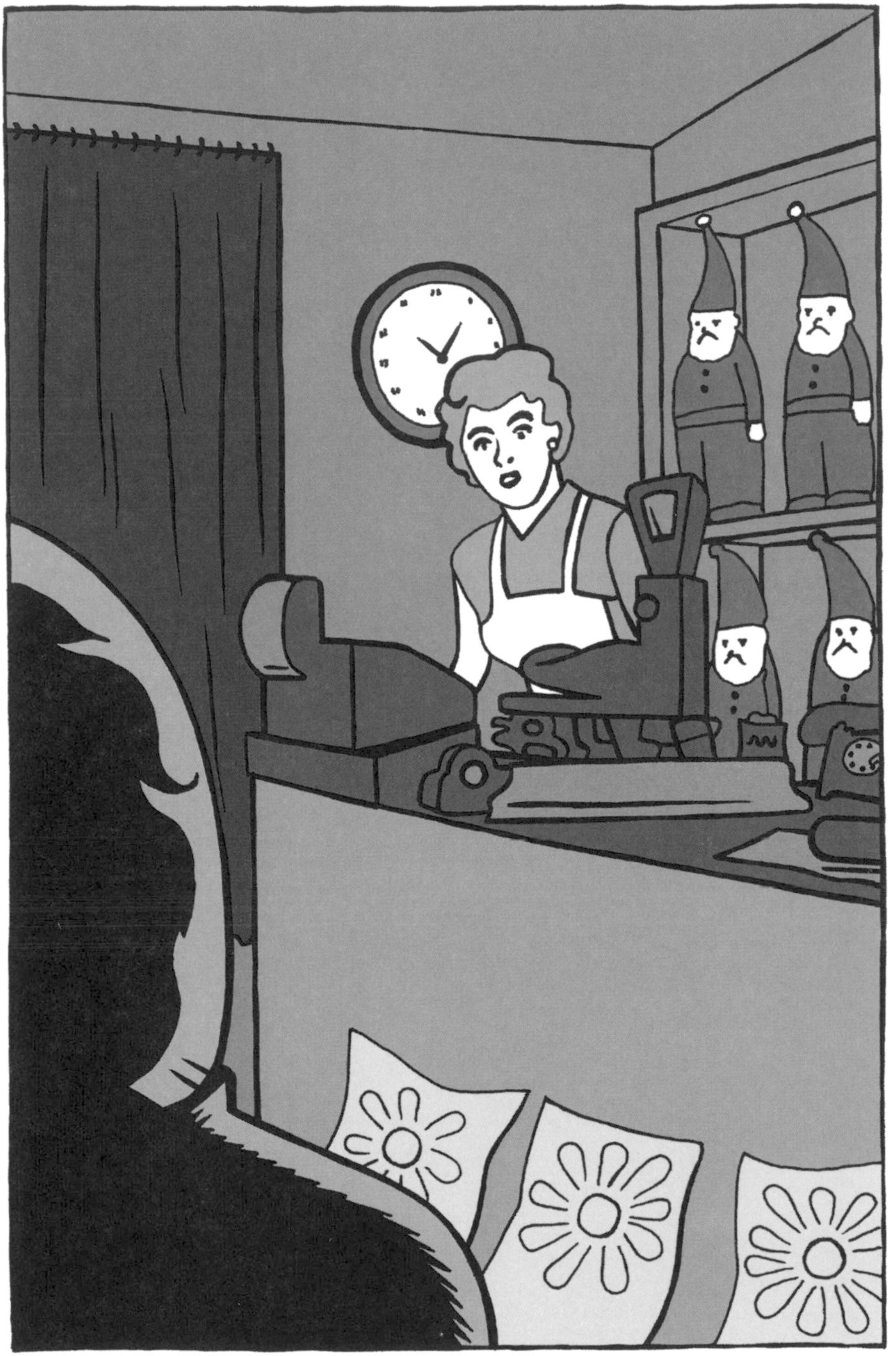

the curtain, and whipping it aside, I leapt into the back of the satellite. There I discovered a Russian thug! He was bent over a telescope which was trained on the Earth, and to my horror, as he stood up in surprise, I recognized the image on the lens: it was my beloved Mame, washing her breasts in lemon juice as she did every day. Little did she know she was being observed from space by an agent of the Kremlin!

Sensing my presence, he turned, and on seeing me his eyes lit up with a cruel glee. He seemed to recognize me, and his space-gloved finger came up to point at me. "Cockamamie!" he sneered, and I realized that he recognized me from his surveillance. "She is wery lovely."

"Get your filthy eyes off her!" I yelled, and in my excitement I got too close to him. His foot lashed out at my wrist, and the gun went spinning, and then he was on me like a thousand pounds of commie ham. We stumbled back through the curtain and backwards through the shop, and as his punches rained on my torso a garden gnome fell off the shelf; the gnome shell disguise fell off, and it was revealed as an atomic bomb. "For dropping on America!" he grinned, and I rammed him in the stomach with my head and we went spinning out the door into orbit. There, in the zero gravity, we faced each other as best we could, and our slow-motion punches bounced each other's helmets and spacesuits. He was the stronger, younger man, though, and he knew it. "I will crush you," he grinned, and he moved relentlessly forwards as I skipped backwards, desperately looking for a tool I could use against him. And then I saw it: a patch of gravity directly behind us. I maneuvered him towards it, and then I jumped backwards just as his massive arms were about to grab me and choke my life out. He stumbled onto the gravity, and then there was a terrible moment before it took effect, when his eyes showed the realization of what had happened, and he cried out: "Nyyyeeet!" he yelled, and then he was moving swiftly downwards, toward the Earth. I stood in orbit and watched as gravity did its terrible work, his body transformed into a smoking meteorite as it hurtled through the Earth's atmosphere. Gravity is like fire, both a friend and an enemy to man.

I loaded all the garden gnome bombs into my rocket, and the young lady too; her name was Marcia Wallace, and she had been kidnapped by the Soviets from Akron, Ohio, to staff their phony garden store. Later she played Bob Newhart's receptionist on *The Bob Newhart Show*. Before we left orbit I succeeded in buying a gallon of good space moonshine from the liquormakers, and wished them luck. Then I returned to the White House, and gave Ike the good news. "That's splendid, Twain," he said, beaming. I didn't tell him about the Russkie spying on his wife's breasts, but I was longing to see them myself.

For the next couple of years Mame Eisenhower and I had a crazy, reckless, off-again and on-again affair, which only ended when she and Ike left the White House in 1960; I was actually caught naked hiding in the Lincoln Bedroom by the Kennedys when they moved in. Luckily Jack, a notorious ladies man, saw the funny side and granted me a pardon and a pair of pants.

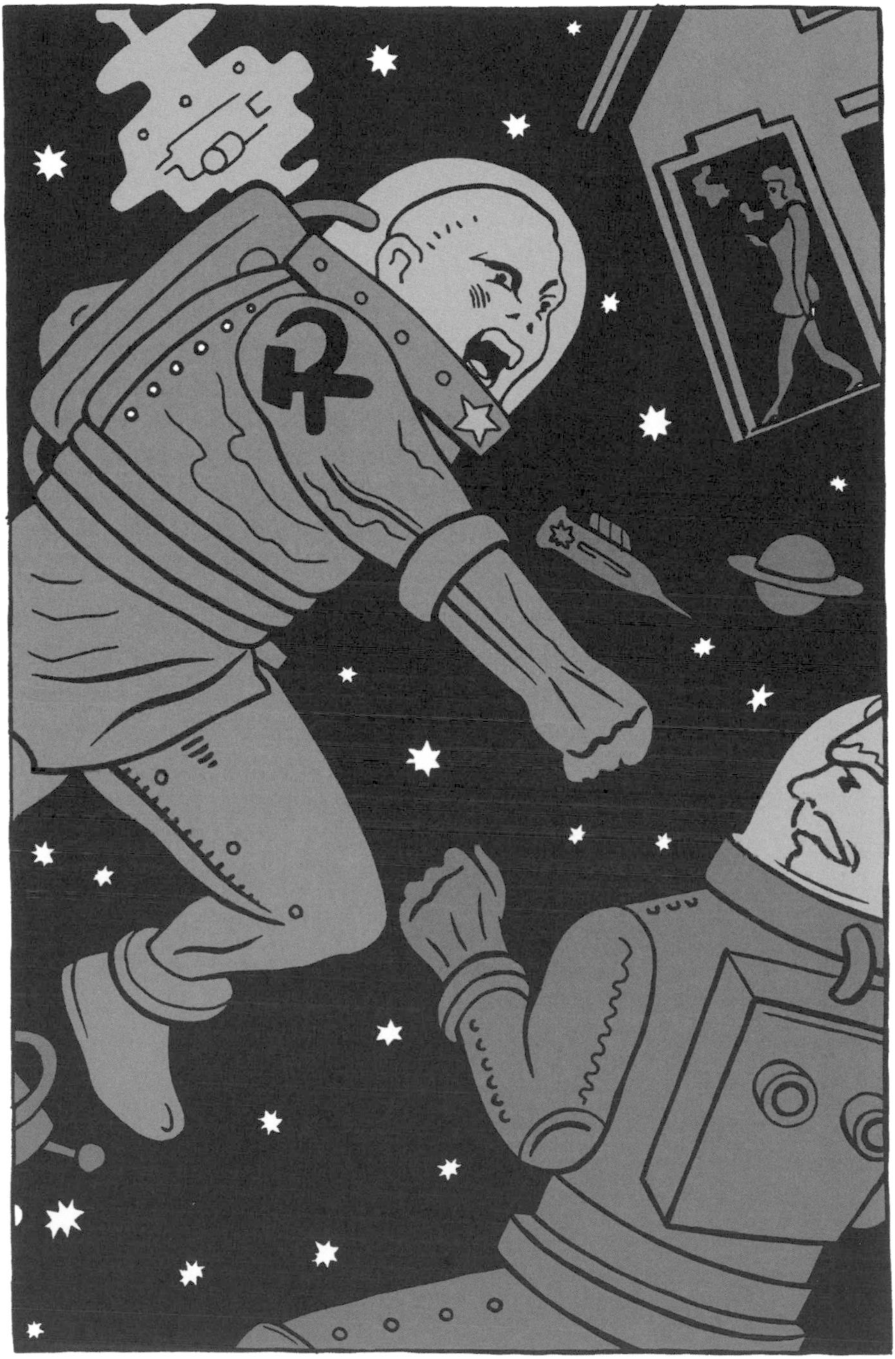

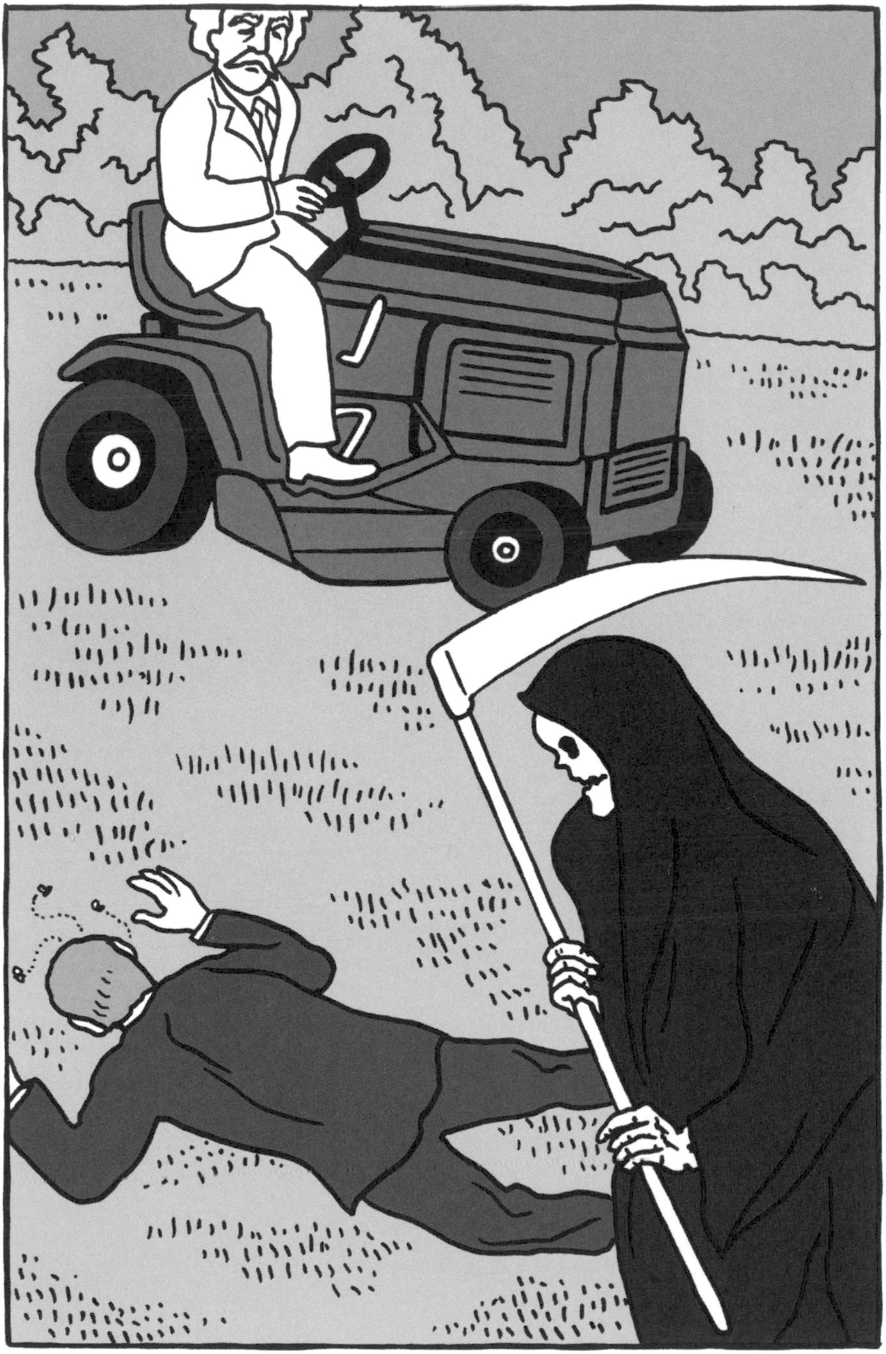

CHAPTER NINETEEN

I'D LIKE TO RETURN THIS GHOST

I had made so much money from advertising that I was able to indulge one of my fondest dreams, and buy a dirigible. Unfortunately, it was haunted, by the ghosts of a Nazi polar expedition team. I returned it to the dealership, and they gave me a blimp in replacement… and that was haunted too!

Products I buy are frequently haunted. All of the refrigerators I've bought have been haunted, several sweaters, five cars, and one thousand three hundred and twenty-seven TV Dinners, all haunted. I ain't afraid'a no ghost (to coin a phrase), but I will give an earful to the complaints department of any business that sells me a haunted appliance. And don't get me started on used furniture, which is so often cursed it should be regulated by some sort of supernatural governing body. I'm tired of chuckling beds and mirrors that show you being murdered, and I think the great American public must be, too.

Recently I purchased a riding lawn mower, and it didn't take long before I noticed that the Headless Horseman was appearing every time I started the engine, and every time he appeared he claimed another victim with his enormous scythe. I tried not to start and re-start the engine too many times after noticing this, but the phone kept ringing and I have a huge lawn. Now the mower couldn't get to all of it because of the corpses. Not worth the time or effort—I rate the Ridecut™ Haunted Riding Mower two stars out of a possible five. (Internet product reviews allow me to express my frustration with supernaturally saturated merchandise.)

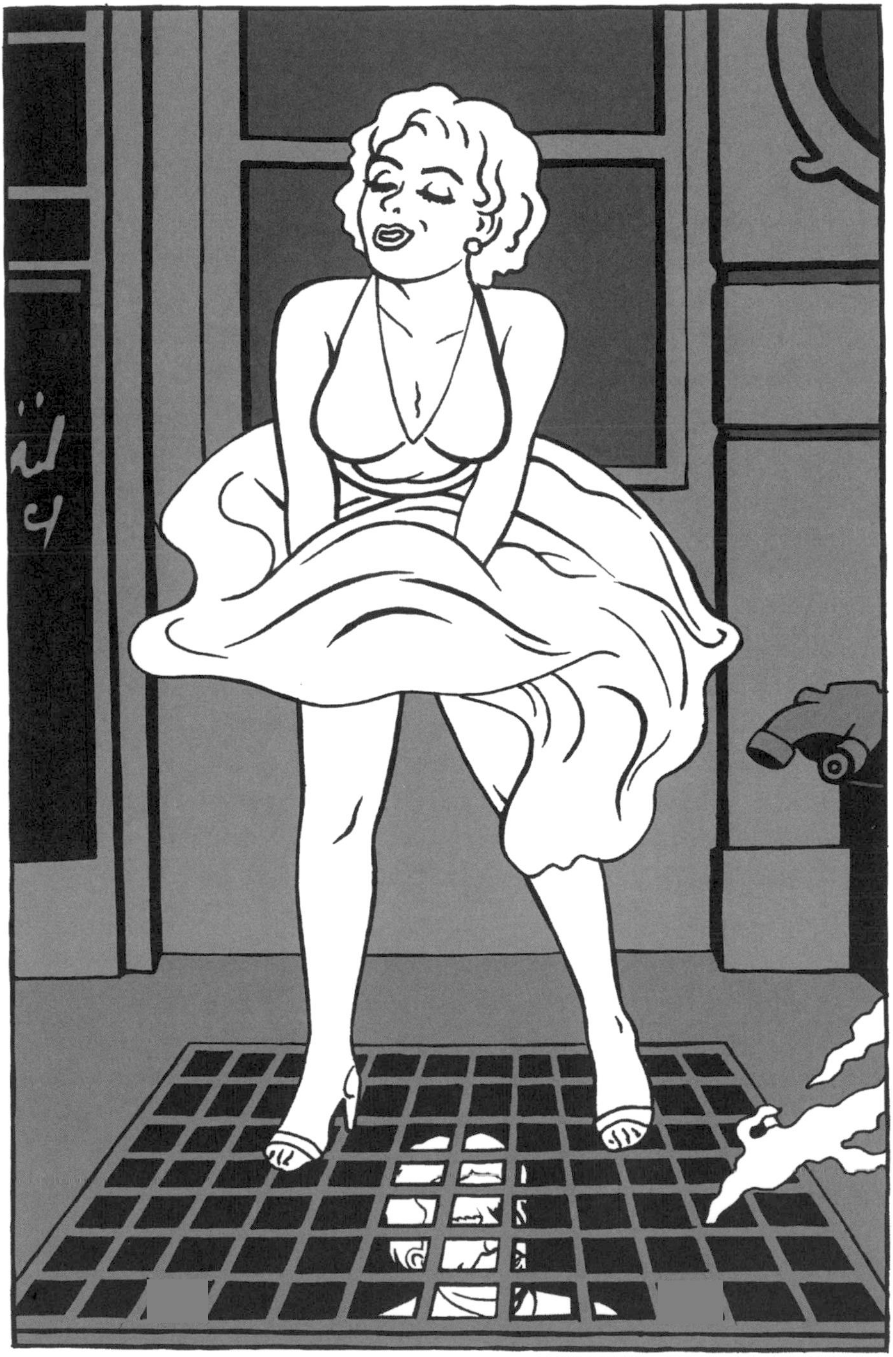

CHAPTER TWENTY:

THE CANDLE NEVER WINS

In 1955 I met Marilyn Monroe. We had a brief but desperate love affair, and I visited her on the set of *The Seven Year Itch*; if you look closely you can see me in the famous "blown dress" still (I'm under the grate). She moved on to Arthur Miller, and I compensated for my broken heart by flinging myself into a cockeyed marriage to soft-soap heiress Mozella Wapsinger.

When I next saw Marilyn it was 1961, and I was newly single again, having recently split with Elizabeth Taylor, whom I had married following my Mamie Eisenhower heartbreak. Marilyn and I spotted each other across the room at a party at Sy Yorkville's Hollywood pad (Yorkville was the producer of the popular *Devil Dogs* series). We exchanged playful banter for a while, and I believe we might have rekindled our romance, but just then she spotted JFK entering with his poodle Millie. JFK was imitating FDR in public at the time, and he looked so dashing in his wheelchair, with pince-nez and cigarette holder clenched in his jaws, that Marilyn rushed right over and had an affair with him. I compensated for my disappointment by entering into my own affair with Harangua Gabor, the most verbose of the Gabor sisters. We soon broke up when I became tired of getting an earful, and I moved on to Moolah Witherstein, the money heiress (her great-grandfather invented the stuff).

It was a deeply saddening when I heard of Marilyn's death and JFK's assassination over the next two years. There have been many conspiracy theories and fictions promulgated, but I believe they were both killed on the orders of United Fruit, who were upset because the price of grapefruit had declined slightly, from 85c a pound to 79c. It was a great tragedy for our country, and I think it is completely ridiculous that a fruit company should be assassinating world leaders and movie stars just because their citrus sales have dipped a little.

My friend Frank Sinatra, seeing how upset I was, invited me to join The Rat Pack. This was a group of the swingingest cats you could ever imagine, all behaving like rats. I met them in Las Vegas; besides me and Frank, there was Sammy Davis Jr., Joey Lawrence, Dean Martin, Shirley MacLaine, and Ernest Borgnine. We promptly created an underground "nest" or "burrow" with multiple tunnel entrances, then started raiding local garbage, chewing our way through the toughest enclosures and leaving our telltale droppings everywhere. We were all crawling with disease-carrying insects, and it wasn't long before the city sent in an exterminator and we all had to scurry out of town.

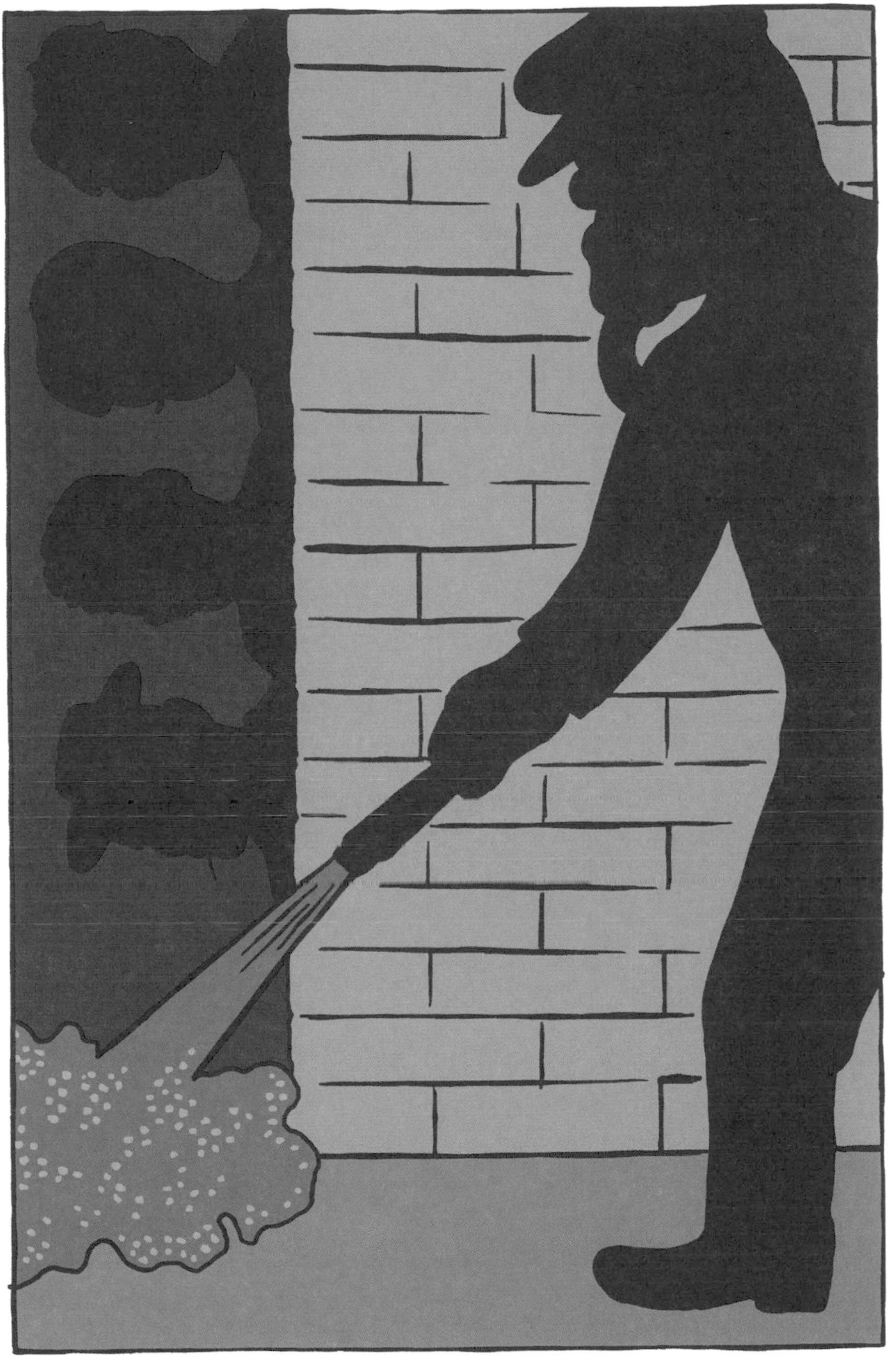

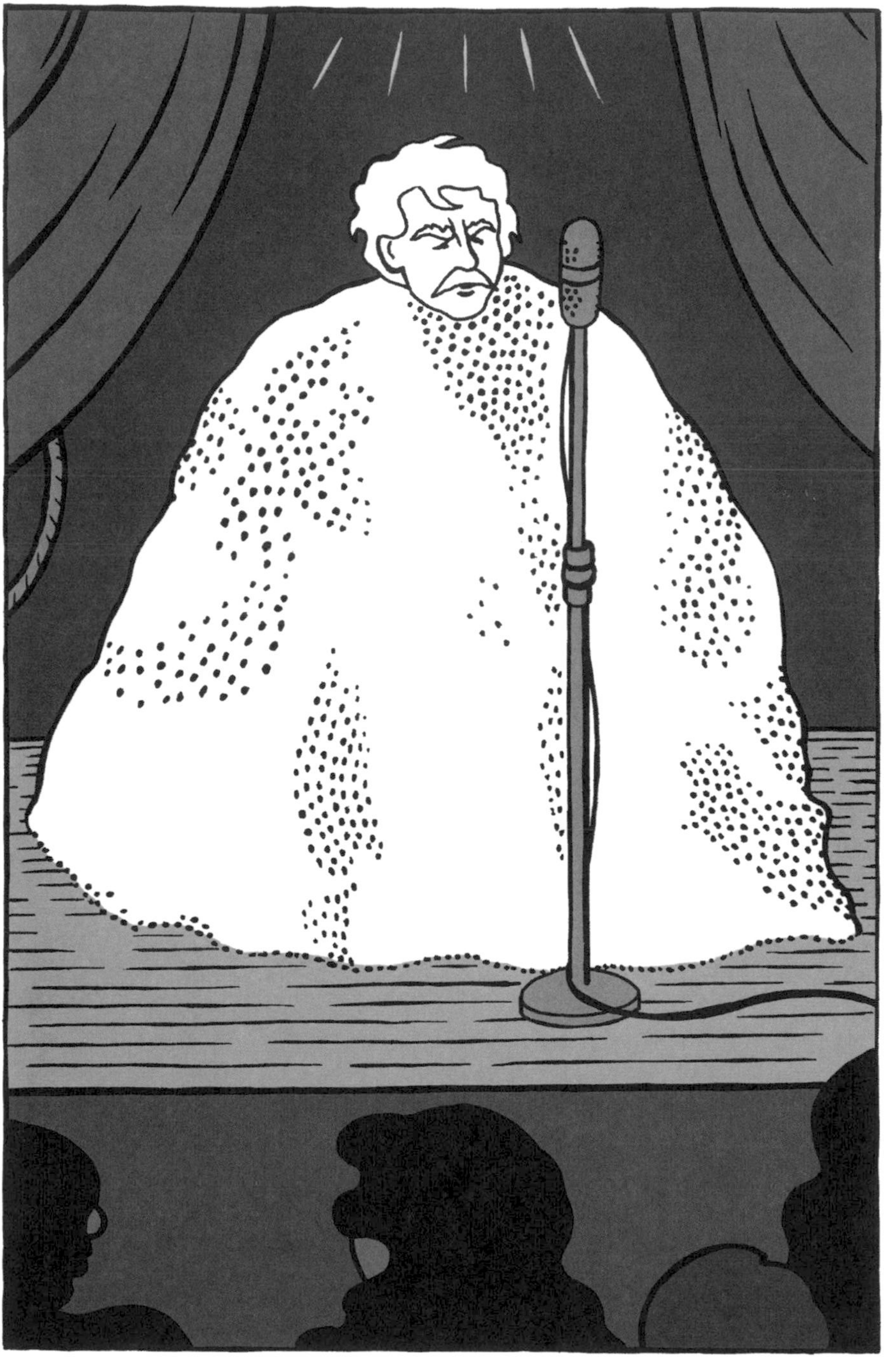

CHAPTER TWENTY-ONE

YUKKY BUSINESS

America in the Sixties was undergoing a comedy explosion, eagerly devouring stand up acts ranging from well-behaved comics to "potty mouth" ones, which were very popular at the time. I've never personally understood why jokes about a mouth being a toilet should be so uproarious, but there you go. I try to understand all kinds of people, but going to the bathroom in someone else's mouth, that's a little beyond my powers of comprehension, and I do not consider it fit subject matter for comedy.

Many comedians, however were not talking about their mouths being toilets, but laying down some very heavy stuff about America and the hypocrisy it was laying down. Like, what is "jumbo shrimp"? That's a complete contradiction in terms, and so is a lot of other stuff these days. I really admired those comics who used the monologue form to explore new territory in poking societal hypocrisy, and this is the kind of comedy I wanted to do.

I worked for months on my standup act, and tested it repeatedly on my good friend, playwright Samuel Beckett. It is very hard to make Sam laugh, let me tell you. When, after hours of trying, I saw his lips curl slightly in reaction to one of my gags I knew I was ready for a real audience. I scheduled my first "gig" at the Thirsty We on a Monday night, and when the curtain opened on Monday night I was buried in a mound of sand up to my chin (Sam's suggestion). I had a full set of hypocrisy-derailing jibes prepared to unleash on the audience, with the intention of not only making them laugh but also making them question their perspectives. I was going to rock their world!

But, as I opened my mouth to deliver the first one, I felt the bite of an ant, and my agony began. The sand was full of ants! Suddenly they were all there, crawling and biting. Never have I felt such uncomfortableness. They spoke an different language from the ants that Einstein and I had encountered, and all my efforts to reason with them were fruitless. I was helpless until the fire department showed up with a shovel.

My set that night was recorded, and made into a record album, against my wishes. *Mark Twain at the Mercy of Ants* contains none of the satiric material I had worked so tirelessly to perfect. Instead there is a whole lot of cursing, yelping, snarling, thrashing and other noises. The audience, damn their hides, thought it was all some elaborate joke, and sat laughing at me as I was devoured, ignoring my fervent pleas for almost three quarters of an hour. The entire experience so embittered me that I vowed never to attempt a stand-up comedy appearance again.

CHAPTER TWENTY-TWO:

DOUBLE THE COUPLE

In 1965 my current wife, the actress Whoopee Wagner, threw me out, suggesting that I not return. At the same time my old pal Albert Einstein's wife also threw him out, likewise dictating that he should not come back. Our old friends Oscar Mendelsohn and Felix Unkler had already been living together, because their wives similiarly had declared "begone"; they had become known as the Odd Couple, due to their contrasting habits of neatness and sloppiness. We decided to move in with them and became known as the Awkward Quartet. Oscar and I both enjoyed smelly cigars and all-night poker games; Felix and Albert preferred reading and atomic experimentation. Felix and I enjoyed cultural stimulation, while Oscar and Albert liked wrestling and corned-beef sandwiches. Special guests like Paul Williams were always dropping in, and at times it was almost like a TV show. I'll never forget the night that I got stuck in the building's elevator with the Harlem Globetrotters during a blackout.

One of our acquaintances was Murray the cop, an amiable shmo who was always loafing off and shirking his duty. The idea of having such an easy career appealed to me; I liked the idea of wearing a uniform and doing nothing. With Murray's help, I passed the police exam and became a street cop in Hell's Kitchen. But what I witnessed turned my stomach. I saw the corruption that let murderers go free while cops turned the other way, their pockets fattened by money earned from the blood of the innocents that they hadn't protected against the scum that were paying them off to walk free. I grew bitter and brooding. I decided to leave the police force and work outside the system as a private eye.

My first client was a man whose shoes hurt him. I saw how ill-fitting shoes made men bitter and unhappy, and how corrupt the big shoe companies had become. I decided to start a shoe company, to make honest shoes for good men and women, and immediately went home to find Oscar loafing around our apartment, eating soup... out of a shoe. "How was your first day as a cop?" he gurgled. I just stared at him. "Want some soup? It's a little feety," he conceded.

This experience made me realize, again, that our society is very complex, and there are no easy, quick-fix solutions. Or are there?

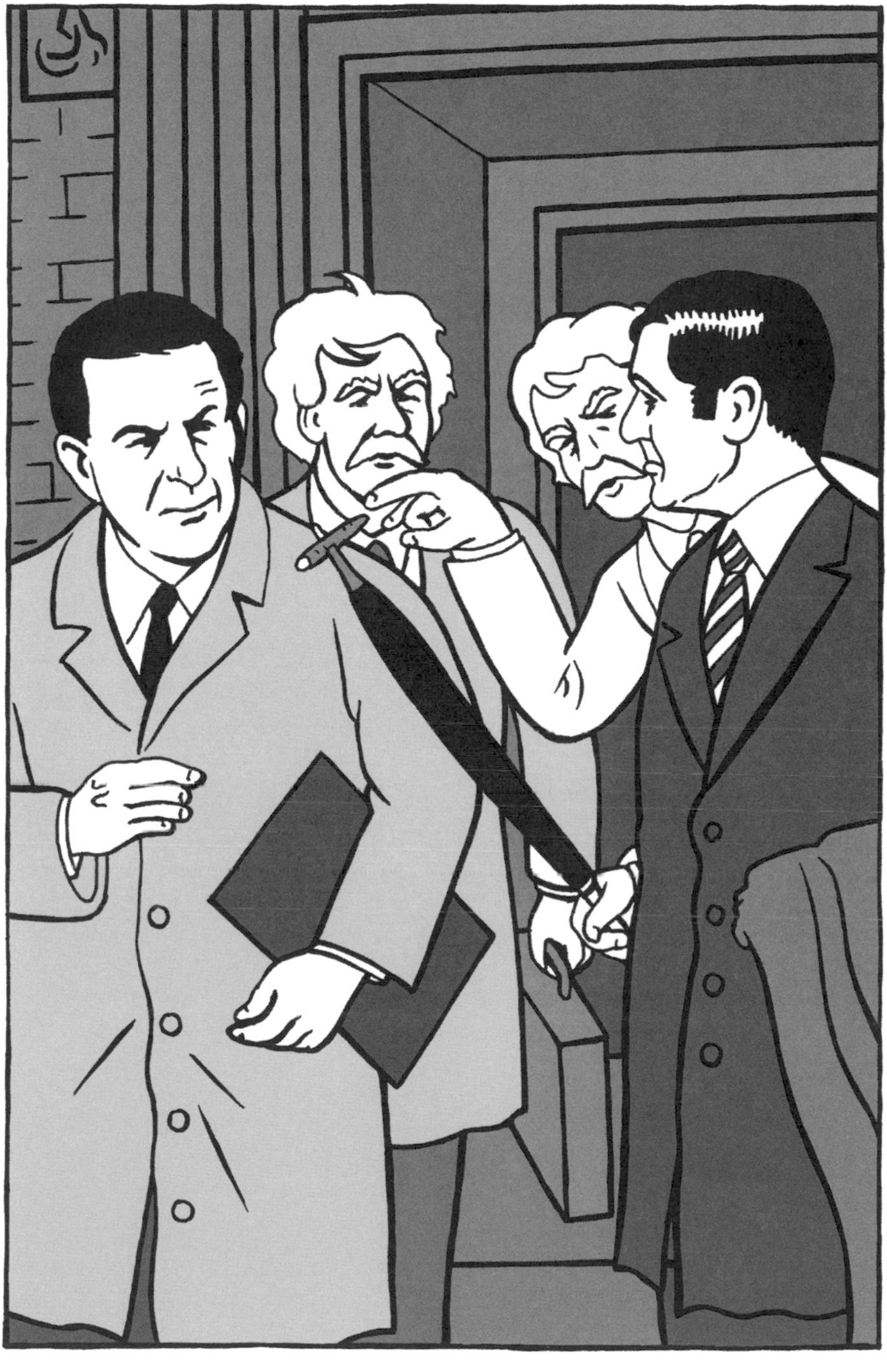

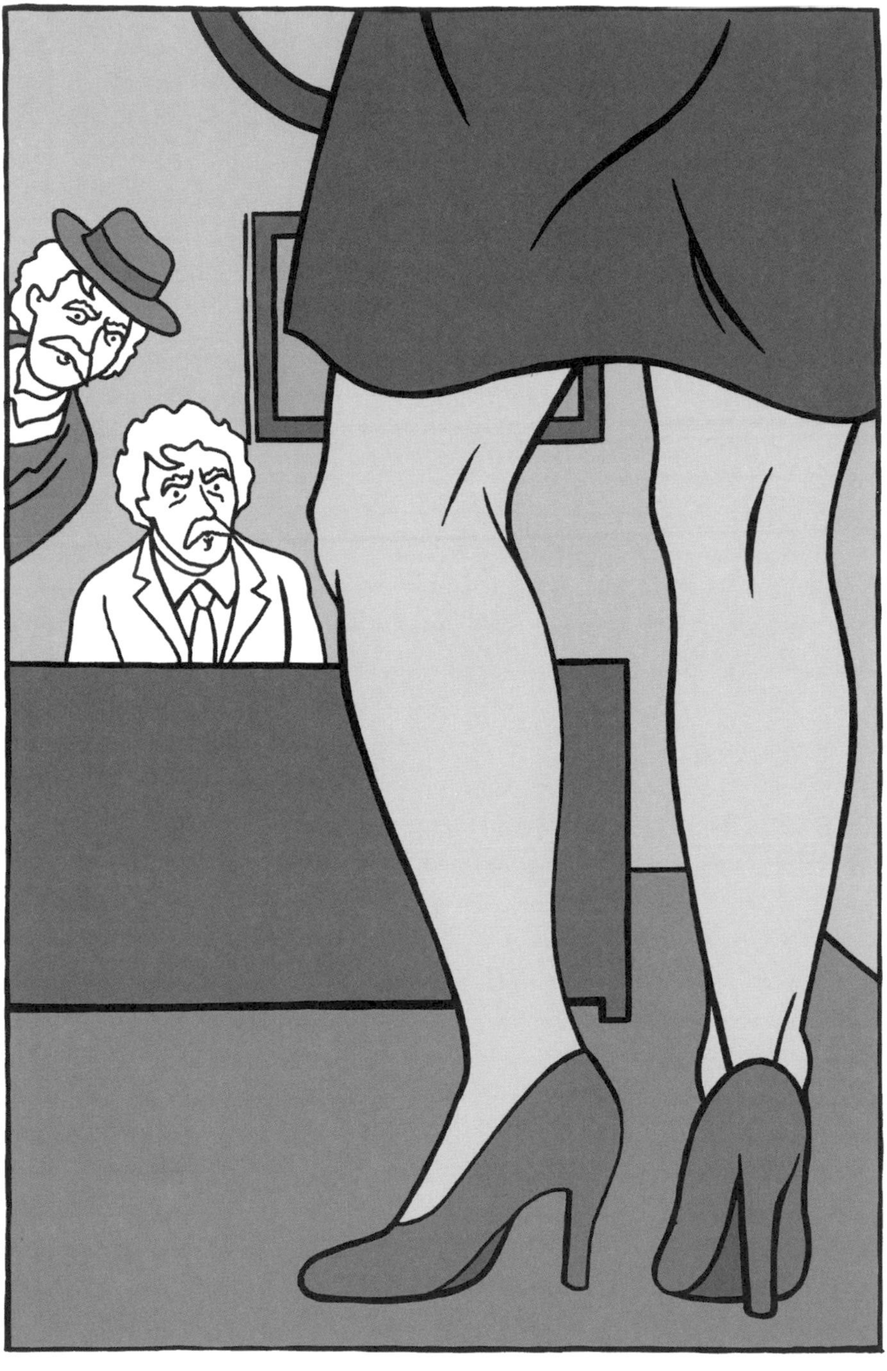

CHAPTER TWENTY-THREE

THE LOIN GOODBYE

I decided to go on being a private detective, as I had already paid two months' rent on the office. I invited Al to join me as a partner, and we quickly became Twain and Einstein, Privates of Eye.

For the first few weeks we mostly handled seedy divorce cases, and quickly learned how to handle distraught spouses seeking painful confirmation (by being greasy and sanctimonious and sniggering a lot). I grew calluses on my shoulders in the shape of Al's shoes, from all the time he spent using me as a human ladder to peer over transoms. No longer were we the idealistic crusaders we had started out being.

Then one morning there was a slight knock on the door, and in sashayed the gamsiest broad I'd ever steam cleaned with my eyes. Her pipes were two long stems that hit the ground walking, and atop her two bulging orbs were lashes that a prisoner would've begged for. In short, she was one hot tomato. Al clamped both hands onto his hat and steam came out of his ears. "Whoooooooo!" he howled. "Pardon my partner, Miss," I said suavely, and ushered Al none too subtly out the door, locking it behind him. "What can I do for you?"

"Is this the language school?" she asked innocently. It turned out she was in the wrong office, but it sure was exciting, a sexy woman coming in like that. Just like in the movies!

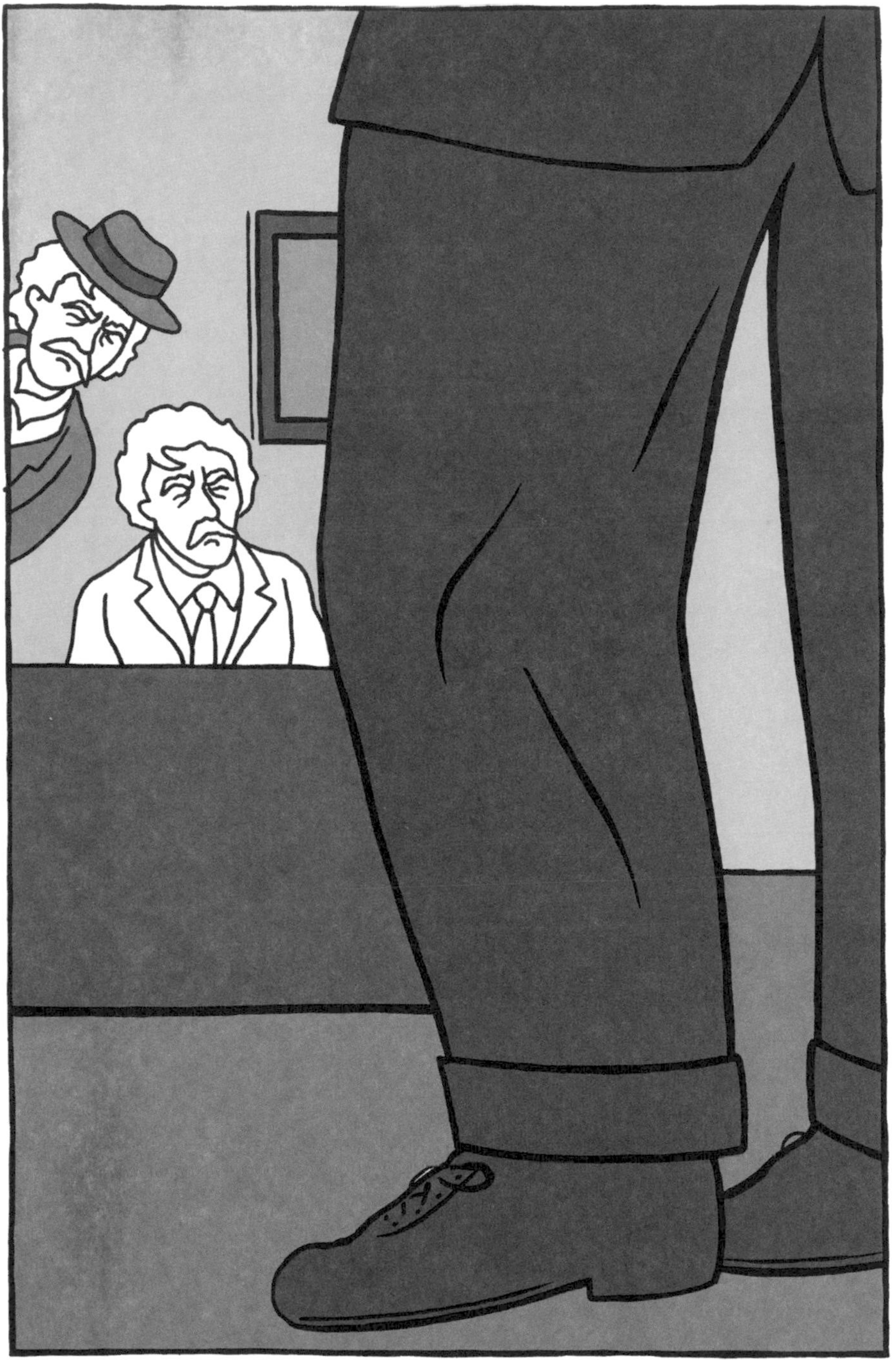

CHAPTER TWENTY-FOUR

WHO'S THE GODFATHER?

Al and I continued to work as private detectives. One day we had a most unusual visitor: Moe Sylvester, the famous head of Allied Reprobates, a notorious criminal organization. For every illegal dollar made or spent on the west half of Manhattan, so the story went, he saw half. I wondered if he had come to threaten us, but it turned out he wanted to hire us.

"Someone in my organization is trine kill me!" he complained vividly. If it wasn't for the thousand-dollar suit and the expensive mahogany eyeglasses, you would have taken him for an ordinary middle-aged head of a gangster consortium. "Me! Moe Sylvester, who brought peace to Canarsie and made all the families see reason, that there was no profit in the killing without reason, that it made our enemies in law enforcement sit up and take notice! But in the old days they had respect! They used bombs and guns and knives and pipes and brass knuckles and dynamite and table legs, the occasional crossbow, sure, but only when they needed to! Now you got these hot-blooded young bloods, they're drawn' the heat!" He stopped yelling and reached for some pills. "Excuse me, my heart," he groused. "You got any water?" I poured some in a glass and he swallowed the pills. "My doctor says I gotta calm down." His face was shiny with sweat. "Someone blew up my car yesterday. And they poisoned my dinner the day before that. And also put deadly chemicals in the swimming pool the previous afternoon. My car tester, food tester, and swimming pool tester are all dead! Thank God I'm an excessively cautious man."

I had a feeling I knew where this was going, but I let him go on without interrupting. "It's someone close to me, that's all I know. I don't know who to trust anymore! That's why I need you. You'll come in as an outsider and scope the situation out, find out who's makin' the moves on me. Then you let me know, and I'll take care of it." His eyes had a steely look to them, like a man who had been served a hot dog he did not like.

"You and your pal Eisenstein, you'll dye your hair black and also your eyebrows and mustaches. You'll be a fiery-tempered pair of guys from somewhere in Eastern Europe, you don't know no English. Imported talent." He smiled thinly.

He was offering too much money to refuse. Soon, we were at Sylvester's private mansion, driving through the wrought-iron gates onto his enormous drive.

"Okay, boys," said Sylvester, showing signs of nervousness, "Remember what I told you. You don't speak English, you don't do nothing. You just look menacing!" And we were rather fierce-looking, Al and I, our hairs now dark as night, and wearing red silk blouses and flared trousers with enormous daggers stuck through our belts. We got out of the car and went into the house, which was blazing with light and full of people.

Several burly men rushed over to us. "Boss! We had no idea where you was! We was gonna throw a council of war!" declared the largest. The next largest butted in. "Is everything okay, boss? You want I should take care of these guys?" he growled, giving us menacing looks. We glared right back at him, and I decided to test out my newest improvised language. "Akoonahok melba tittiform!" I hissed through my teeth. "Stvbrooba wroslawopa! Stzimenek!" Sylvester pushed us away from each other. "There's no need for any of that! You young hotheads... These two are hired muscle from somewhere in Eastern Europe, they're here to help out for a bit. Their names are Starky and Melarky," he lamely improvised. I wished then we had decided on names beforehand. "Yeah, well okay," muttered the hothead. "Starky, Melarky, this is Joe Hotnoggin. And next to him are Steam Cranius and Lawrence Faceburn." The three men nodded hello, sullenly and without real friendliness. Then a vision in feminine radiance came rushing over, a real hot patootie. "Oh Momo, I was so worried," she cried. I felt a stab of jealousy as she embraced him—she was a real creamy dish, all blonde silky hair and expensive frilly clothes.

"All I did was go to the airport to pick up these guys! I felt like a drive on my own," Moe sighed. "C'mon, boys, we got business to do!"

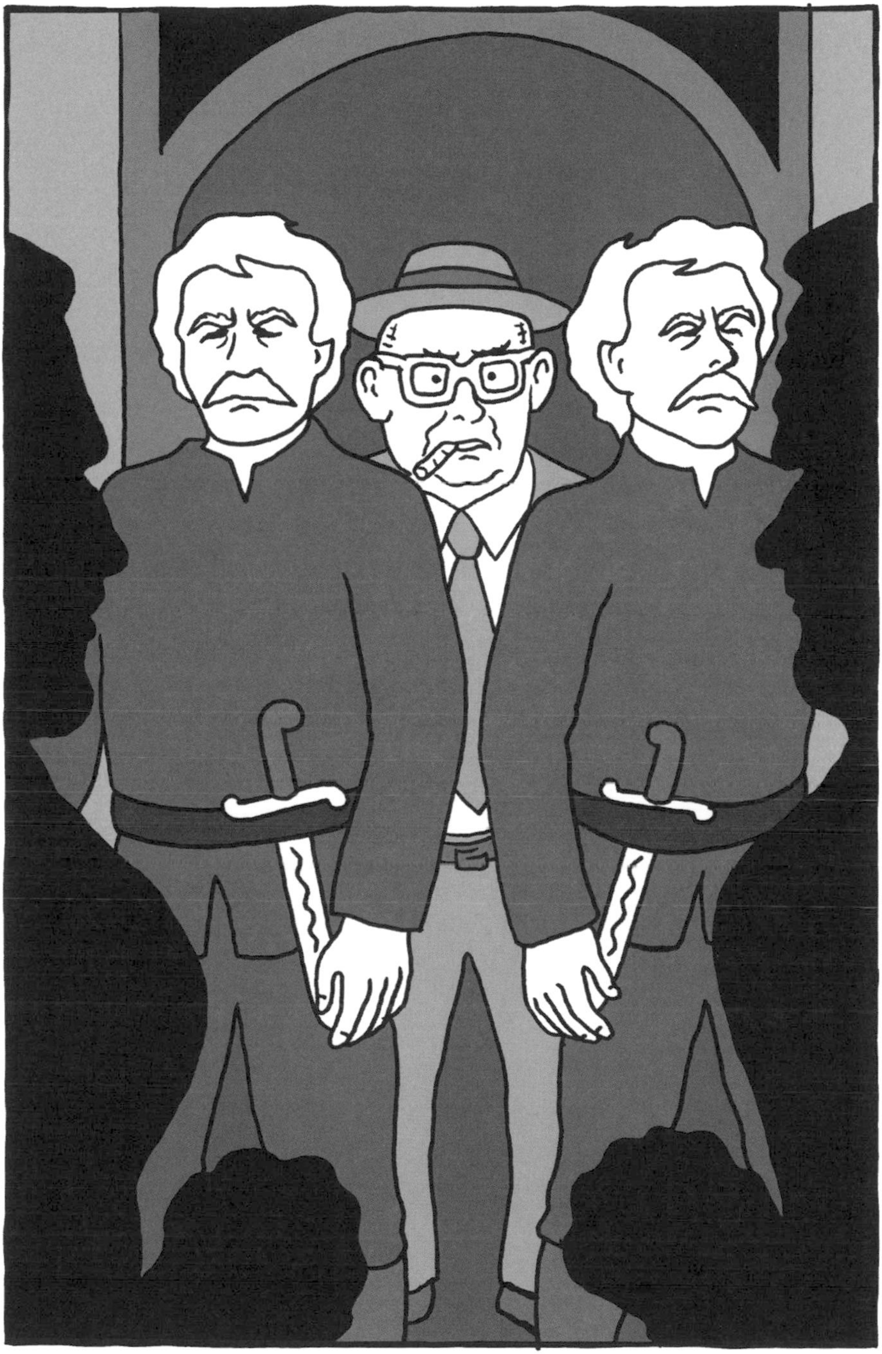

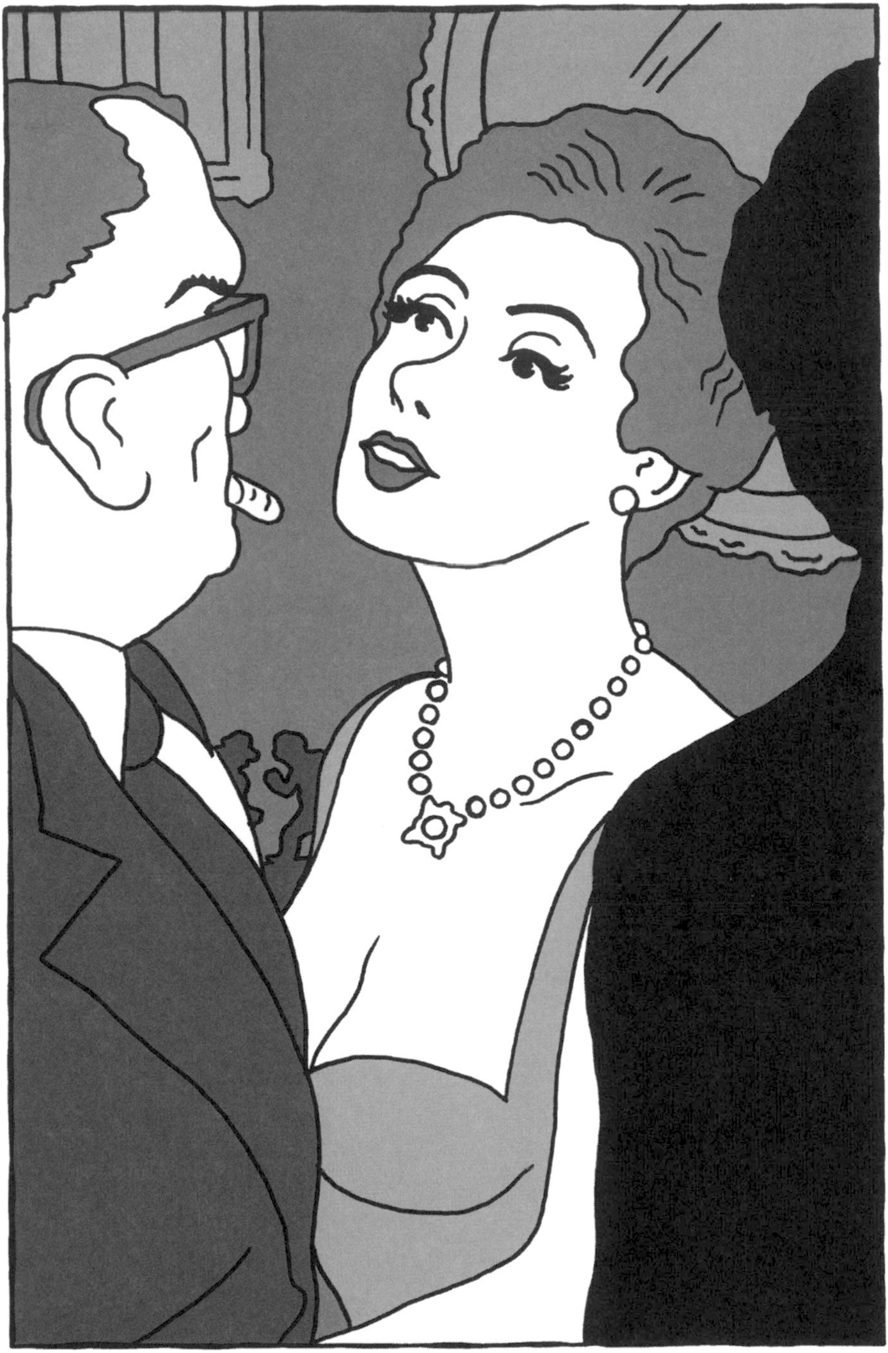

They all headed into his office, and the wife and servants went into various rooms. We were left on our own.

"I wish we could hear what they're saying to each other," I muttered, only to see Al grin mischievously. "I put a bug on him," he told me. "What, you mean a listening device, or one of those itch beetles you keep pranking people with?" "Alright, I put two bugs on him." We turned on the transmitter and listened to the voices of the boss and his underlings. "I told those two someone was tryna whack me," Moe was saying. "We'll murder the Mayor and pin his murder on those two clowns."

"We'd better get out of here," I hissed, but Al had another mischievous glint in his eye. He winked at me and pulled out an envelope of red powder. "All we need to do is get them to drink this Goodness Punch." The Goodness Punch was the result of years of research and Princeton; it was a powdered drink that made people repent and confess their bad deeds. Going into the kitchen, we mixed up a big pitcher of the stuff, and carried it on a tray with glasses into the gangsters meeting room. "Frekvelokroif, fekllkweagre freer!" exclaimed Al, handing the drink around. "Thanks boys, I was beginning to get thirsty," crowed Moe as he drank it, and the rest followed suit. Soon the effects were apparent. "I've been a terrible person," sighed the crime boss, and his subordinates were quick to declare themselves worse. "Let's all go to the police station to confess to our crimes," suggested Lawrence Faceburne, a suggestion which pleased them all mightily, and they ran out of the house and drove away.

"That's some powerful punch," I commented. "Thanks, the government is going to suppress it," Al responded.

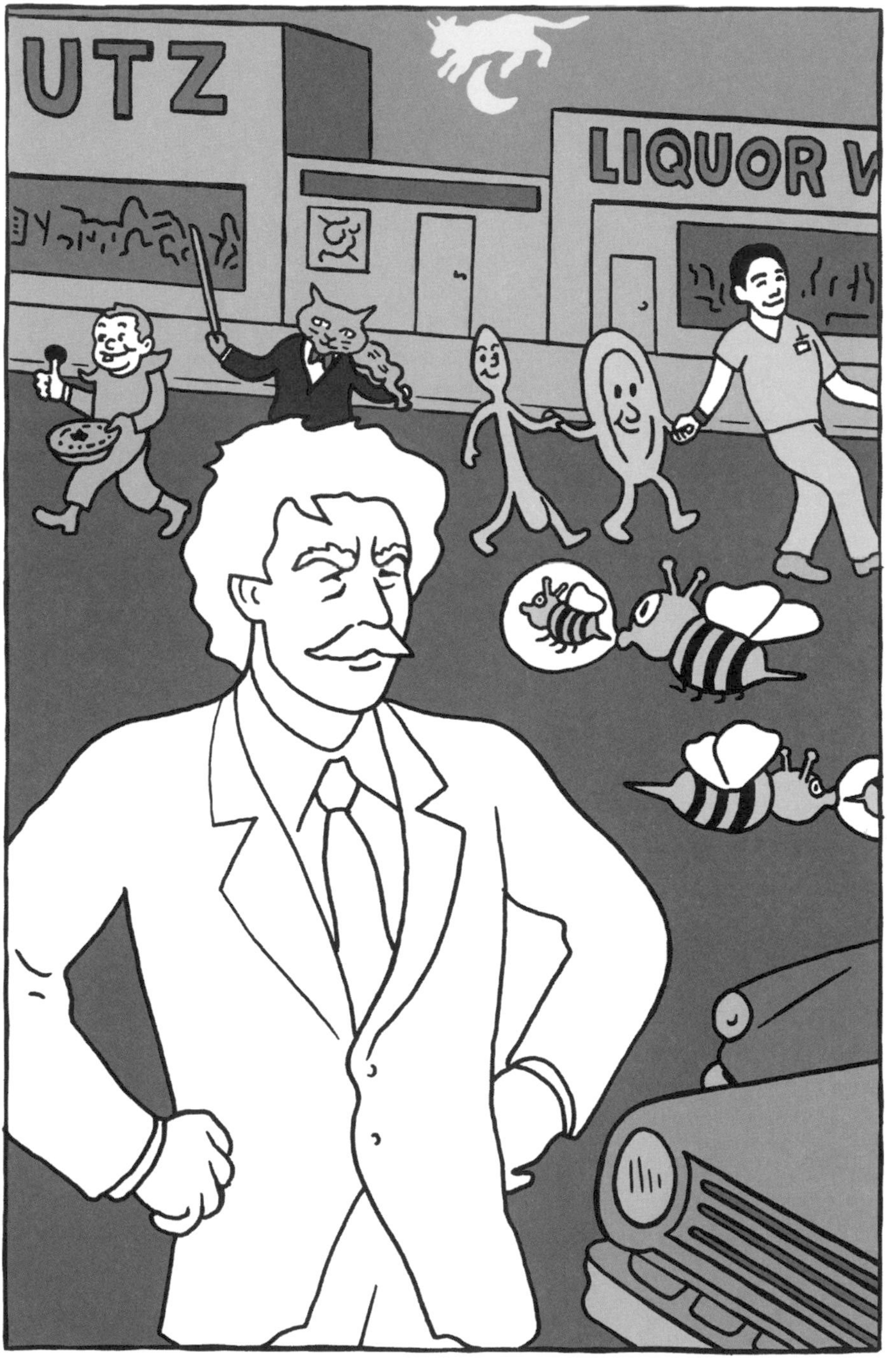
UTZ
LIQUOR

CHAPTER TWENTY-FIVE

MY WIT GETS MORE ACID

In 1967 I went to a doctor for a checkup—I was 132 years old and my knee was hurting a bit (it turned out to be nothing). But I didn't realize what I was letting myself in for when I went to see Doctor Swami Volcano Rabbit. "You should do acid, it's groovy," he told me. I swallowed the pill he gave me without question; after all, he was a doctor, wasn't he? (It turned out he wasn't.)

As I was leaving his office, my feet turned into canoes and my hands became flamingoes. I turned to go back in but at that moment I realized I had been transported to the land of nursery rhymes and fairy tales. Little Jack Horner, the Plate and the Spoon, Sam from *Quincy*, and many other beloved characters were capering around right in front of me! I have always wanted to meet that celebrated rascal Jack Sprat, and when I spotted him cavorting on the other side of the parking lot I made a beeline towards him.

The beeline, however, was full of bees, and they were blowing bubbles, which had more bees in them. I realized that these bubble-blowing bees were just what I needed to resume my vaudeville career, and I started to try to gather some of them into a paper bag that was lying nearby. The bag, however, was laughing at me and refusing to cooperate in any way. In anger I grabbed my cigar lighter and tried to burn the bag, to teach it a lesson. And it was then that the acid hit me.

As the LSD flooded my system my third eye gained perspective and I was able to see that it was all meaningless, the bees and the paper bag, the fairy tale characters, all of it, all ego games that society had set up for me and which I had used to ensnare and blind myself. So-called rational existence was like a void, but not empty, it was full of "no." I called it the Noid. "Avoid the Noid," I whispered to myself, and later I was able to sell this concept to Domino's Pizza for some commercials for a large sum of money. That was one profitable acid trip! I might have gone to see Doctor Rabbit again, but he had unfortunately been raided and gone underground; when I met him again he was the President of Columbia University.

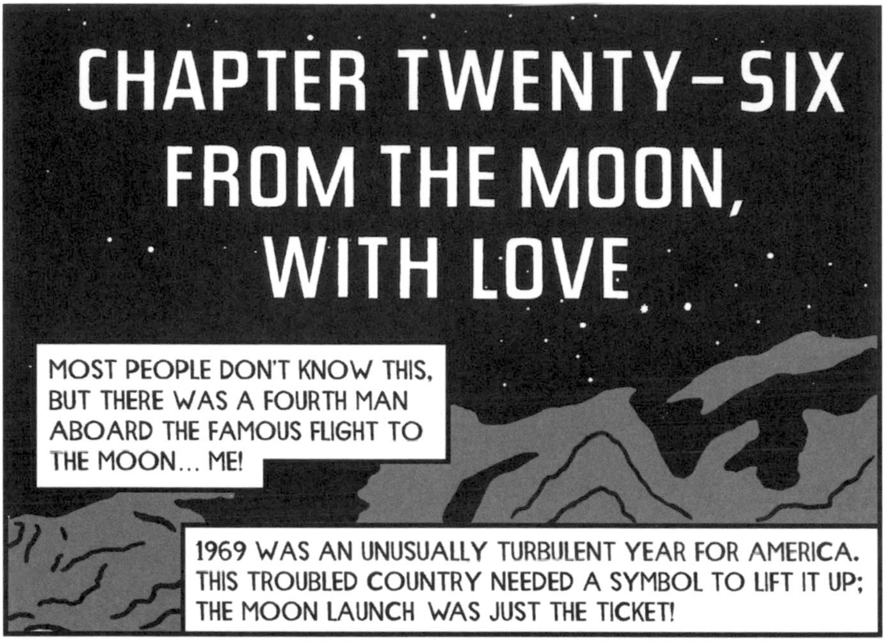
CHAPTER TWENTY-SIX
FROM THE MOON, WITH LOVE
MOST PEOPLE DON'T KNOW THIS, BUT THERE WAS A FOURTH MAN ABOARD THE FAMOUS FLIGHT TO THE MOON... ME!
1969 WAS AN UNUSUALLY TURBULENT YEAR FOR AMERICA. THIS TROUBLED COUNTRY NEEDED A SYMBOL TO LIFT IT UP; THE MOON LAUNCH WAS JUST THE TICKET!

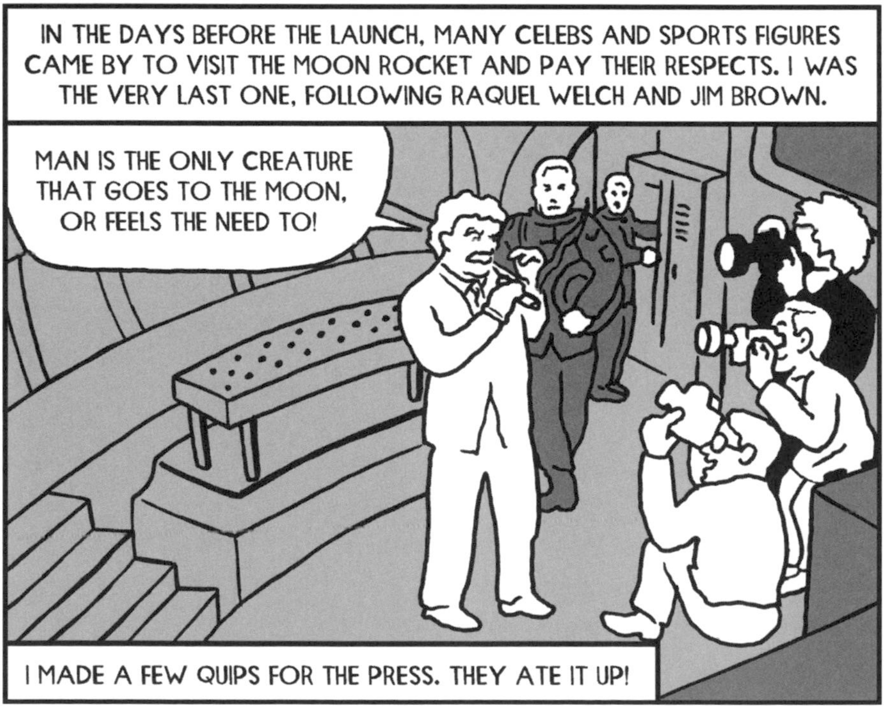
IN THE DAYS BEFORE THE LAUNCH, MANY CELEBS AND SPORTS FIGURES CAME BY TO VISIT THE MOON ROCKET AND PAY THEIR RESPECTS. I WAS THE VERY LAST ONE, FOLLOWING RAQUEL WELCH AND JIM BROWN.
MAN IS THE ONLY CREATURE THAT GOES TO THE MOON, OR FEELS THE NEED TO!
I MADE A FEW QUIPS FOR THE PRESS. THEY ATE IT UP!

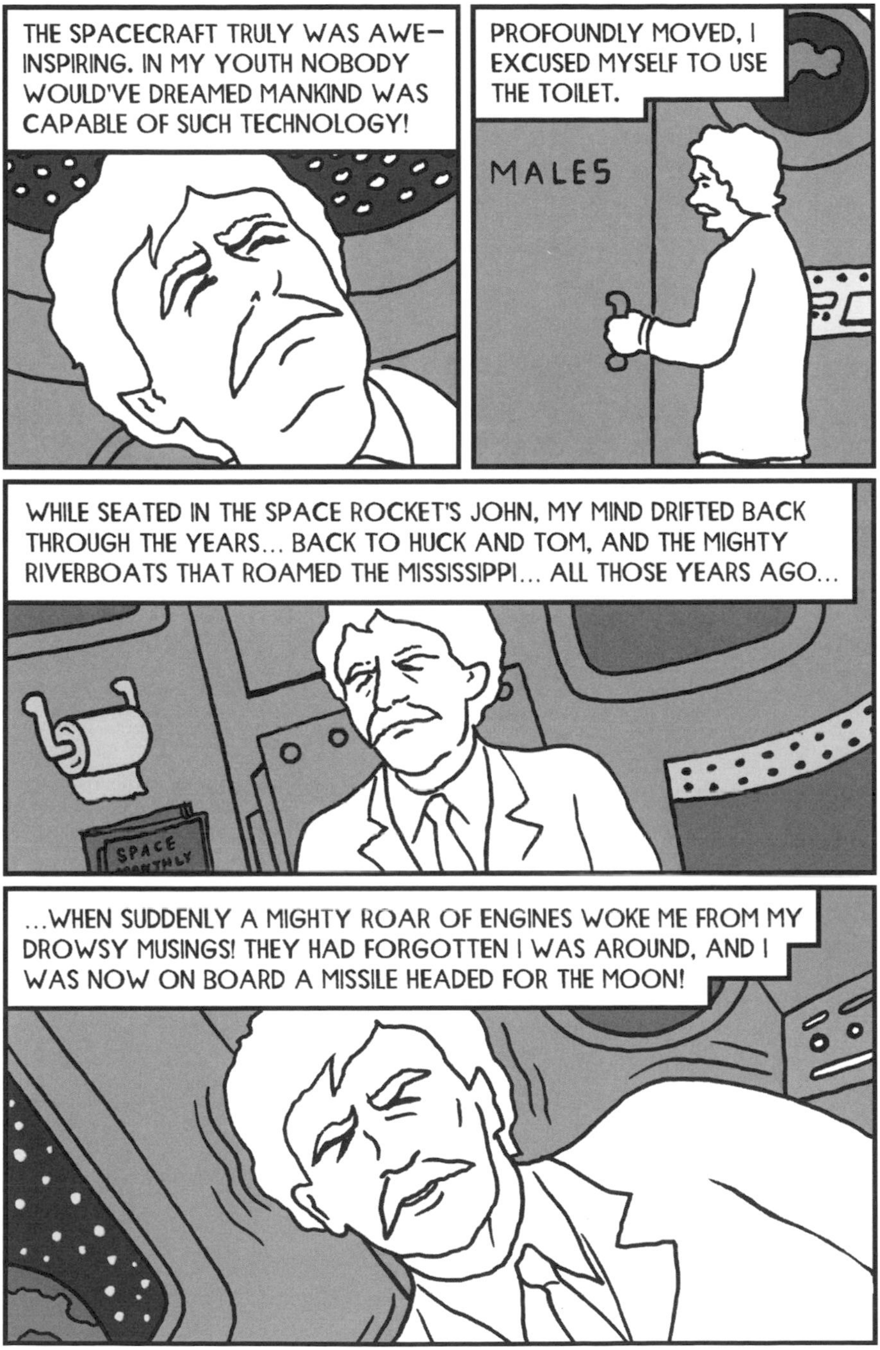
THE SPACECRAFT TRULY WAS AWE-INSPIRING. IN MY YOUTH NOBODY WOULD'VE DREAMED MANKIND WAS CAPABLE OF SUCH TECHNOLOGY!
PROFOUNDLY MOVED, I EXCUSED MYSELF TO USE THE TOILET.
MALES
WHILE SEATED IN THE SPACE ROCKET'S JOHN, MY MIND DRIFTED BACK THROUGH THE YEARS... BACK TO HUCK AND TOM, AND THE MIGHTY RIVERBOATS THAT ROAMED THE MISSISSIPPI... ALL THOSE YEARS AGO...
SPACE
...WHEN SUDDENLY A MIGHTY ROAR OF ENGINES WOKE ME FROM MY DROWSY MUSINGS! THEY HAD FORGOTTEN I WAS AROUND, AND I WAS NOW ON BOARD A MISSILE HEADED FOR THE MOON!

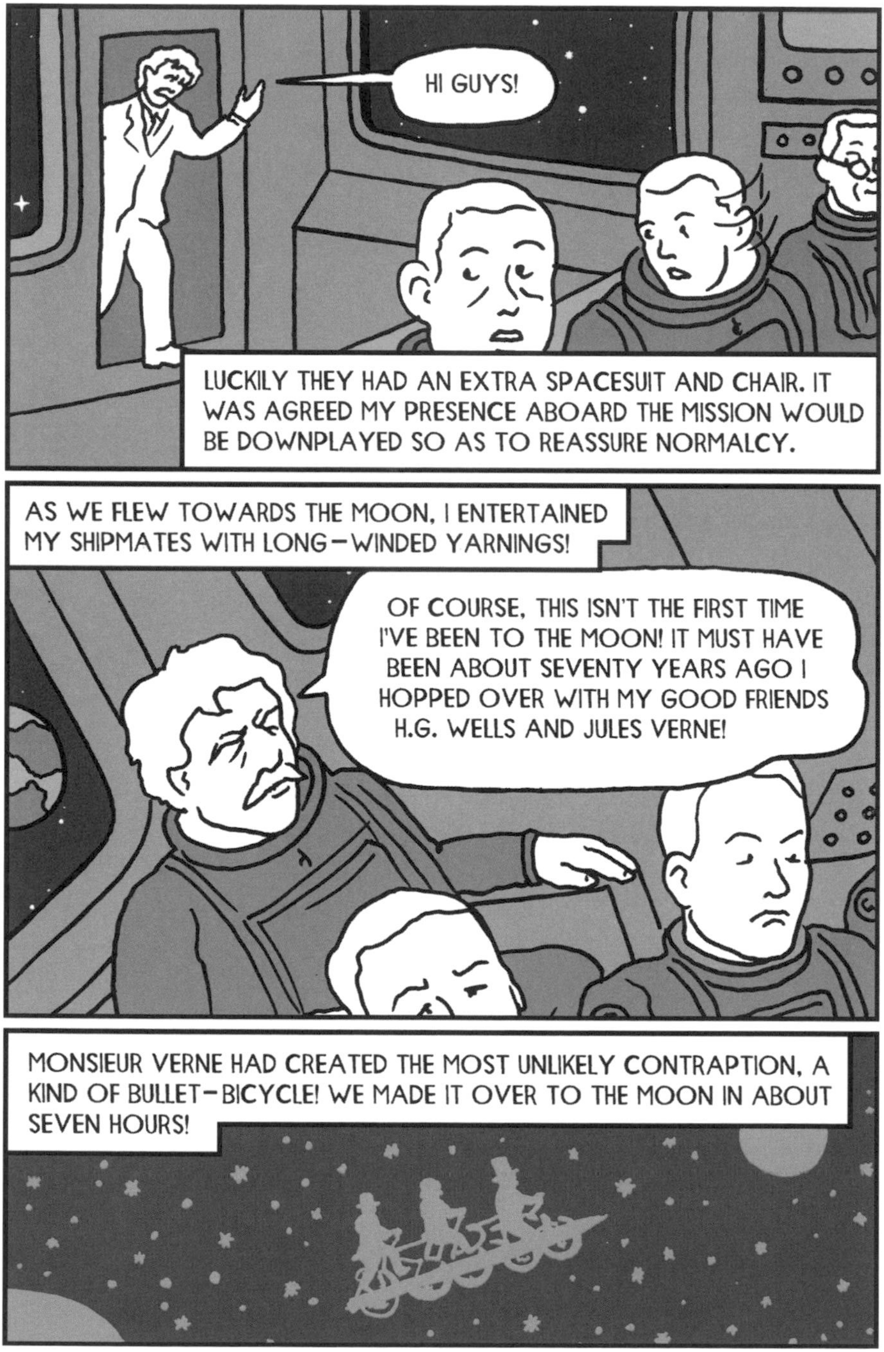
HI GUYS!
LUCKILY THEY HAD AN EXTRA SPACESUIT AND CHAIR. IT WAS AGREED MY PRESENCE ABOARD THE MISSION WOULD BE DOWNPLAYED SO AS TO REASSURE NORMALCY.
AS WE FLEW TOWARDS THE MOON, I ENTERTAINED MY SHIPMATES WITH LONG-WINDED YARNINGS!
OF COURSE, THIS ISN'T THE FIRST TIME I'VE BEEN TO THE MOON! IT MUST HAVE BEEN ABOUT SEVENTY YEARS AGO I HOPPED OVER WITH MY GOOD FRIENDS H.G. WELLS AND JULES VERNE!
MONSIEUR VERNE HAD CREATED THE MOST UNLIKELY CONTRAPTION, A KIND OF BULLET-BICYCLE! WE MADE IT OVER TO THE MOON IN ABOUT SEVEN HOURS!

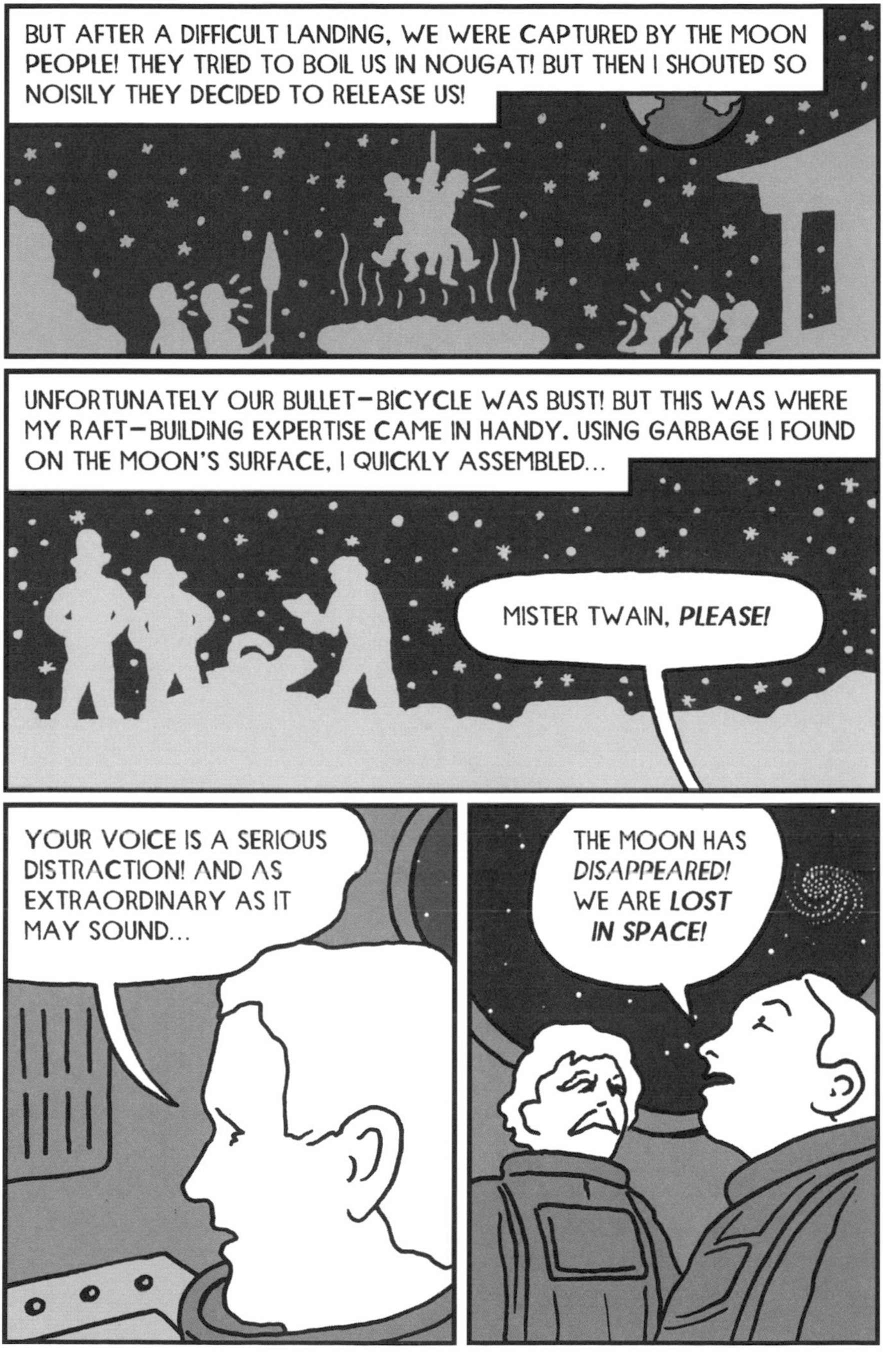
BUT AFTER A DIFFICULT LANDING, WE WERE CAPTURED BY THE MOON PEOPLE! THEY TRIED TO BOIL US IN NOUGAT! BUT THEN I SHOUTED SO NOISILY THEY DECIDED TO RELEASE US!
UNFORTUNATELY OUR BULLET-BICYCLE WAS BUST! BUT THIS WAS WHERE MY RAFT-BUILDING EXPERTISE CAME IN HANDY. USING GARBAGE I FOUND ON THE MOON'S SURFACE, I QUICKLY ASSEMBLED...
MISTER TWAIN, ***PLEASE!***
YOUR VOICE IS A SERIOUS DISTRACTION! AND AS EXTRAORDINARY AS IT MAY SOUND...
THE MOON HAS *DISAPPEARED!* WE ARE ***LOST IN SPACE!***

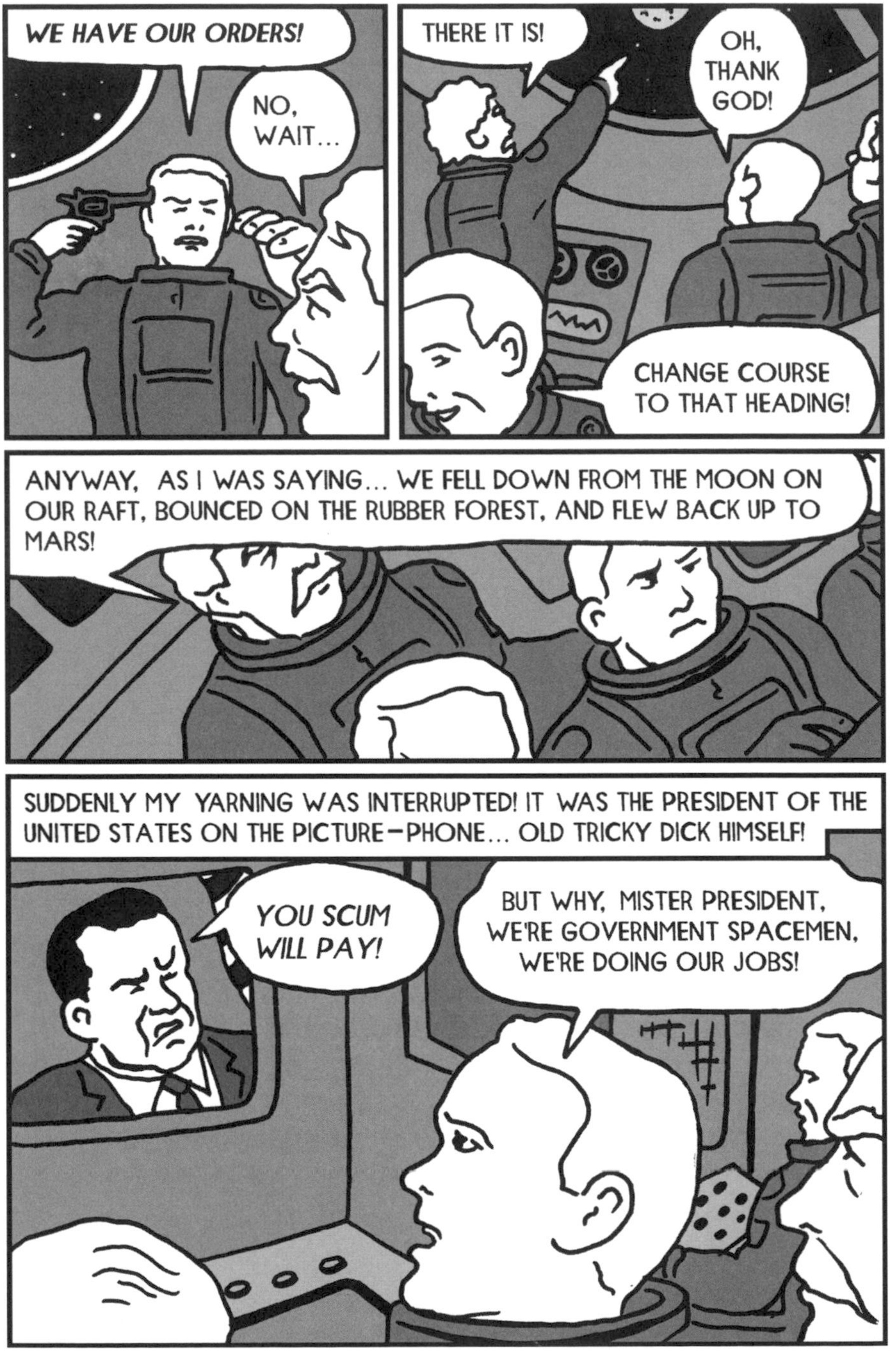
WE HAVE OUR ORDERS!
NO, WAIT...
THERE IT IS!
OH, THANK GOD!
CHANGE COURSE TO THAT HEADING!
ANYWAY, AS I WAS SAYING... WE FELL DOWN FROM THE MOON ON OUR RAFT, BOUNCED ON THE RUBBER FOREST, AND FLEW BACK UP TO MARS!
SUDDENLY MY YARNING WAS INTERRUPTED! IT WAS THE PRESIDENT OF THE UNITED STATES ON THE PICTURE-PHONE... OLD TRICKY DICK HIMSELF!
YOU SCUM WILL PAY!
BUT WHY, MISTER PRESIDENT, WE'RE GOVERNMENT SPACEMEN, WE'RE DOING OUR JOBS!

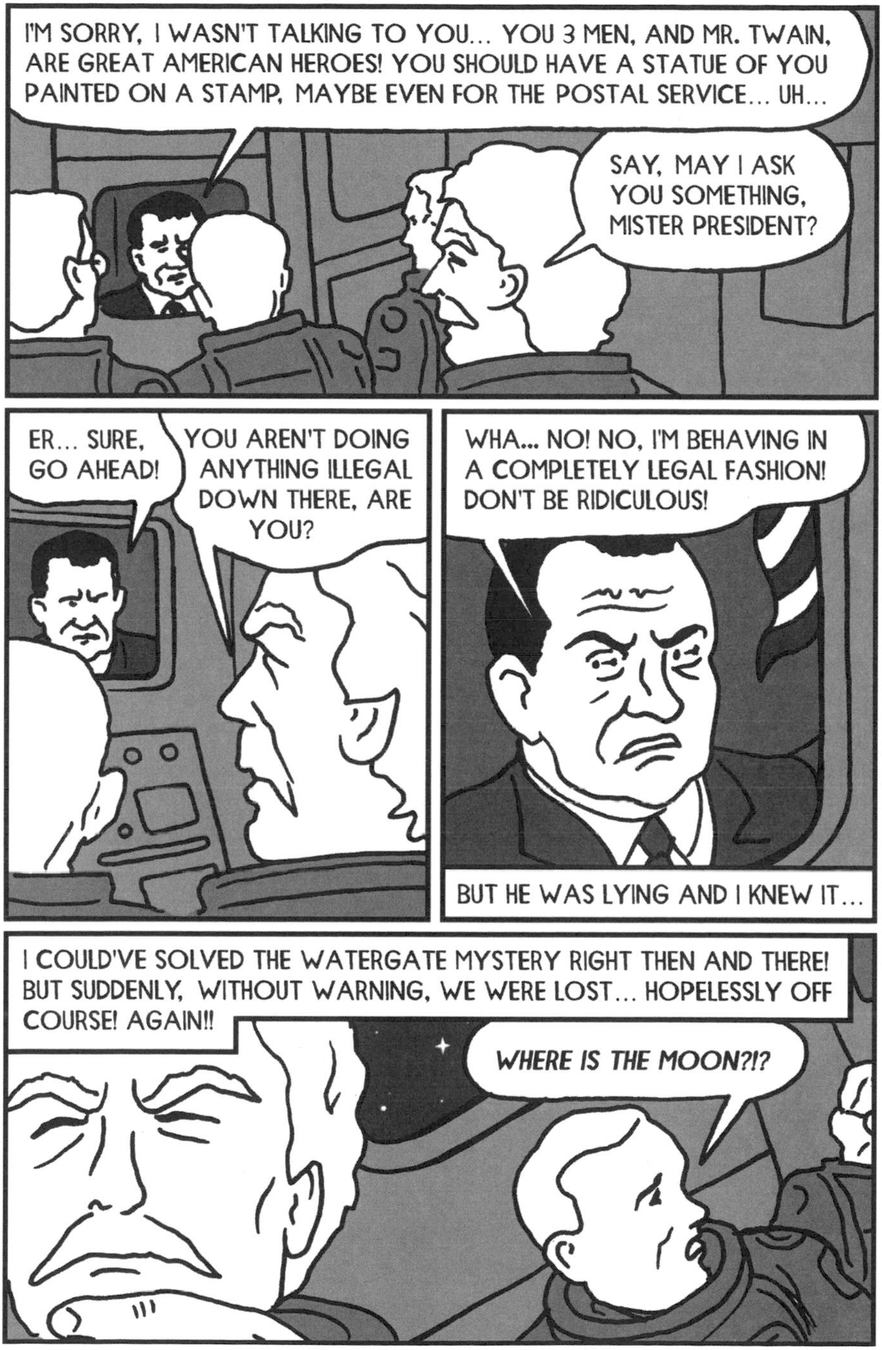

I'M SORRY, I WASN'T TALKING TO YOU... YOU 3 MEN, AND MR. TWAIN, ARE GREAT AMERICAN HEROES! YOU SHOULD HAVE A STATUE OF YOU PAINTED ON A STAMP, MAYBE EVEN FOR THE POSTAL SERVICE... UH...
SAY, MAY I ASK YOU SOMETHING, MISTER PRESIDENT?
ER... SURE, GO AHEAD!
YOU AREN'T DOING ANYTHING ILLEGAL DOWN THERE, ARE YOU?
WHA... NO! NO, I'M BEHAVING IN A COMPLETELY LEGAL FASHION! DON'T BE RIDICULOUS!
BUT HE WAS LYING AND I KNEW IT...
I COULD'VE SOLVED THE WATERGATE MYSTERY RIGHT THEN AND THERE! BUT SUDDENLY, WITHOUT WARNING, WE WERE LOST... HOPELESSLY OFF COURSE! AGAIN!!
WHERE IS THE MOON?!?

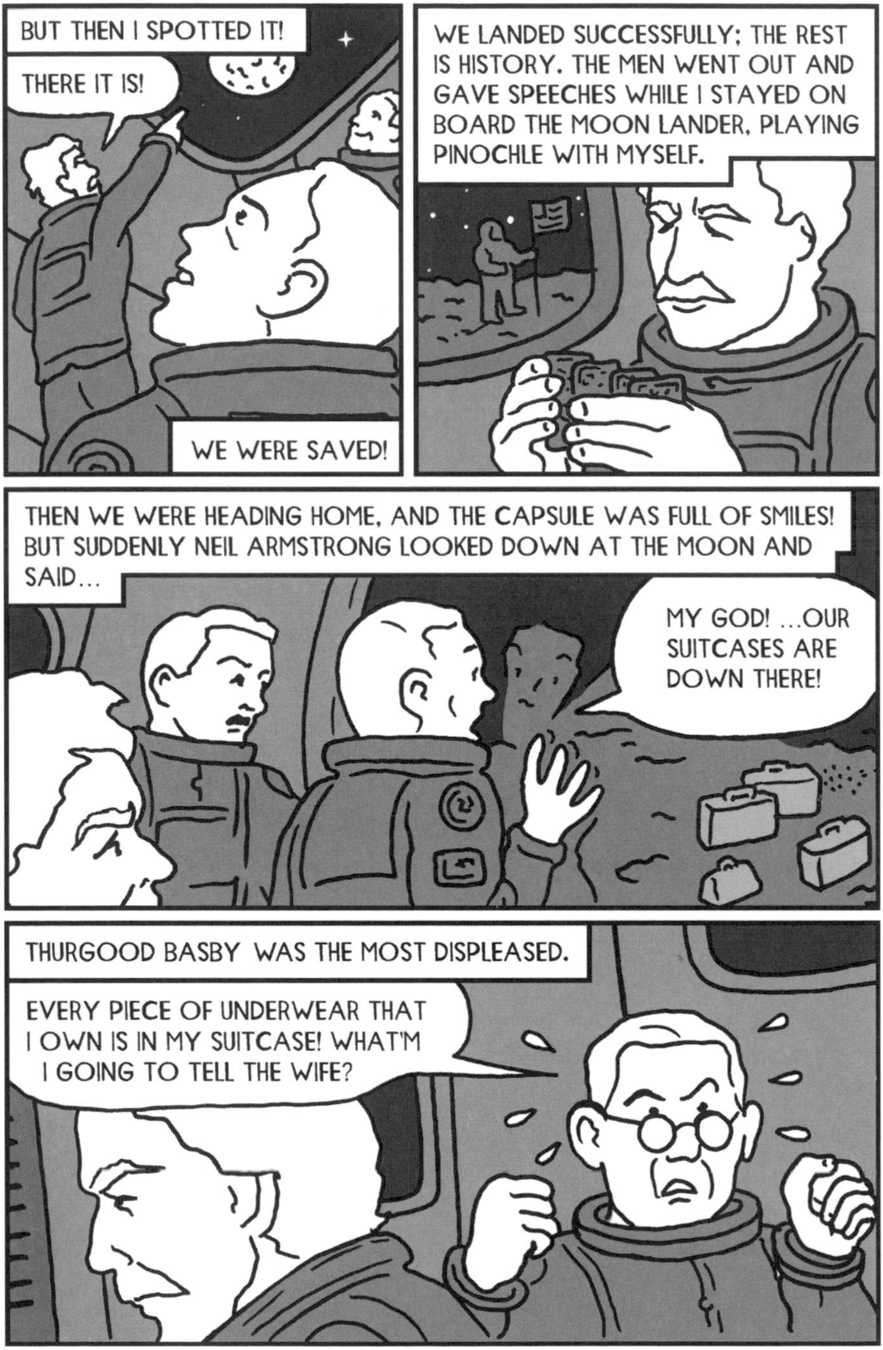
BUT THEN I SPOTTED IT!
THERE IT IS!
WE WERE SAVED!
WE LANDED SUCCESSFULLY; THE REST IS HISTORY. THE MEN WENT OUT AND GAVE SPEECHES WHILE I STAYED ON BOARD THE MOON LANDER, PLAYING PINOCHLE WITH MYSELF.
THEN WE WERE HEADING HOME, AND THE CAPSULE WAS FULL OF SMILES! BUT SUDDENLY NEIL ARMSTRONG LOOKED DOWN AT THE MOON AND SAID...
MY GOD! ...OUR SUITCASES ARE DOWN THERE!
THURGOOD BASBY WAS THE MOST DISPLEASED.
EVERY PIECE OF UNDERWEAR THAT I OWN IS IN MY SUITCASE! WHAT'M I GOING TO TELL THE WIFE?

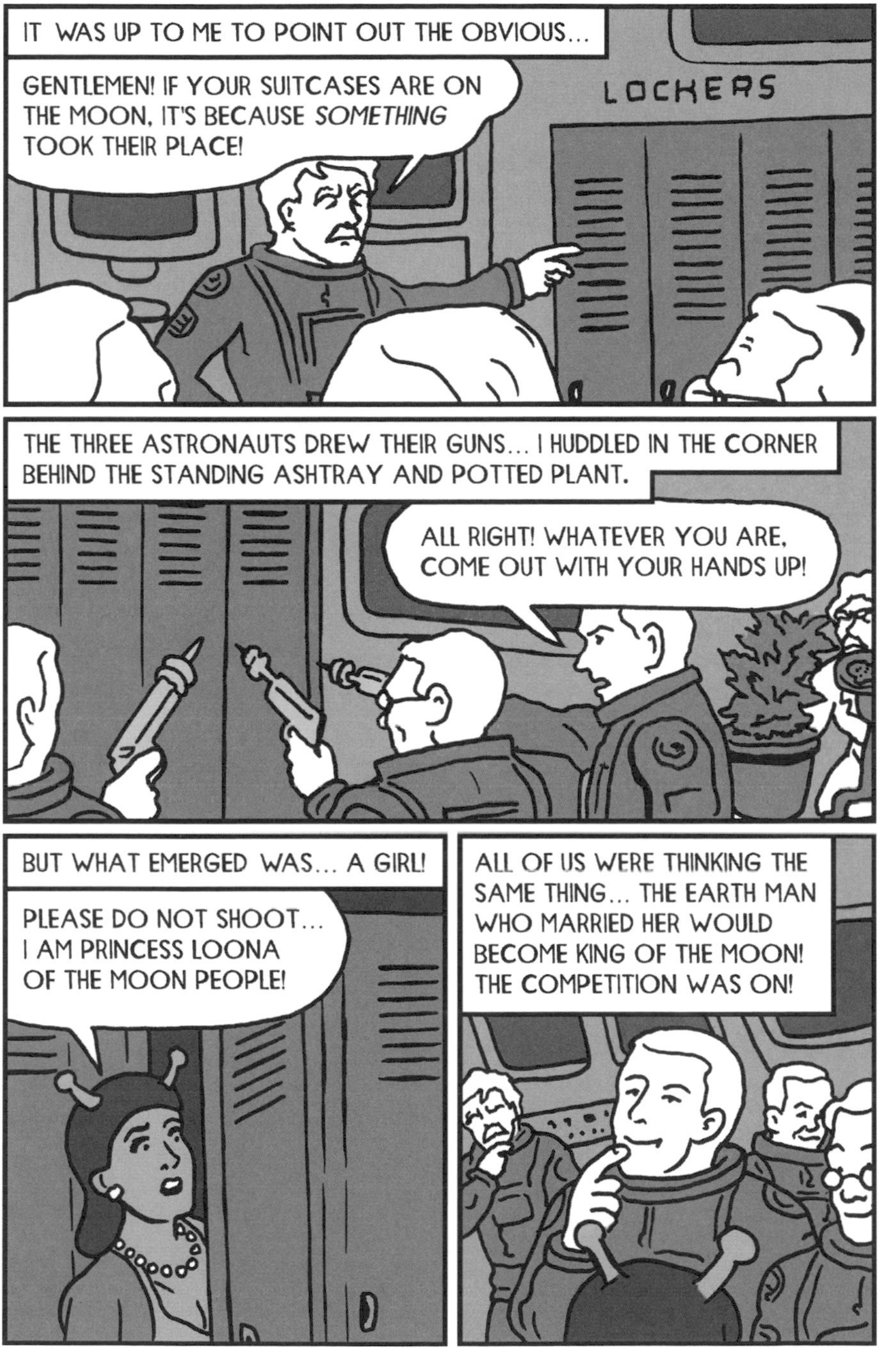
IT WAS UP TO ME TO POINT OUT THE OBVIOUS...
GENTLEMEN! IF YOUR SUITCASES ARE ON THE MOON, IT'S BECAUSE *SOMETHING* TOOK THEIR PLACE!
LOCKERS
THE THREE ASTRONAUTS DREW THEIR GUNS... I HUDDLED IN THE CORNER BEHIND THE STANDING ASHTRAY AND POTTED PLANT.
ALL RIGHT! WHATEVER YOU ARE, COME OUT WITH YOUR HANDS UP!
BUT WHAT EMERGED WAS... A GIRL!
PLEASE DO NOT SHOOT... I AM PRINCESS LOONA OF THE MOON PEOPLE!
ALL OF US WERE THINKING THE SAME THING... THE EARTH MAN WHO MARRIED HER WOULD BECOME KING OF THE MOON! THE COMPETITION WAS ON!

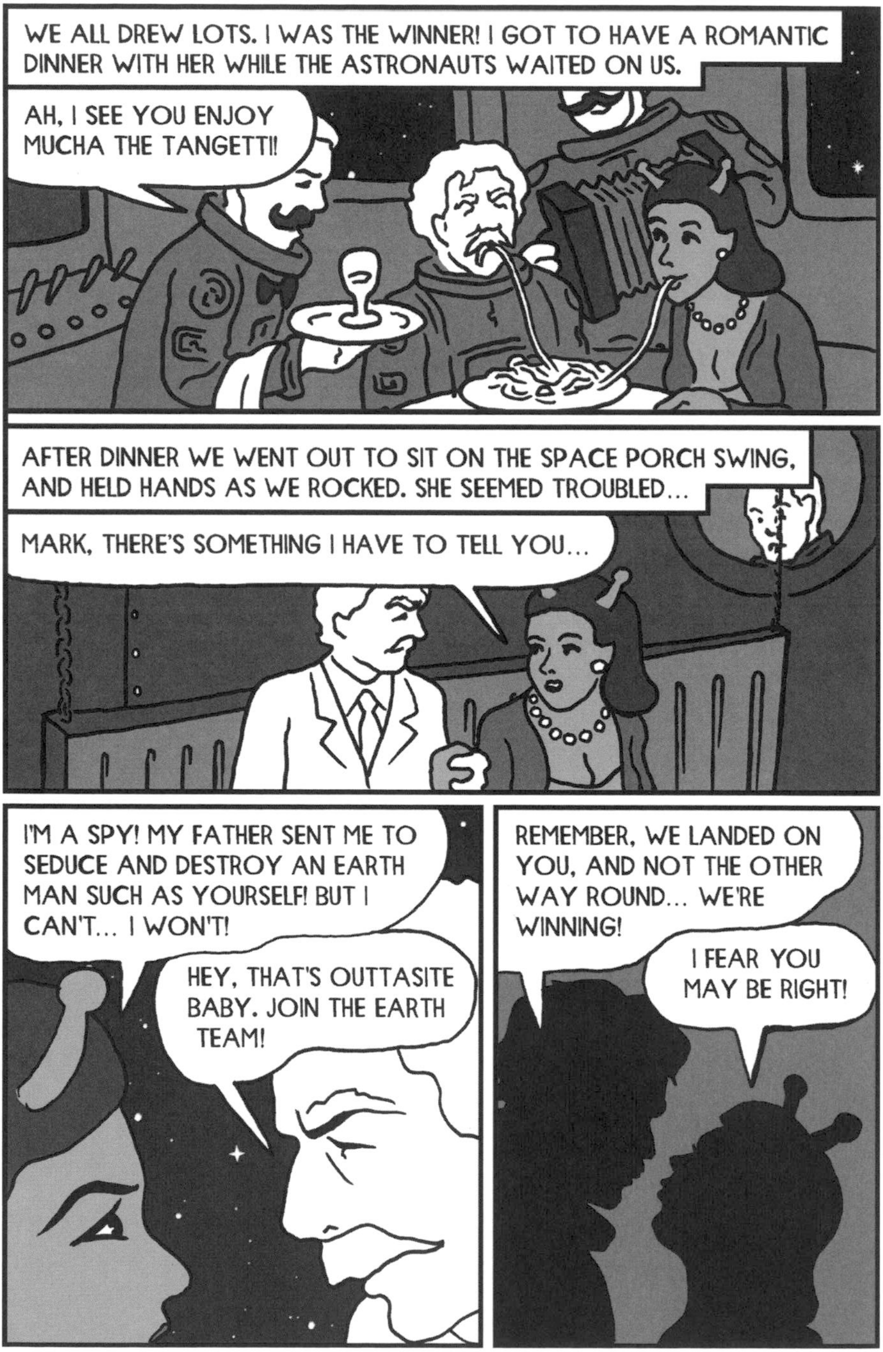
WE ALL DREW LOTS. I WAS THE WINNER! I GOT TO HAVE A ROMANTIC DINNER WITH HER WHILE THE ASTRONAUTS WAITED ON US.
AH, I SEE YOU ENJOY MUCHA THE TANGETTI!
AFTER DINNER WE WENT OUT TO SIT ON THE SPACE PORCH SWING, AND HELD HANDS AS WE ROCKED. SHE SEEMED TROUBLED...
MARK, THERE'S SOMETHING I HAVE TO TELL YOU...
I'M A SPY! MY FATHER SENT ME TO SEDUCE AND DESTROY AN EARTH MAN SUCH AS YOURSELF! BUT I CAN'T... I WON'T!
HEY, THAT'S OUTTASITE BABY. JOIN THE EARTH TEAM!
REMEMBER, WE LANDED ON YOU, AND NOT THE OTHER WAY ROUND... WE'RE WINNING!
I FEAR YOU MAY BE RIGHT!

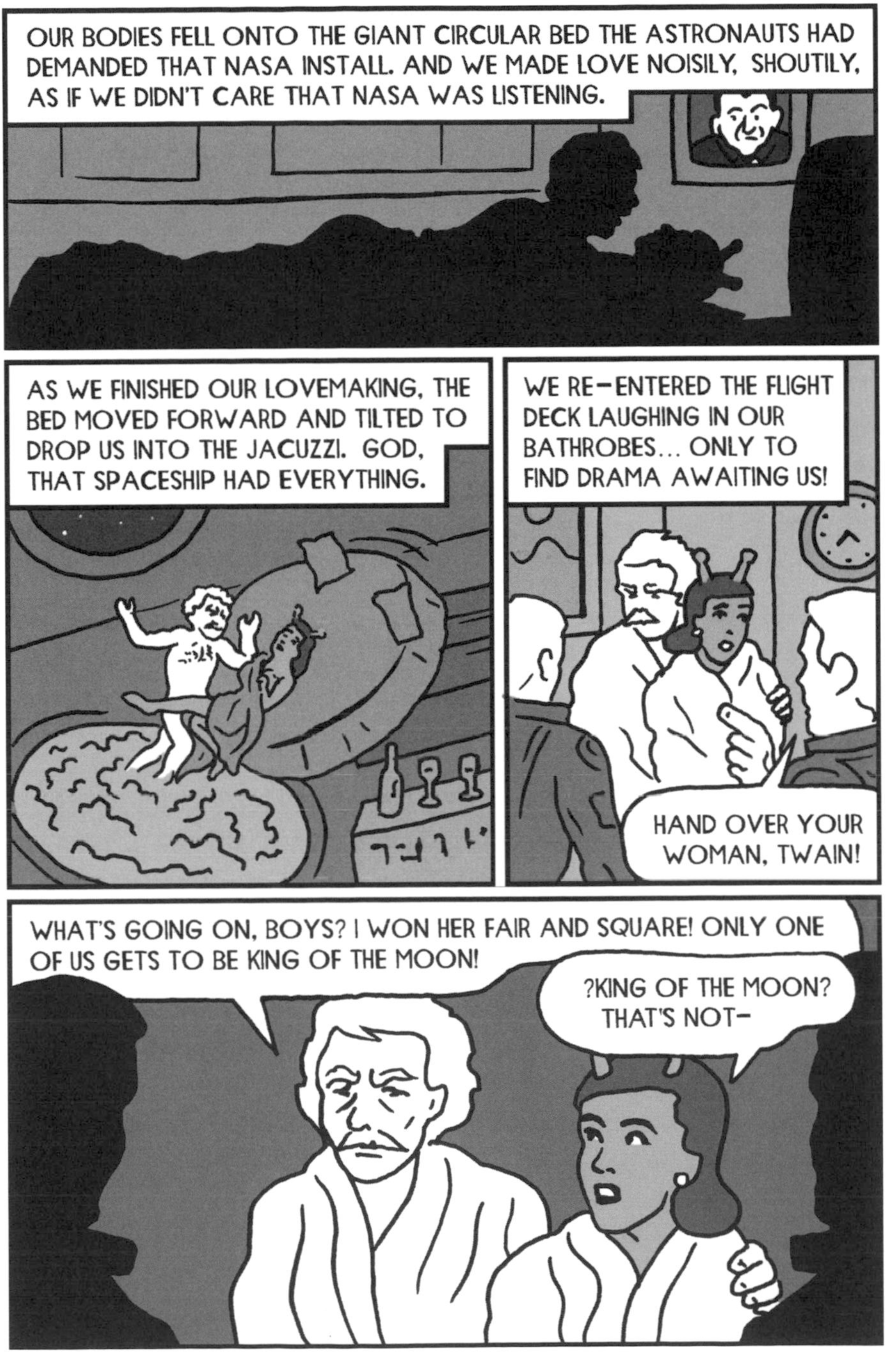
OUR BODIES FELL ONTO THE GIANT CIRCULAR BED THE ASTRONAUTS HAD DEMANDED THAT NASA INSTALL. AND WE MADE LOVE NOISILY, SHOUTILY, AS IF WE DIDN'T CARE THAT NASA WAS LISTENING.
AS WE FINISHED OUR LOVEMAKING, THE BED MOVED FORWARD AND TILTED TO DROP US INTO THE JACUZZI. GOD, THAT SPACESHIP HAD EVERYTHING.
WE RE-ENTERED THE FLIGHT DECK LAUGHING IN OUR BATHROBES... ONLY TO FIND DRAMA AWAITING US!
HAND OVER YOUR WOMAN, TWAIN!
WHAT'S GOING ON, BOYS? I WON HER FAIR AND SQUARE! ONLY ONE OF US GETS TO BE KING OF THE MOON!
?KING OF THE MOON? THAT'S NOT-

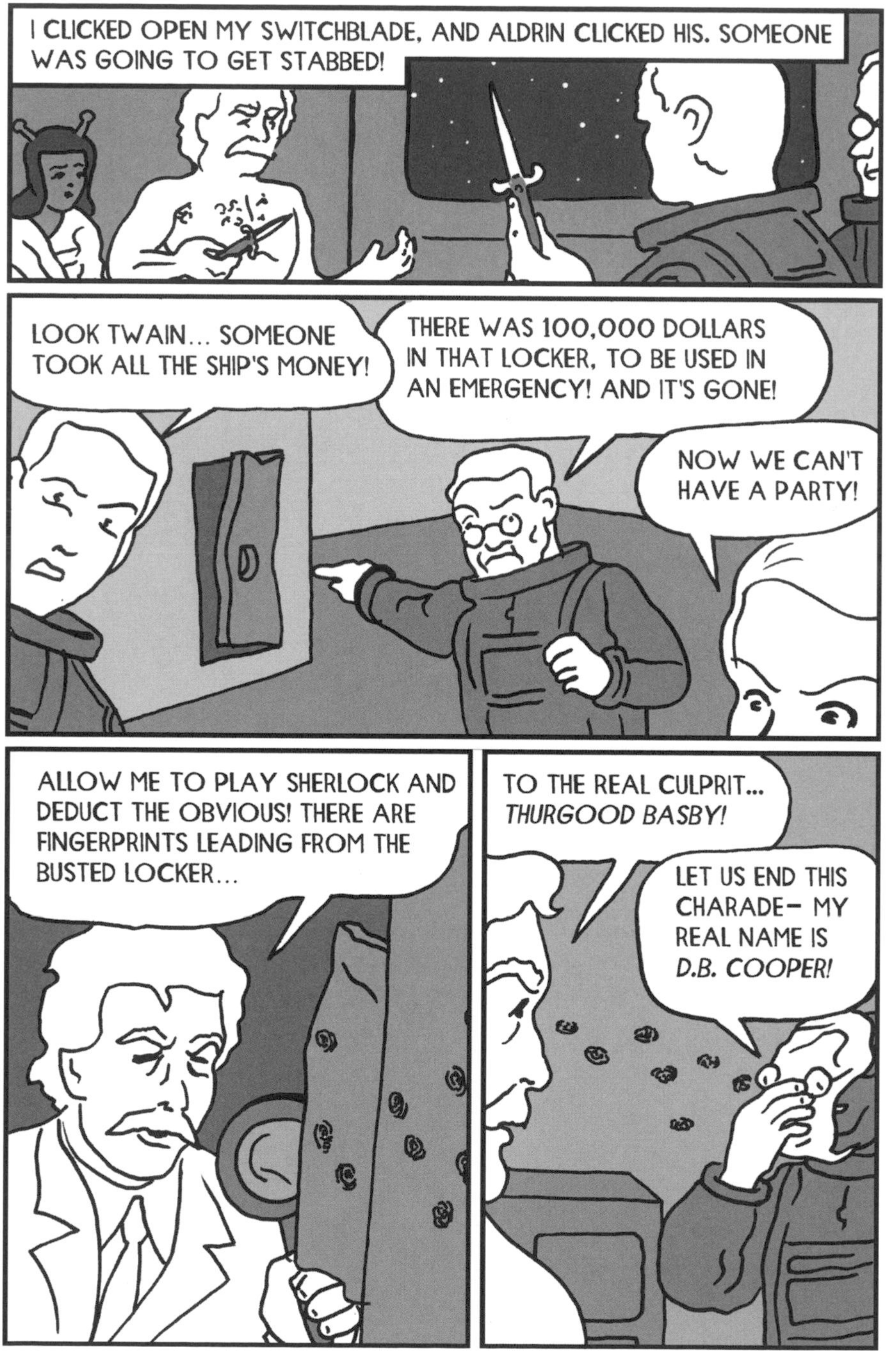
I CLICKED OPEN MY SWITCHBLADE, AND ALDRIN CLICKED HIS. SOMEONE WAS GOING TO GET STABBED!
LOOK TWAIN... SOMEONE TOOK ALL THE SHIP'S MONEY!
THERE WAS 100,000 DOLLARS IN THAT LOCKER, TO BE USED IN AN EMERGENCY! AND IT'S GONE!
NOW WE CAN'T HAVE A PARTY!
ALLOW ME TO PLAY SHERLOCK AND DEDUCT THE OBVIOUS! THERE ARE FINGERPRINTS LEADING FROM THE BUSTED LOCKER...
TO THE REAL CULPRIT... *THURGOOD BASBY!*
LET US END THIS CHARADE– MY REAL NAME IS *D.B. COOPER!*

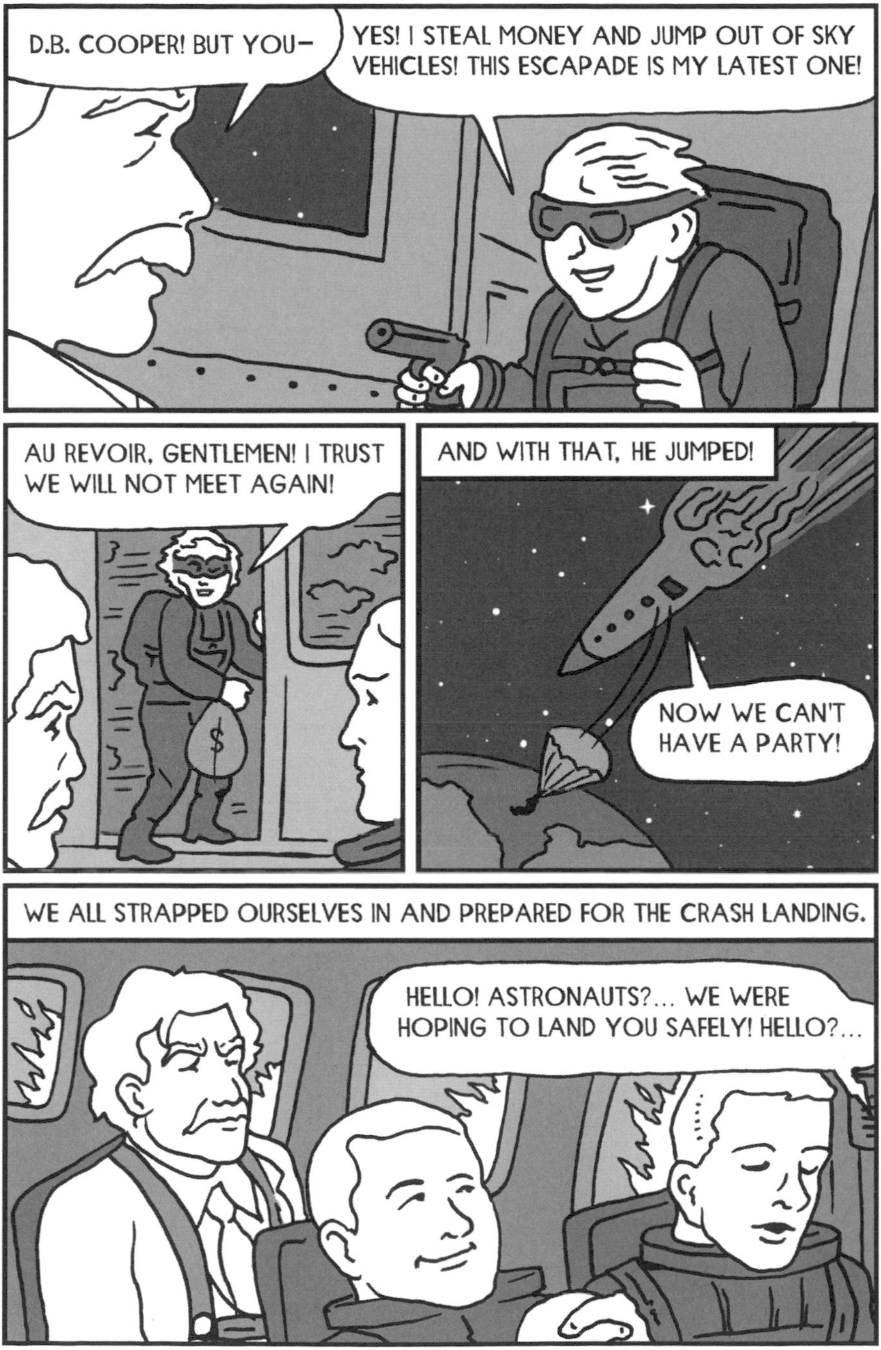
D.B. COOPER! BUT YOU–
YES! I STEAL MONEY AND JUMP OUT OF SKY VEHICLES! THIS ESCAPADE IS MY LATEST ONE!
AU REVOIR, GENTLEMEN! I TRUST WE WILL NOT MEET AGAIN!
AND WITH THAT, HE JUMPED!
$
NOW WE CAN'T HAVE A PARTY!
WE ALL STRAPPED OURSELVES IN AND PREPARED FOR THE CRASH LANDING.
HELLO! ASTRONAUTS?... WE WERE HOPING TO LAND YOU SAFELY! HELLO?...

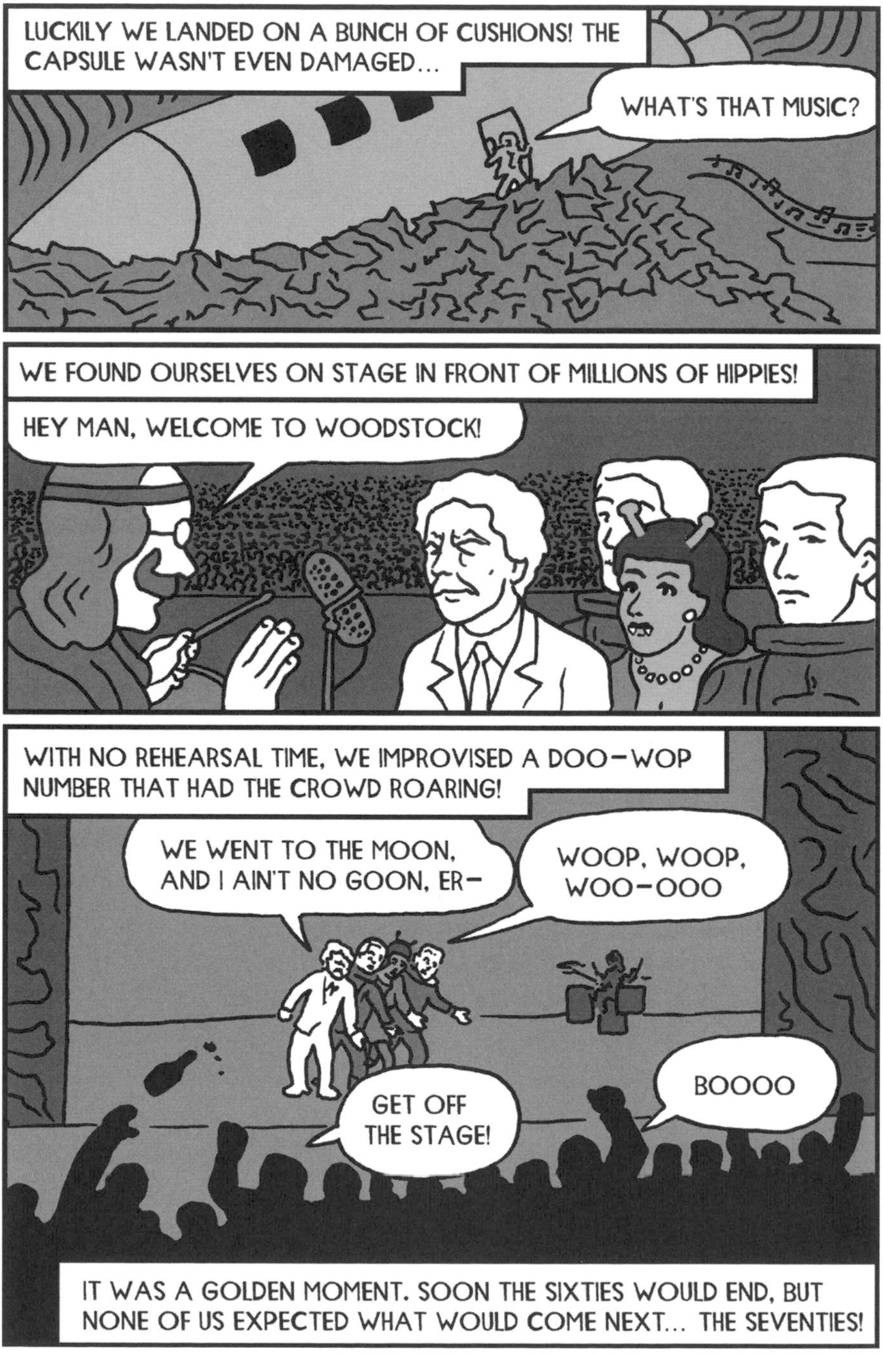
LUCKILY WE LANDED ON A BUNCH OF CUSHIONS! THE CAPSULE WASN'T EVEN DAMAGED...
WHAT'S THAT MUSIC?
WE FOUND OURSELVES ON STAGE IN FRONT OF MILLIONS OF HIPPIES!
HEY MAN, WELCOME TO WOODSTOCK!
WITH NO REHEARSAL TIME, WE IMPROVISED A DOO-WOP NUMBER THAT HAD THE CROWD ROARING!
WE WENT TO THE MOON, AND I AIN'T NO GOON, ER-
WOOP, WOOP, WOO-OOO
GET OFF THE STAGE!
BOOOO
IT WAS A GOLDEN MOMENT. SOON THE SIXTIES WOULD END, BUT NONE OF US EXPECTED WHAT WOULD COME NEXT... THE SEVENTIES!

CHAPTER TWENTY-SEVEN

AN ICY DUNKING

"Come out here and face me, you snow-covered coward!" I shouted at the snowy waste. The place was Tibet, and the year was 1971. I had accepted a job as host of "Hidden Monsters," a TV series where myself and a film crew travelled the globe, investigating supposed beasts who hid from mankind, like the Loch Ness Monster or the Duluth Dinodingus. Mostly, we saw a lot of murk and fog. But on our last endeavor, a search in Tibet to find the Yeti, that mythical man-beast of nether yore, I was determined to strike paydirt.

We set out from Tibet City on August 8th, as we thought it was best to make the attempt when it was pretty snowy but not too snowy. Fifteen days out into the mountains we struck gold—or rather scat, Yeti scat (poos). We tromped around for days after that looking everywhere but no dice, and that's when I started shouting abuse. I was hoping the Yeti would somehow understand me and come out to challenge this affront to his dignity. Or something like that. I fortified myself with brandy and continued bellowing. "I can stay here all day, stupid cold weather monkey!" I sighted one particular cavehole and made it my target of abuse. "Yeti, come out and play!" There was no sign of life. "I know you're in there, you damn dirty ape! What are you doing, playing pinochle? I've got your favorite kind of candy here," I continued, switching tactics. All of a sudden I slipped and fell into the river. As I was carried along in the rushing, icy cold water I could swear I saw the smiling face of the Yeti looking down at me.

The water I was in was headed to the North Pole, and it was getting colder by the second. I could tell I was becoming encased in a block of ice. Soon everything below my waist was solidly frozen and my left hand was already trapped. While my right hand was still free I hurriedly wrote "FAMOUS AUTHOR" on the growing icy outside of the block which held me in its grasp—then I was completely frozen, and my ice-block bobbed out into the icy sea to join thousands of others at the top of the Earth.

It was several years before I'd be found and defrosted, and I remember having some very colorful dreams during that period, including one where I was King of the Owls and lived in a chocolate egg.

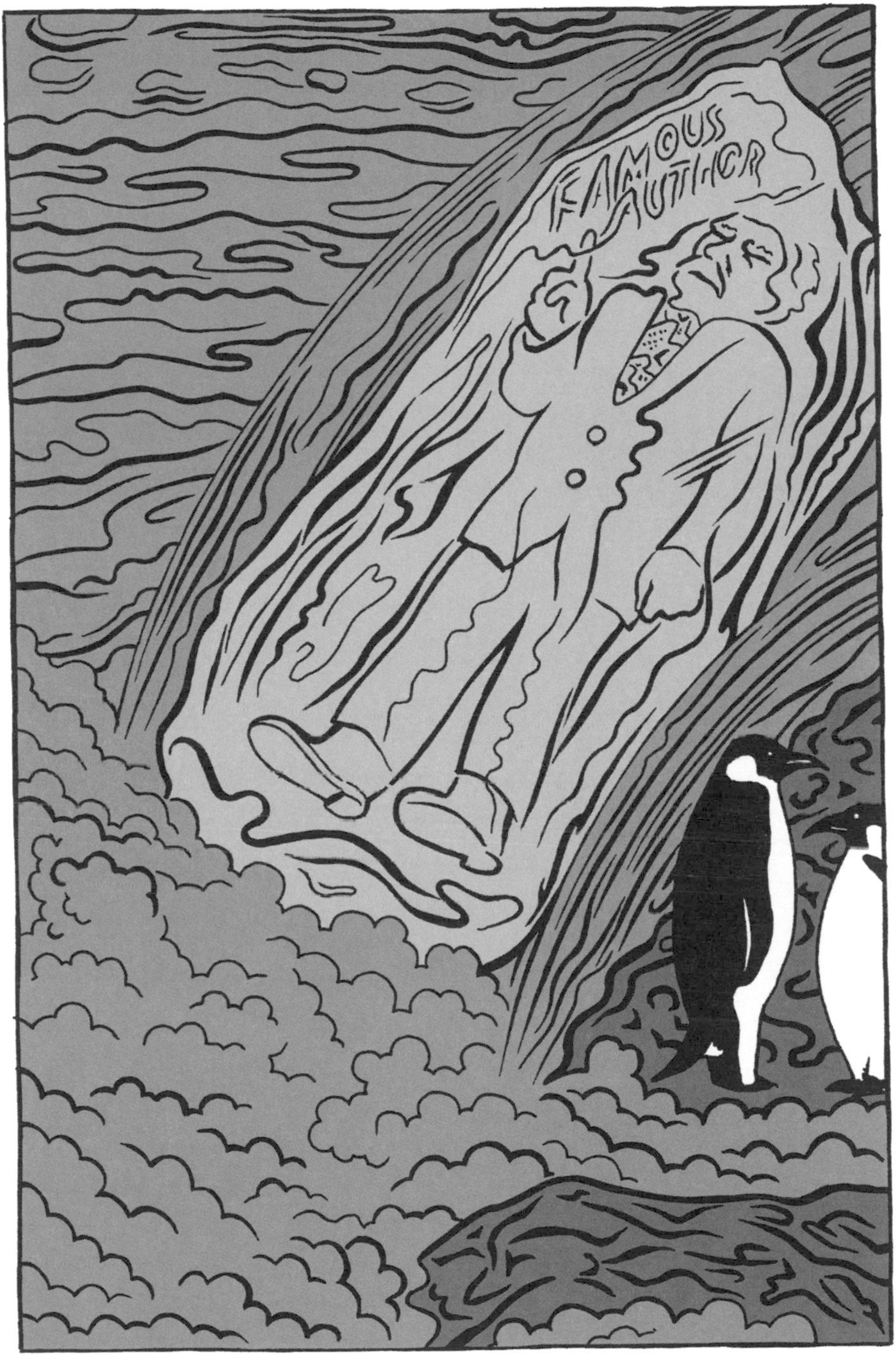
FAMOUS AUTHOR

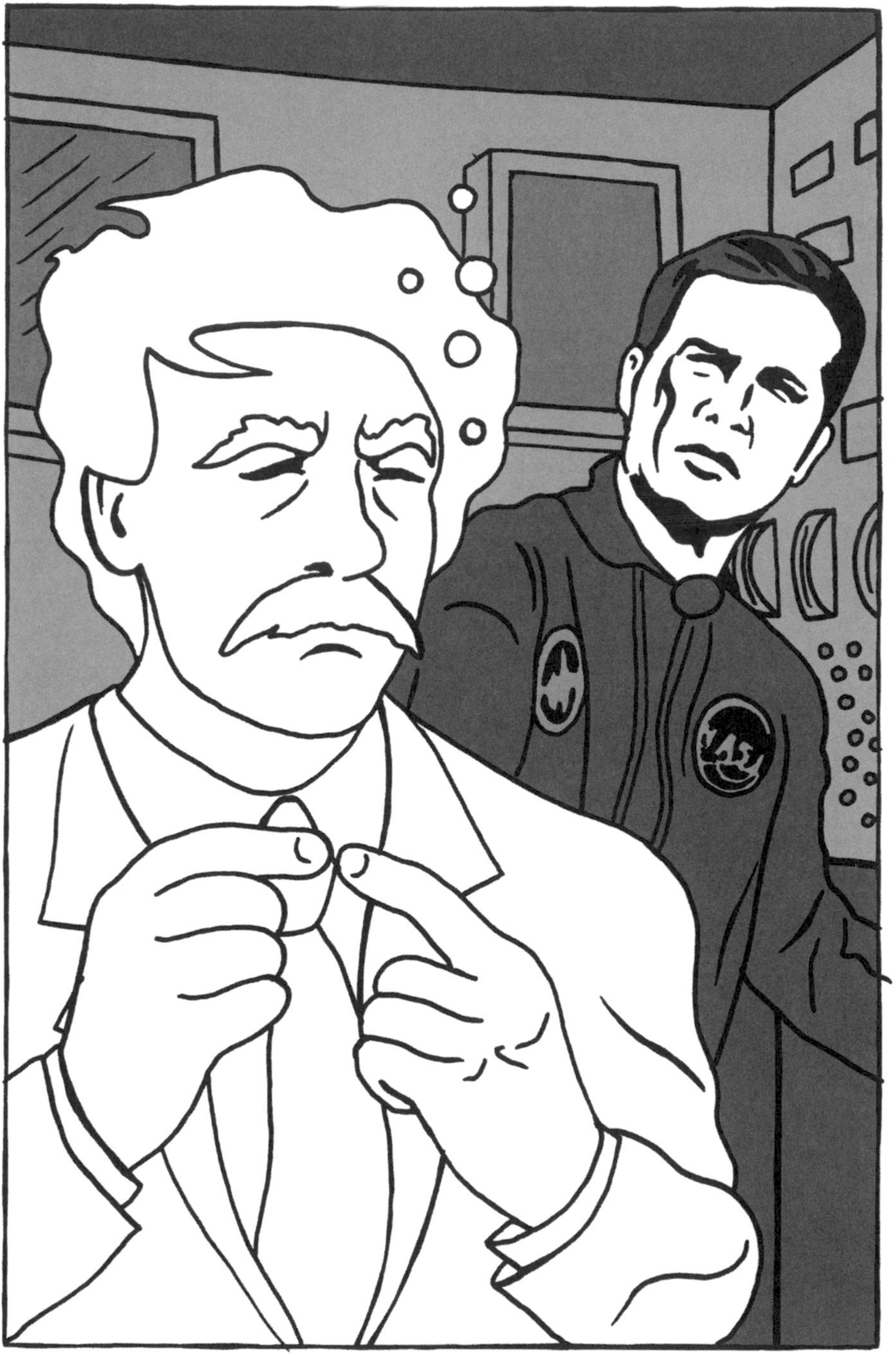

CHAPTER TWENTY-EIGHT:

THE SLEEPER GETS AWOKEN UP

The next thing I knew it was 1974, and I was getting woken up. There was a man standing in front of me who I soon found out was Steve Austin, The Six Million Dollar Man, because he told me, "I am Steve Austin, the Six Million Dollar Man." I somewhat unsteadily stood up to my full height and puffed out my chest. "Well then, I am worth ten thousand dollars" I riposted. "Mister Twain, you've been asleep a long time. A million is more than a thousand," he informed me. He was right. I realized I was still drunk from three years earlier.

"You'll be interested to know," he informed me, "the President has just resigned, because he was implicated in criminal malfeasance." Richard Nixon had quit! I knew he was a crook the moment he accidentally chastised his thugs over the radio during my Moon launch adventure. It turned out I had missed out on a lot during the last three years, including the end of the Vietnam War, the launch of Skylab, and the final episode of *Bewitched*. Oh well.

Austin informed me that I had been unfrosted in perfect health, except for the big toe on my right foot, which had developed frostbite and had had to be removed. They had taken their scientific initiative and replaced it with an ultra-modern hydraulic version. "It can lift great weights up stairwells" he explained. "You can probably lift a thousand pounds with this toe." I said I wasn't using it and I never have. Hydraulic big toe! What's wrong with these people? They should have made my big toe a magnet that would attract bad guy's guns—*that* would be useful.

Steve was an ex-astronaut and half-robot, as I'm sure most of you know. At that time they were doing a TV series based on his life. I made a guest appearance in one episode as the villain, the nefarious Mansquito; I wore a yellow and green bug costume with an enormous stinger, and did a lot of chuckling and rubbing my hands, although finally I was flattened beneath a giant fly swatter.

I always respected Steve for his mechanicalness, but he smelled faintly of motor oil.

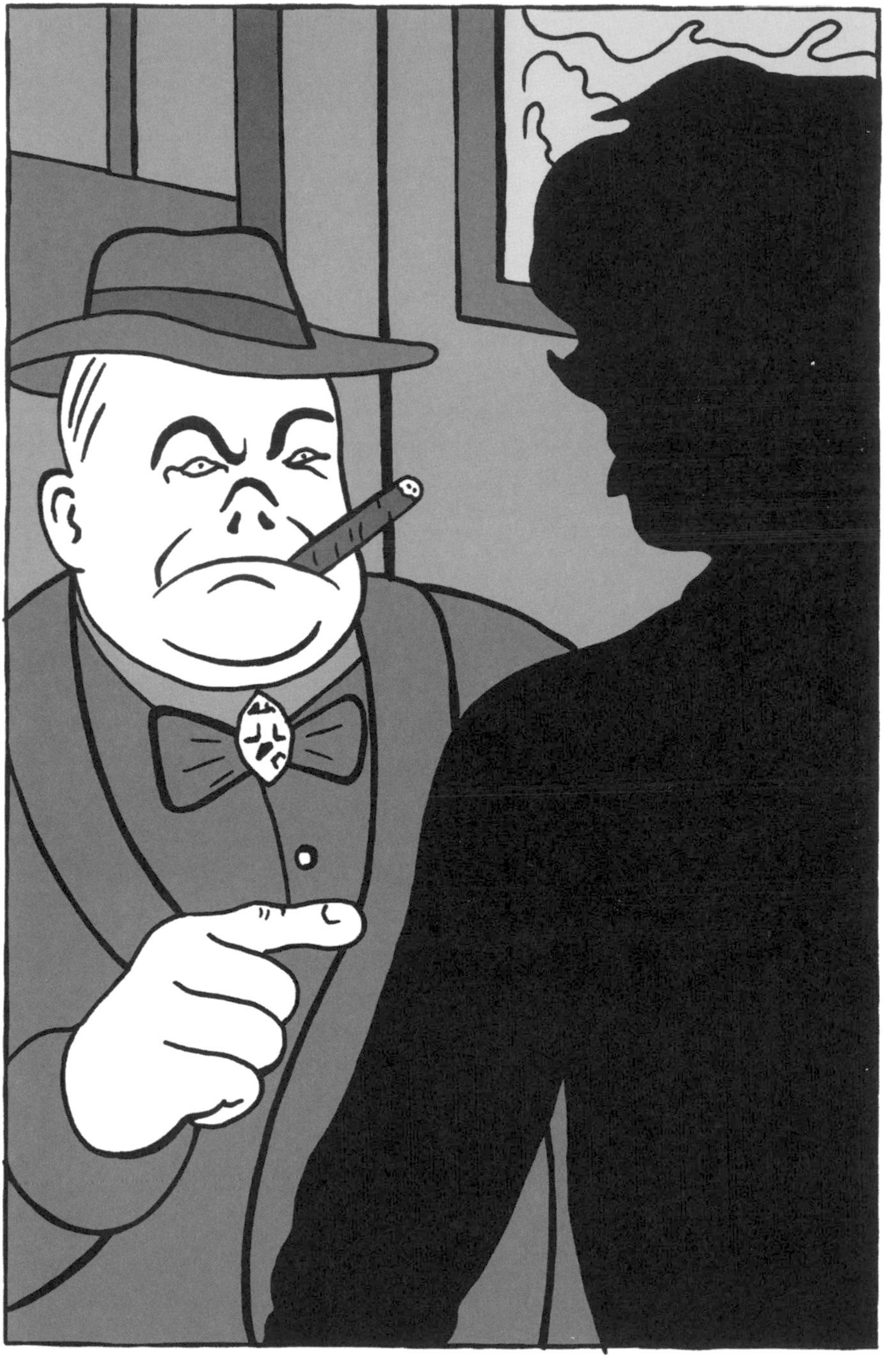

CHAPTER TWENTY-NINE:

I TINGLE AMERICA'S DINGLE

In 1976 America was feeling sexier than ever before. Jimmy Carter was campaigning with lust in his heart, and key parties and swing clubs had completely transformed suburban neighborhoods. I stood by, bemused; if my Victorian ancestors could only have seen this, they who became so aroused at the sight of an exposed ankle! Now films like *Ankles Away* showed them being used in the most sexually explicit manner filmable. I had no idea that soon I was to be on display in this particular arena, of that you may be sure!

I had returned to writing, and had a number-one bestseller in 1978 with *Spank My Donkey Ass Lust*, a rollicking, ribald picaresque slice of life roman à clef set in the advertising industry. Inspired by the book's success, the *New York Times* came a-calling to ask me to do an editorial on any subject which inspired passion in my heart or brain. I decided to write an article deploring Mammon, the hypothetical deity of materialism and riches, whose greedy influence has so weakened the American brain.

Unfortunately the *Times*'s copy editor misunderstood the name and changed it to Mammo. Mammo was the notorious gangster who ran a topless-lady "Mammogram" service in most urban centers. This was like the old singing-telegram business but with bare breasts instead of vocalization. Mammo had been imported in his youth from the harsh docks of Marseilles and had risen to become a feared vice lord—imagine my surprise when I opened the Sunday *Times* and saw that I had just written a public editorial denouncing him! I went to the police for protection, but they said without evidence their hands were tied. I went home and sat quivering, awaiting his approach. Sure enough, soon I heard footsteps. The door opened and there he was: Mammo! His flat, slit-like eyes glared at me from their position in his blocky head atop a massive body—fists the size of hams swung at his sides. He grunted for a few minutes, then spoke. "You no like Mammo? What Mammo done to you?" he demanded. I explained about the mixup at the *Times* and promised to issue a correction. He nodded, then pointed his sausage finger at my face. "You make it up to Mammo? You be in Mammo's movie!" I agreed without considering, as I have always enjoyed doing a bit of acting, and how bad could his film be? Well, I soon found out!

"Man is the only animal that blushes, or needs to" I wrote quite a long time ago. Imagine my blushes when I got to the set Monday morning and was greeted by bare butts. It was a porno movie! I almost ran for it, but Mammo emerged from his office and explained that I wouldn't have to take my clothes off, unless of course I wanted to. I was to be playing a professor of literature named Dixton Mulberworthy, who would resemble myself and tell a group of assembled co-eds that they would receive extracurricular credits for doing the simplest of all acts that humans can do with their conjoined nether regions. I completed my lines and exited gracefully, although I did stay to watch the filming for the rest of that day. I also came back and watched the filming for the rest of the week as well. The film turned out pretty well, I think, it's called *Switching Positions* and by today's standards it's pretty tame, apart for the constant close-ups of entwined genitals moistly conjoining. The *New York Times* raved about the sex, which they called "masturbatorially inspiring," but they derided my "sixth-rate Professor Irwin Corey imitation." Ouch!

Unfortunately, that sneaky Mammo had another trick up his sleeve. Taking outtakes of me sitting around staring into space, he combined them with footage of a disguised stand-in to produce a new film called *The Erotic Adventures of Mark Twain*. I sued to prevent its release, but to no avail. The movie was cunningly constructed to withstand legal action, but made it appear as if I was a horny fellow who doffed his duds and literally leapt into every sexually consummative situation which life offered. I would like to emphasize, I have never had sex with a dozen women at once, nor have I ever shared a woman with Henry Kissinger. Such was the licentious spirit of the day that the film brought me literally dozens of sexual offers, only a few of which I accepted.

The fellow who played me in the movie had the nerve to change his name to Mack Twain, and to star in an increasingly shameful series of stag reels and videos throughout the 1980s—titles such as *Twainal* and *Yank My King Arthur Pork*, with laughable production values and nonsensical storylines. It was painful for me to be associated with such tawdry dross, although I met Mack later and he was a delightful fellow, and good company for a night's drinking.

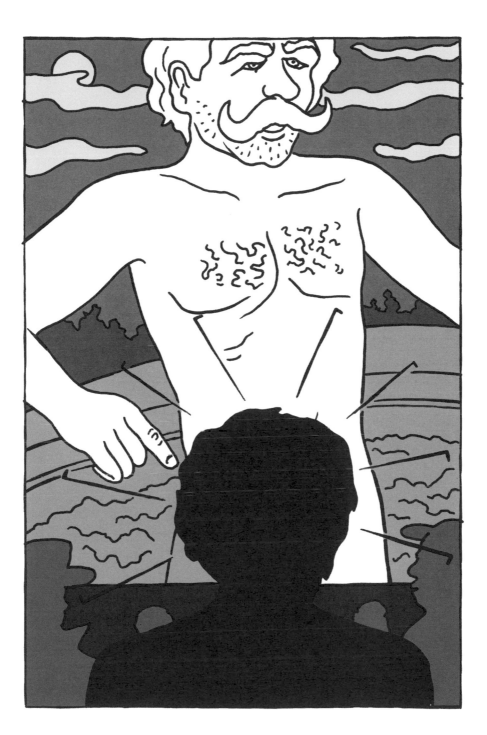

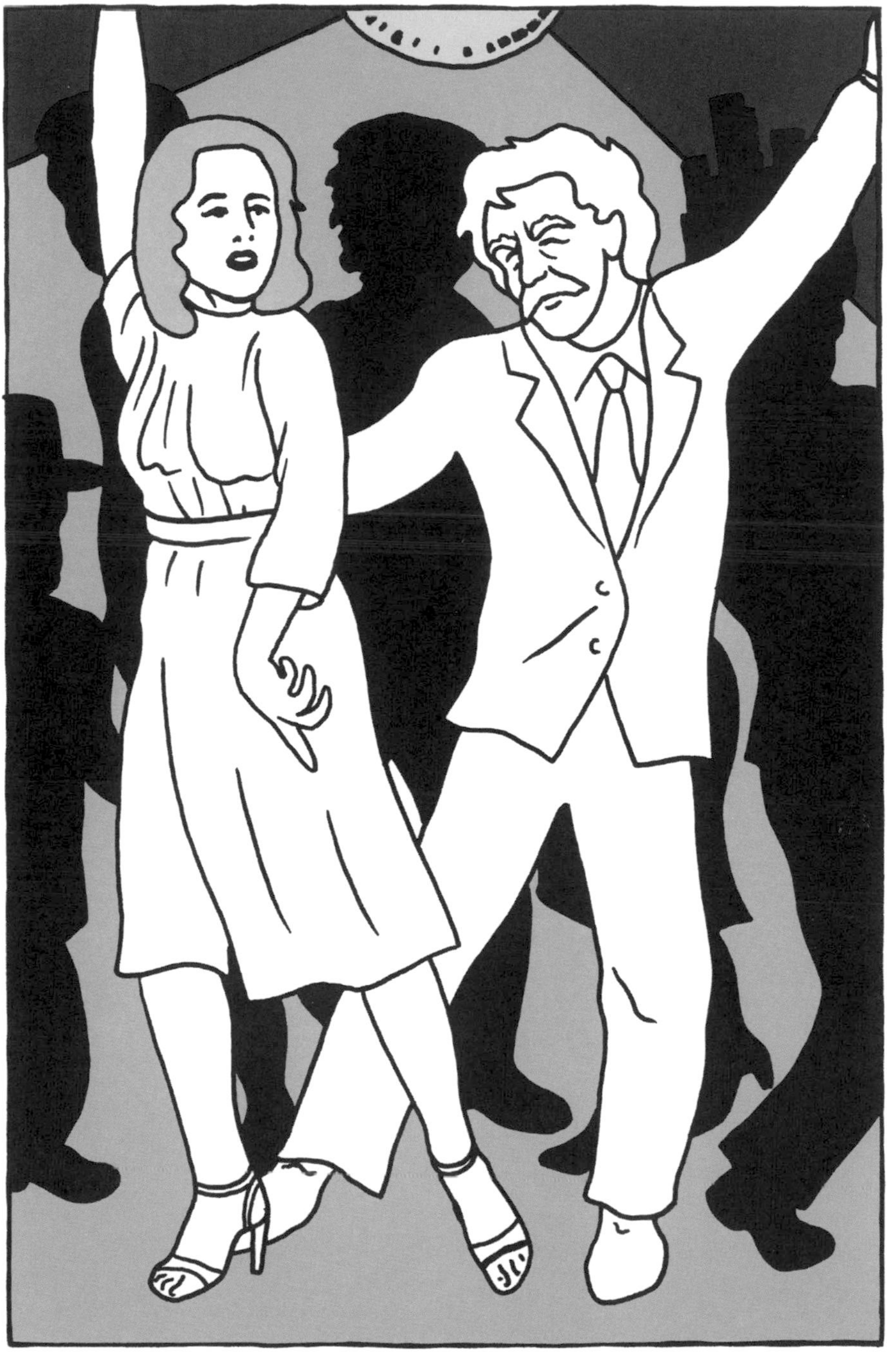

CHAPTER THIRTY

DANCING THE NIGHT AWAY

In the 1970s New York City faced the darkness and partied on. Bankruptcy and blackouts plagued the Big Apple, yet notable writers, artists and performers such as myself made it their home because of its fantastic discos. Hotspots such as Basement 69 and The Waffle Club more than made up for the rats that nipped at our ankles as we boogied.

An average evening might see me venturing from my brownstone penthouse at 10 PM and heading to Mr. Discos. There I'd enjoy a fabulous buffet of party shrimp with luminaries such as Hobnobberella, Princess Fragrance, Salvador Dali Jr. and Bronx impersonator Bronxwell. Around 11:30 I would make my move to Party City, where I'd usually see Pepper Wepperling, Mazooma Bronson, Shields and Yarnell, and President Carter, who flew down many evenings to boogie his woes away. At 1 AM we might go to the Thrill Hole, to disco vigorously with the likes of Witchina, Norman and Bubbles Mailer, Delighter Jones, Swami Salami, Boss Hogg, and Wooga Mackenzie. At 3 AM I'd slow down at a mellower disco such as Muttley's Infernohole, where I'd enjoy the company of Rollerhoncho, Lauren Bacall, Lauren Hutton, Lauren Order, Mister Cholesterol, Mimsy Frimpton, Faboola, Hairy S. Truman, Napoleon Gynomite, Oops Van Whoopee, Peter Fonda, Fonda Peters, Peter Falk, Jonas Salk, Jonah the biblical character, and Tempest Hurricane. At 5 AM I'd stop at Moochy's for a small brandy—Woody Allen or Idi Amin would usually be there—and then I'd finish the night having breakfast at a diner with friends such as Toni Basil, Meatloaf, Mashed Potatoes, Hot Chocolate, Stacka Pancakes, Alfalfa, Potatoes Browning, Soupy Sales, Khoffi Annan, Juice Newton and Melanie. God, those were the days.

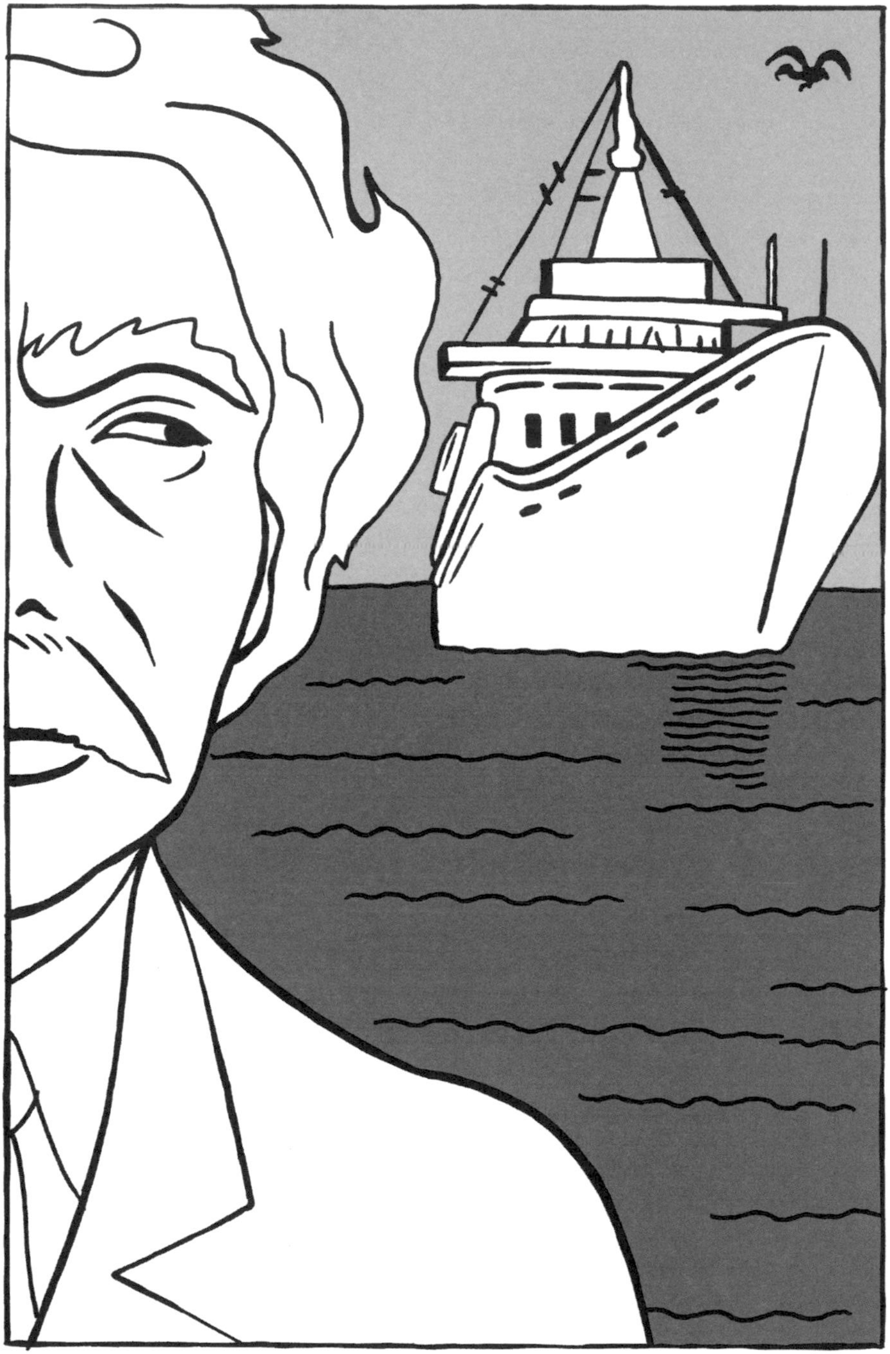

CHAPTER THIRTY-ONE:

I CLIMB INSIDE THE BOX

Doing the *Six Million Dollar Man* show thing had netted me a television agent, and one day in 1979 he called me. "Mark baby, bubbaleh, let's cut through the schmaltz because you give me nachas!" (He was Jewish). "The reason I'm calling is, I got a call from the producers of a show called *The Love Boat*. Don't know if you've seen it (I hadn't, too busy discoing), but it's a show where all these couples go on a boat, or maybe they meet on the boat, the boat is part of it, and they're using a lot of older actors to draw in the senior crowd. Douglas Fairbanks Jr., Lionel Stander, now they want you."

I accepted the job with alacrity—discoing doesn't pay anything and some nights it can be quite expensive—and headed out to California, where I was signed on as part of that week's cruise/episode. Playing my love interest would be Lillian Gish, who I felt was a little too old for me, although of course I'm much older than her. Also sailing were Donny Most, Yakov Smirnoff, Barbi Benton, and the Pointer Sisters. We all remembered to stay "in character" as we straggled up the gangplank merrily, greeted by members of the fictional crew. Everybody was wreathed in smiles, which showed that we had no idea about what was going to befall us.

My character's name was Morgabin Standish, and I was supposed to be an old country doctor struggling to come to terms with the loss of my wife, who had also been elderly and then died. Lillian played Flossie McRossie, a dog portrait painter who was considering a move into painting mustaches. Naturally my magnificent lip mane lured her in, and we started a prickly romance. Also I had been accidentally double-booked in a room with Donny Most, which was upsetting enough that they wrote it into the show. Donny was nice enough but a bit obstreperous. I spent most of the cruise at the bar, chatting with Isaac the bartender or Doc the Doctor. And then the iceberg appeared, looming out of the mist.

An iceberg in the South Pacific ocean? But there it was, bigger than anything anyone could've imagined. It dwarfed the ship we were on. to give you some idea of it's size, it was like thirty five office buildings piled on top of each other. And it headed straight for us.

"We're all gonna die!" screamed Paul Williams (I forgot to mention, he was in this episode too). But then the façade of the iceberg began to melt inwards—there was an opening big enough to swallow our ship, which it did. We were plunged into what seemed like pitch blackness, but then flood lights came on, blinding us. What we saw when we could focus again was an amazing sight.

The Love Boat was one of a dozen ships lined up inside the bay of this enormous fake iceberg... it was in fact a vessel, and we were inside it! Above us, on walkways and platforms, running men in uniform took up their positions, standing above us with machine guns pointed at us ready to rain hot lead. We were prisoners! They herded us into a room and closed the door. Already in the room were all the people from the other ships—it was from them we learned the true extent of our predicament.

We had been captured by the insane millionaire and would-be dictator of Earth, Stavros Helsinki. a millionaire with a lust for power and a zest for acquiring ocean liners. Also in the bay with us were the QEII, The Queen Mary, and The Lady Bigboat. I realized someone would have to do something.

I requested permission to speak to Mister Helsinki. As his goons led me at gunpoint to his office, I did my best to scan for weaknesses, and saw none. The situation appeared hopeless.

The doors opened onto an office that was the most stupendous I've ever seen. It was the size of a football field, with an swimming pool in the middle, and at the end of it sat Helsinki beneath red drapes thirty feet high. His desk was the made of solid marble and had a fountain on it. When he saw me, he put in a fresh monocle and bounded over to shake my hand.

"Mister Twain! It is such a pleasure to have you, such a distinguished man of letters, as a prisoner aboard our ship-capturing iceberg. Guards,

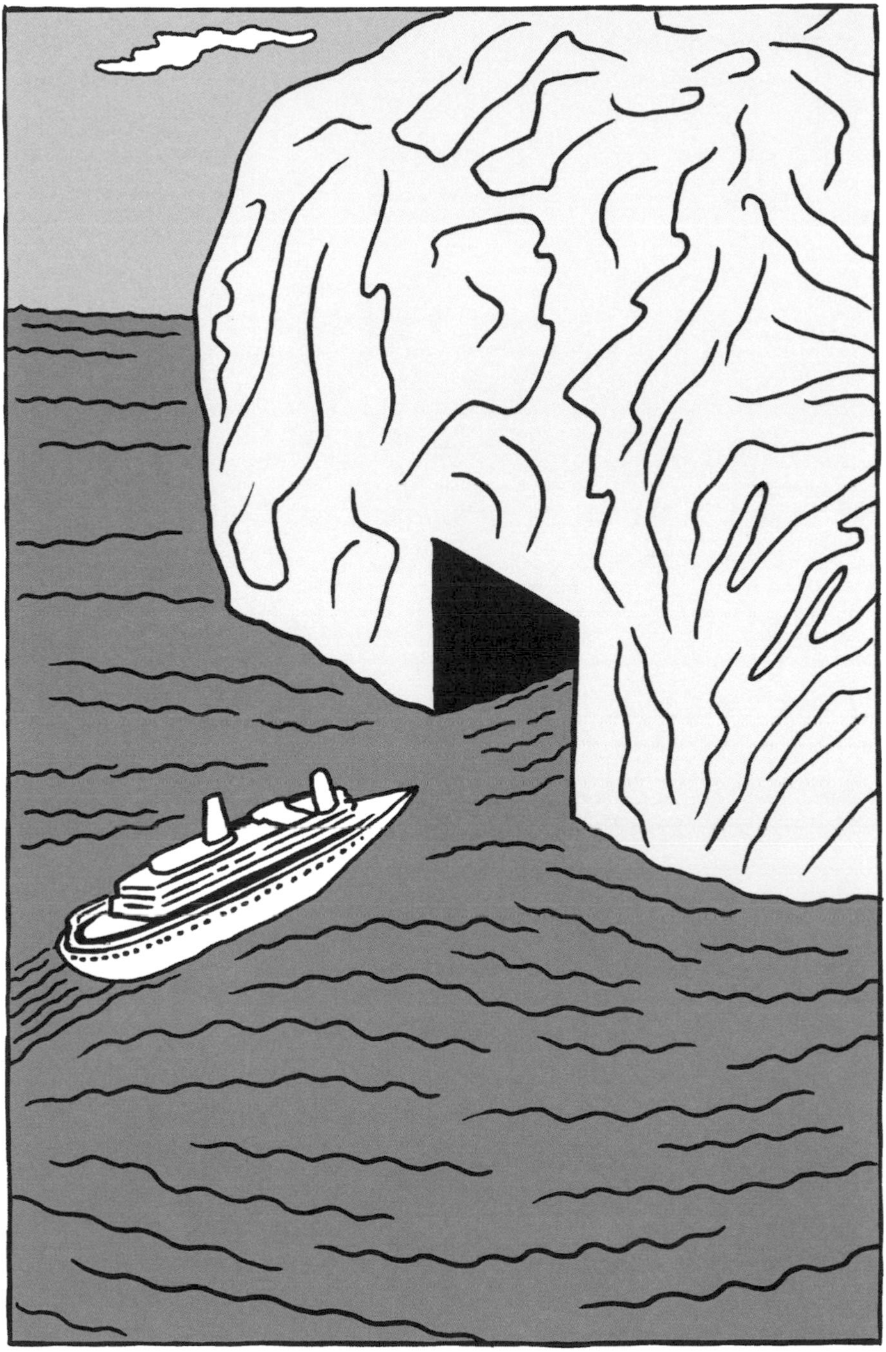

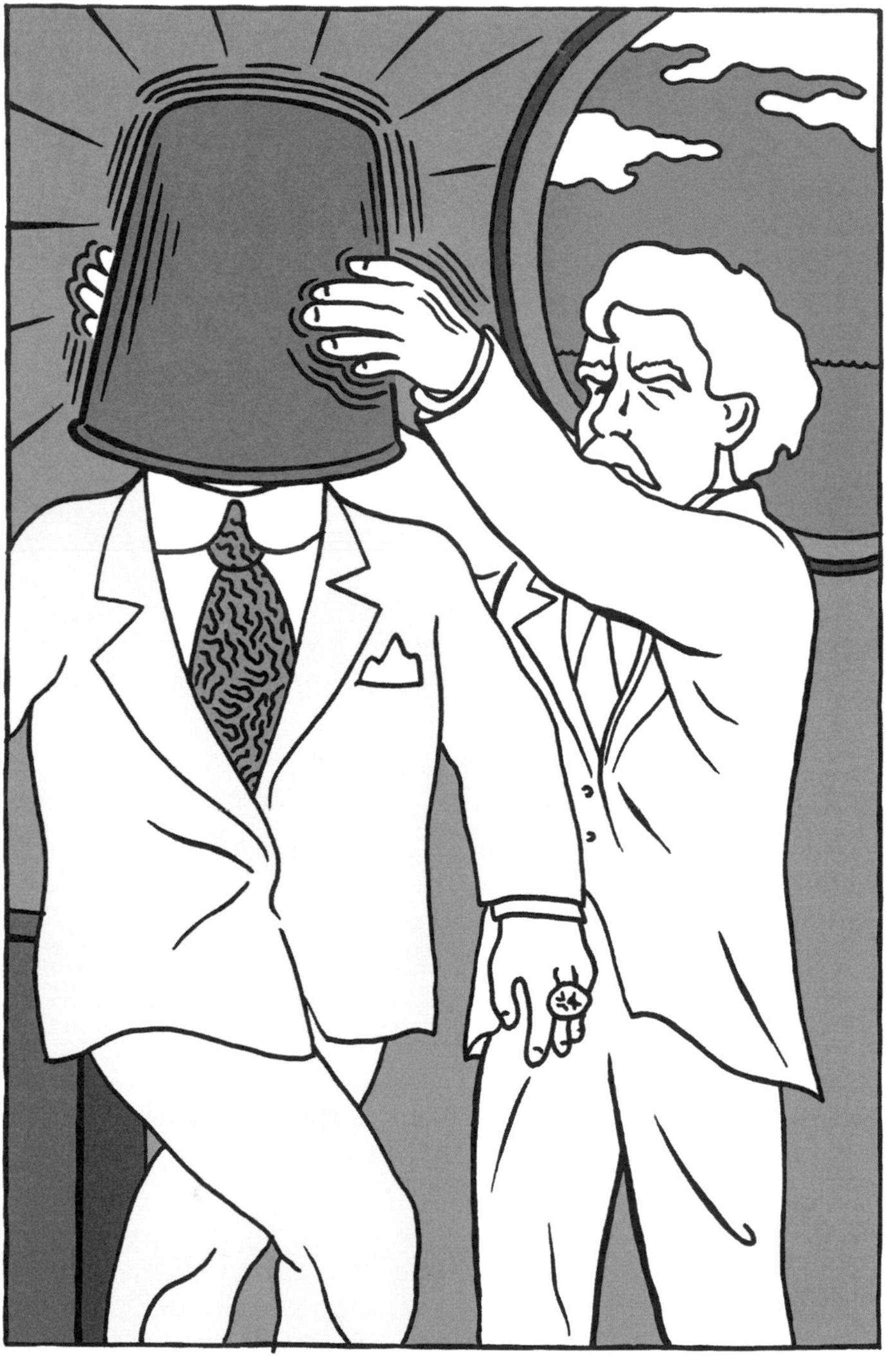

you may leave us. I am sure Mister Twain and I will have quite a delightful discussion."

With his hand, he indicated one of the nineteenth century velvet chairs sitting on the Persian rug, and he took the other.

I looked him straight in the eye as I spoke. "Mister Helsinki, I have come to you with a simple request. There are more than five thousand prisoners in a room together downstairs. I beg of you, we simply must have a bucket."

Understanding flooded his face. "But of course! I do beg your pardon, I have been entirely remiss as a host. Here, I have a bucket right here." He went behind his desk, bent down, and came up with a bucket. "It has been recently cleaned, so it is fresh for use. Here you go." "Thank you," I said, and quickly flipping the bucket over his head, I commenced banging on it with both hands. He staggered around for a bit, then sat down and fell sideways. He was out! I went to his desk and started hunting for a control panel, sure enough there was one with a red button marked "SELF DESTRUCT." Already I could hear shouts from the guards who had re-entered the office and were running towards me; I had only minutes left. I pressed the button. I also saw one that said "OPEN BAY DOOR," and I pressed that too. There was a massive shudder all through the iceberg; then it began to fall apart. A chandelier came crashing down, and rare Chinese vases began to tip off their pedestals. I darted to the left of the room, and finding a small area of rainforest, used it as cover to get back out of the office without the guards capturing me. I ran back downstairs, stairways and gangplanks collapsing behind me, and kicked down the door of the room where passengers and crew huddled cowering. "C'mon everybody, it's time to go!" I shouted. The captains of the big ships jumped in and started their ignitions, with everyone scurrying aboard like reverse rats. All twelve cruise ships shot out of the iceberg a moment before it began to sink beneath the waves. We barely made it before the whirlpool almost sucked us under, but then we were free. Nothing remained of the madman's dreams except a Chinese vase floating on the water.

The rest of our cruise continued incident-free. After the stress we'd been through I even found it possible to enjoy Donny Most's antics, and I found it easier to pretend attraction to Lillian Gish. Our episode was voted "one of the best" by the readers of *TV Guide,* and led to me appearing on shows such as *Fantasy Peninsula, Falcon Hole, Master My Servant,* and *Murder She Ate.* I appeared on the latter show seven times, and was finally offered a featured role in the spinoff *Murder He Painted.* I was Petroonius Spalding, neighbor and fatherly adviser to the show's hero, Raphael Jones, played by Dean Jones. Raphael was an absent-minded landscape painter, and every week he would accidentally paint a murder that was going on the landscape he was painting. I would give him puckish advice and share homilies while he tried to solve it. Unfortunately it only lasted six seasons.

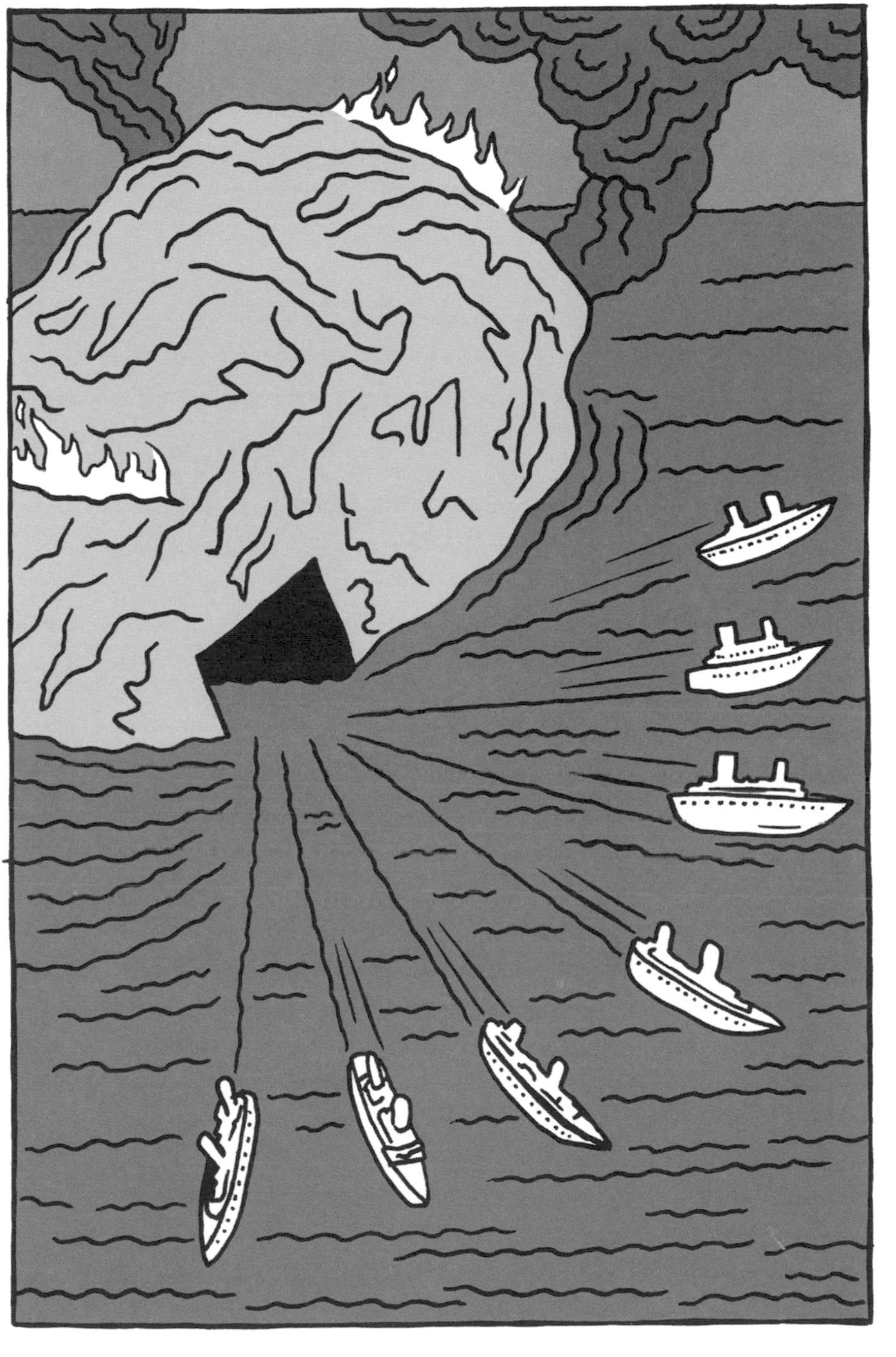

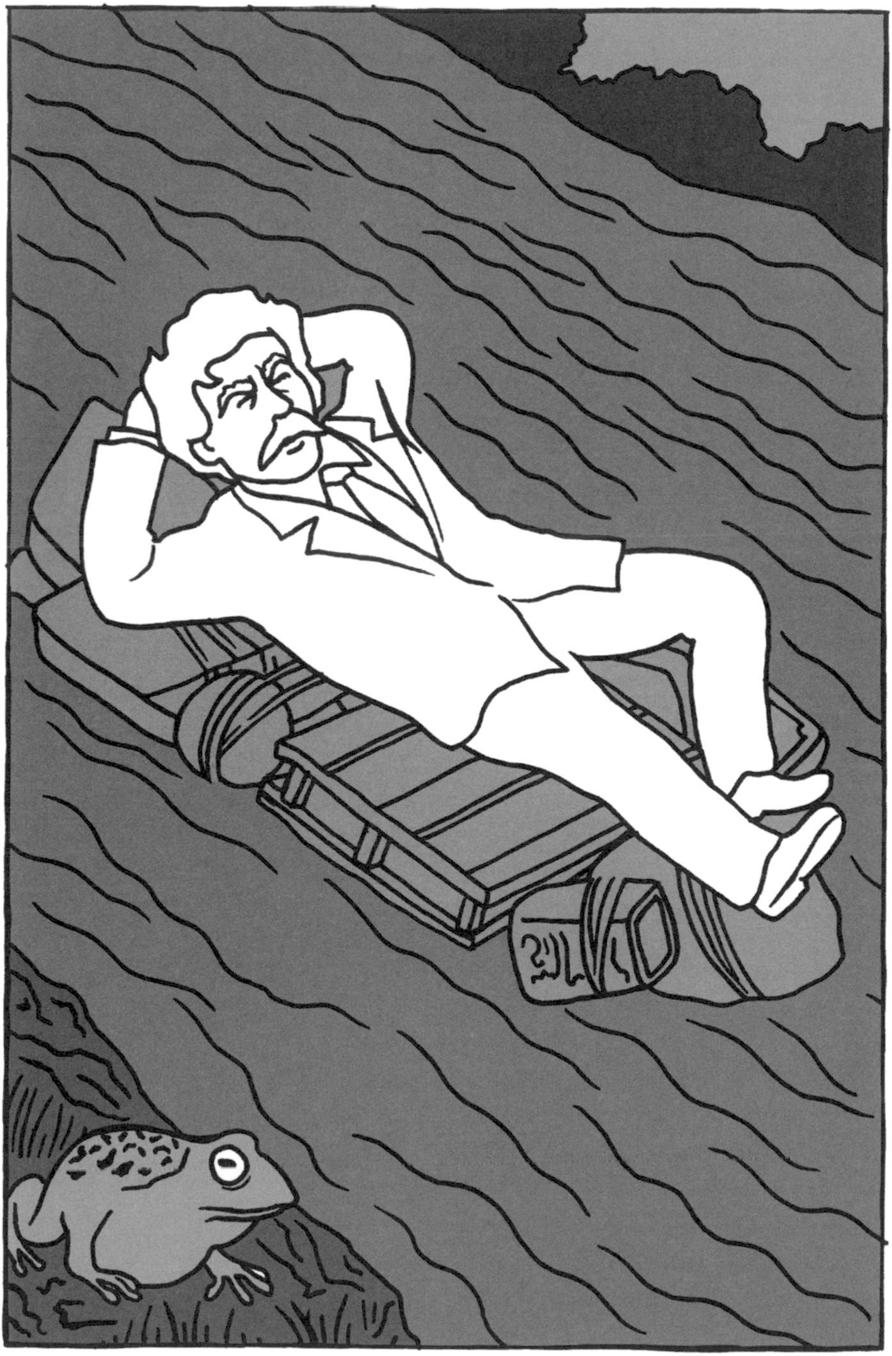

CHAPTER THIRTY-TWO

NOT DONE ROAMING

When my TV series was cancelled I discovered I was also bankrupt, thanks to my latest bad investment, in Horny Ray's Erotic Pizza. Apparently people don't care to have their pizzas covered with simulated genitals and such, it doesn't matter how perverted they are. I wish I'd realized this fact before investing in a chain of 17 stores throughout New York and New Jersey.

Once again I was freed from the burden of possessions or steady residence, so for a while I drifted from job to job. Literally. For three months I worked at Downtown Mike's Lightly Used Cars, then one day I got in an argument with a customer. The boss took her side and accused me of being a "dummy." I wasn't going to take that lying down, and so I marched off the lot to the river at the end of the street, where as they watched, astonished, I quickly assembled what I found there (a car fender, some water bottles, a soiled poncho, and a garbage bag full of inflated balloons) into a passible raft, which I threw into the river with myself on top of it. I bobbed there for ten minutes, which was frustrating, because I was caught on a bicycle tire, but then I freed myself and went floating down the river. Ahhh, sweet liberty! As I bounced along I found enough foodstuffs bobbing along in the current that I was able to make myself an adequate sandwich. Thus the hours passed until I dozed off, awaking to the hubbub of voices and music. "Wha— wuzzat," I slurred, and then came awake. It was night. The river had gotten narrower and deeper; the reflections of neon on the water, the smoke in the air, not entirely tobacco, and the perfumed smells of laughing smiles told me I was passing through a sleazier, more urban town. As my raft passed near a magnolia which overhang the river, I snagged it and pulled myself to dry land. Amazingly, the raft had kept a single drop of water from touching me, and I watched my noble craft depart regretfully. Then I wandered up the slope toward the main drag, looking for a bar and grill.

There was a carnival going in the main park, and I wandered the rows admiring the various grifts and cons being perpetrated. The fortune teller's tent was empty, and there was a sign: "FORTUNE TELLER NEEDED." I applied and was instantly hired; I got on the turban and cape, turned on the crystal ball, shuffled the cards, and sat down and waited. Quite soon a man came in and sat down across from me—the local sheriff, wearing mirrored sunglasses and a greasy sneer. "See here, Mister Twain, all new spiritualists, necromancers, soothsayers and the like in this town gotta pay me a fee for not imprisoning them under the Witchcraft Act. So you better grease my palm if you intend prognosticating in this here constabulary."

I was having none of it, and gazed aggressively into the crystal ball. "I see here a corrupt meatball who'd better knock it off," I opined. "Meatball he? Why I oughtta—" and he was rising from his chair when an arrow shot through the side of the tent and buried itself in his back. He slumped over the table, dead.

I stepped out of the tent and yelled, "Hey! There's a dead guy in here!" Another cop came running over. "Did you see who did this?" I shook my head. "Would you like to take his place, become sheriff and investigate his murder?" asked a judge who had appeared from behind the Shoot-the-Wasp booth. "Okay," I answered. At least I'd have a place to stay that night. Deputy Knudsen took me to the late sheriff's house. "It's yours now," he informed me. "Investigate it, do whatever you want with it. I don't care what you do with it," he concluded, showing surprising bitterness for one so young, and then he drove off, leaving me alone on the front doorstep of a dead man's house.

I went in and inspected the premises. It wasn't as smelly as I feared it would be, even with the large collection of moldy-looking stuffed animal heads lining the living room. The dining room featured a display of dead animal butts. The late sheriff had had a macabre sense of humor. I hoped the house wasn't haunted.

"What are you doing here? Where's my husband?" asked a female voice. I turned to regard the owner of that voice, and was surprised to find an attractive, well-dressed woman.

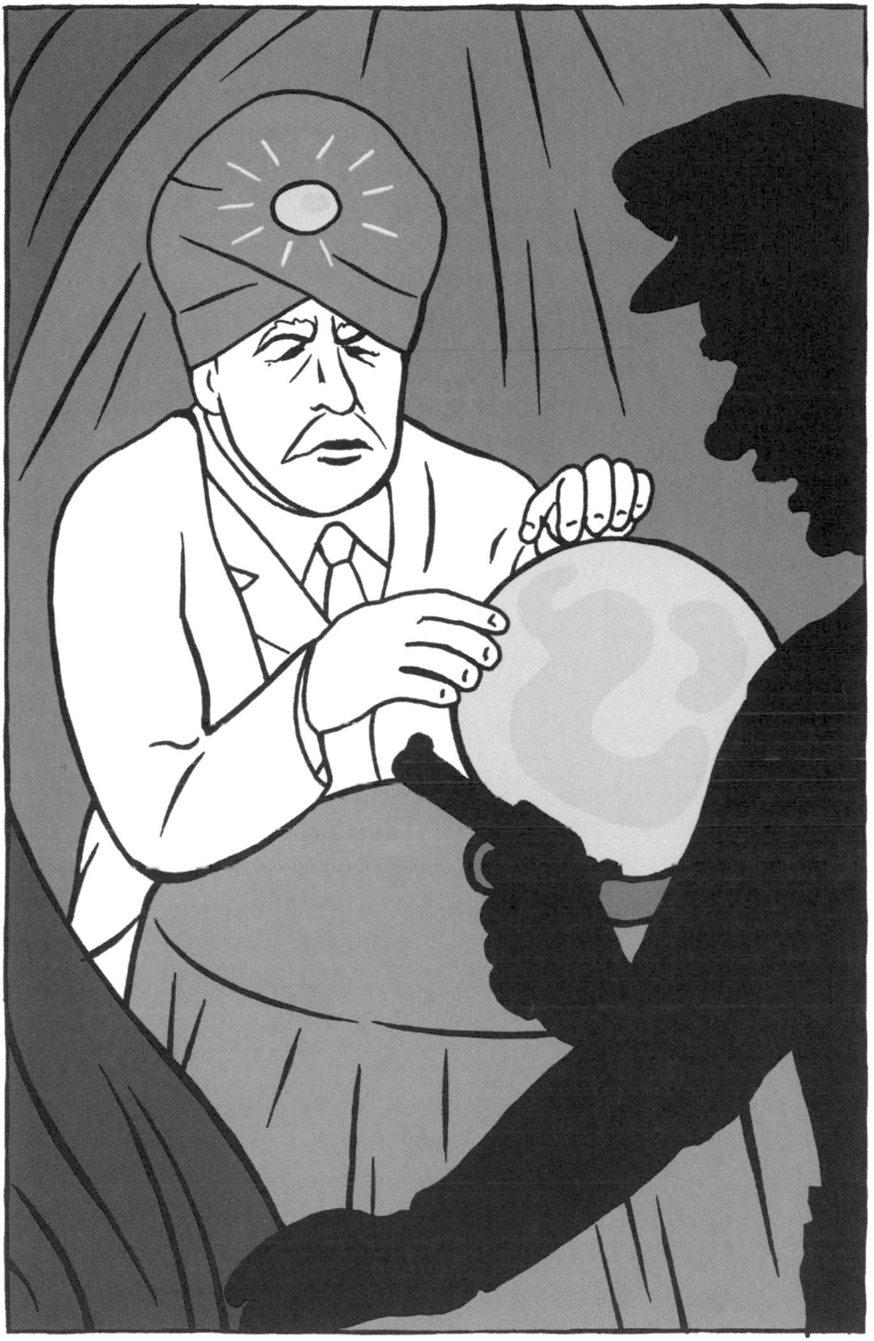

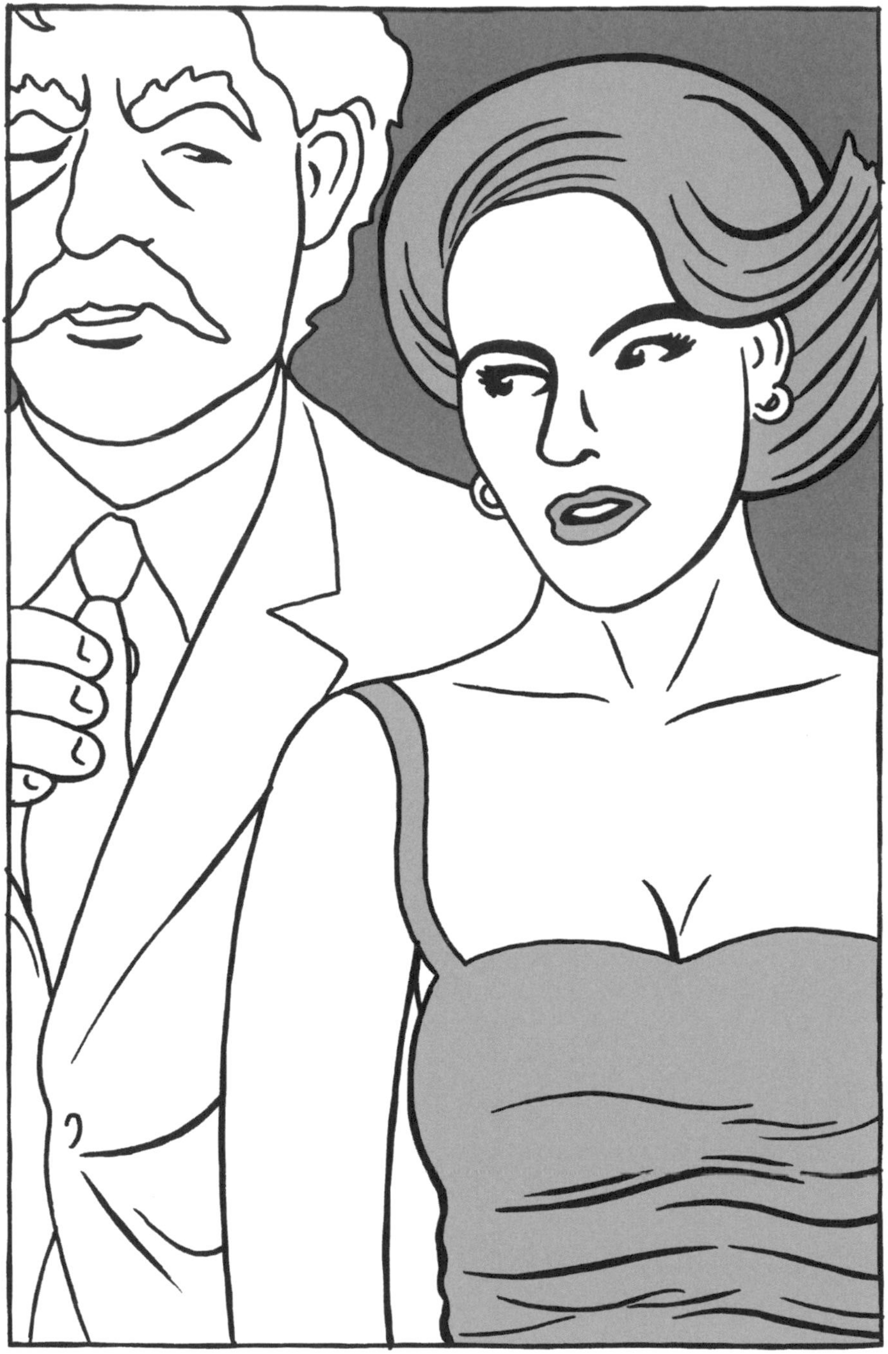

"Your husband's dead, I'm sorry to have to tell you this way," I offered. "Why don't we sit down with some cocktails and I'll tell you about it. Where do you keep the liquor?"

Over martinis I described her husband's passing as sensitively as I could. "I'm the sheriff now, and that means I'll be investigating his murder. And I think this house belongs to me now too. You can move out, if you like, or... you might belong to me too... Hmm. What do you think?" I ventured. She did not appear amused. "I'll sleep on the couch if that's all right with you, Mister Twain." Already sparks were beginning to fly!

The next day I came downstairs to ask her to make me breakfast, but she had already left. I got breakfast at a Snakes 'n' Ladders on my way to the station, and as I drove I mused on the Sheriff's murder. I knew one thing: I would rather find the murderer before I suffered the same fate, although if neither of these things happened I'd be fine with that too.

As I walked into the police station an arrow bounced off the bricks next to my head. I whirled to find the judge, loading another arrow onto his bow. "I thought you were too stupid to figure out that I was the murderer. But then I realized that maybe you're not!" His next arrow came dangerously close, and I sprinted past the station to the woods. "You're crazy! Take this job and shove it!" I shouted over my shoulder. Running to the riverbank, I hastily constructed a new raft out of the materials I found there (a child's piano, a cardboard cutout of Spock from *Star Trek*, a discarded set of speakers, and a cardboard box full of back issues of *People*), and hurriedly launched myself with it as arrows splashed all around me. That town had some serious problems, and I wasn't going to stick around to solve them. It's not like I needed closure or anything.

I drifted pleasantly through two more towns, and at the third I alighted and took a job as a wasp-jam maker. This was pleasantly distracting labor, and I stayed for a few weeks, until wasp-jam season was over. When I took to my next raft, I failed to realize how close I was to the ocean. I was several miles out to sea before I was luckily rescued by a tramp steamer carrying a load of steaming tramps to New York City's Bowery.

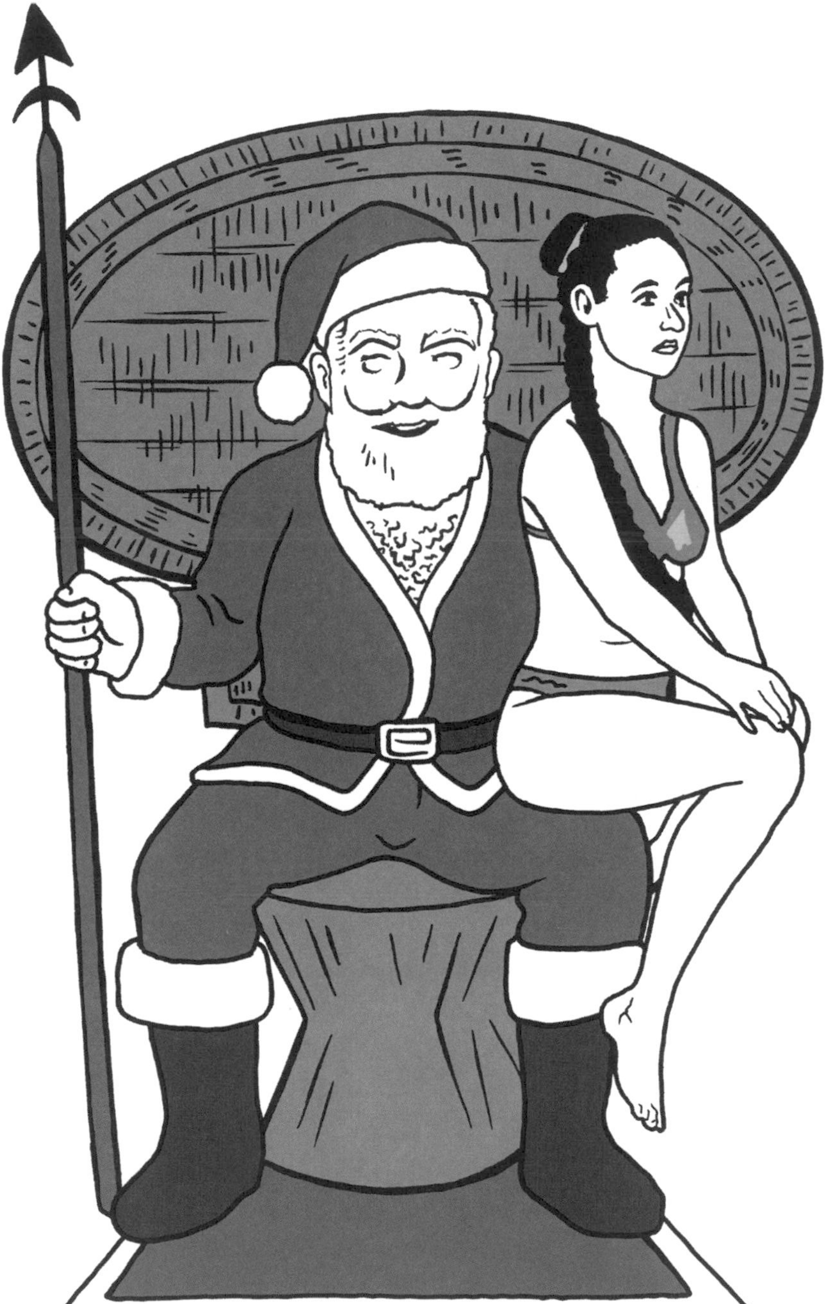

CHAPTER THIRTY-THREE

SANTALANDER

It was later that year that I decided to return to my roots as a newspaperman. I have always had a love of impertinence, and reporting gives one license to be as impertinent as one likes, and to be paid for it. And the trenchcoat and hat with the little card in it are truly groovy, as my great, great, great, great, great, great grand-daughter might have said. I love standing at the bottom of an airplane gangplank, shouting questions and scribbling in my little notebook.

I applied for a position at the *Duluth Times Examiner-Dispatch Press,* and was hired as a junior reporter at $275 a week. At first I was assigned to the interesting dogs beat, but I soon tired of describing funny-looking terriers and schnauzers, and asked my editor if he couldn't give me something more exciting. He could tell that I was serious, because he gave me an assignment that any newspaperman would've gone wild over: he sent me to the mall to interview Santa Claus. The jolly old elf of yore had decided to reveal himself to mankind in the flesh after all these aeons, and had chosen to do it in the central court of Duluth's Shady Whispering Pines shopping center. I dutifully trotted over to investigate.

It took me a while to find Santa's grotto, and when I did I was chagrined to find it closed. But a voice spoke from within: "Enter, foolish mortal." Santa was seated in an enormous wicker chair, one hand caressing an enormous spear, the other on the thigh of a naked woman. "Ho ho ho" he roared. "Who is this that has come to see me?" I wasn't scared and I stood my ground. "It is I, Mark Twain, a humble reporter, here to dig up innuendo and smear your private life," I responded honestly. He considered this for a moment, then clapped his hands together. "Leave us!" he shouted, and his retainers and hangers-on departed swiftly.

Santa inhaled from a massive hookah that was next to his chair. All the while his baleful eyes glittered at me. Then he spoke as he exhaled.

"Mister Twain, of course I know who you are. For you and I are part of a very small society of men who cannot die. And when we meet, we must fight." He stood, and, moving surprisingly swiftly for a man his size, went to the wall, where two enormous swords were mounted. He threw one to me, and I stepped to the side and let it clatter on the floor. It looked sharp! He raised his sword and let out a mighty yell: "There can be only ONE!" "One what?" I shouted back over my shoulder as I ran away. He followed me out of his grotto and all through the mall, waving and slashing his huge sword. "Stand still so I can kill you!" he bellowed. Thinking quickly, I grabbed my lighter and set fire to a cinnabon. The thick, greasy, buttery, sugary smoke helped me to distract Santa and make my escape.

Incredibly, they didn't even fire him at that mall! Can you believe it? He worked there all through that Christmas, the following Easter (local tradition) and the next year's Christmas! But by then I had moved on, and I exaggerated my own death again so he would leave me alone... Hope he doesn't read this book!

CHAPTER THIRTY-FOUR

BACK-TO-BACK HITS

I have always wanted to be a wacky radio DJ—the type of fellow who is having such a good time yelling and barking and making poo-poo noises that he doesn't know which way to turn for the delight he is giving himself and his millions of listeners. I wanted to be the blaring voice of the nasal oaf who is spread all over the airwaves honking and braying with joy at his own half-witted antics. I have always dreamed of playing juvenile, moronic pranks on slow-witted phone answerers, and broadcasting the results on the public frequencies as I fart and honk my way through some nasal dribble. So imagine my happiness when WKXB Minneapolis called me in to fill in for their Morning Zoo man Travis Buckle, who had collapsed under the weight of his own ego. I would be collaborating with local radio legend Hoagie "Basket Case" Skunch, as we lightened the mental and emotional burdens of weary commuters bending over their steering wheels and desks. Of course I said yes and the next morning we commenced jabbering.

Basket Case and I were perfect together, a real "dream team" of shouting and zany sound effects. We played records, we interviewed celebrities, an we did skits. I developed characters such as The Farting Moron and Johnny Poo-Poo Head, and Basket had his own creations such as Foreign Pete and Fartin' Sheen. During the drive-time hours we would shout out traffic information combined with fart noises and sound effects. And we pranked area residents relentlessly, using our skills at voicework and fart noises to weave a web of annoyance and troublemaking. It was too good to last, and so of course it didn't.

We were scoring with all the major demographics and we knew it. But in retrospect, it's clear we went too far. The power of ruling the radio waves went to our heads, making us twisted and cruel. We became known as "The Killer Jocks" due to our habit of killing people, thanks to our cruel pranks and deliberately misleading traffic information. People became terrified to turn on the radio or pick up the phone. The straw that broke the camel's back came when we pranked the governor, convincing him that Minnesota was being invaded by communists disguised as senior citizens. He ordered out the National Guard and three old people were killed during the ensuing confusion. We were suspended from the air and imprisoned as an act of public safety.

It was my first time in prison, and I'd be lying if I said I enjoyed it. But the foolish prison authorities made the mistake of putting me and Basket Case on the air again on the prison radio station—it wasn't long before we incited a riot and made good our escape. B.C. was recaptured and died in prison, but I made even gooder on my escape by exaggerating rumors of my own death again, till my most recent peccadilloes were forgotten.

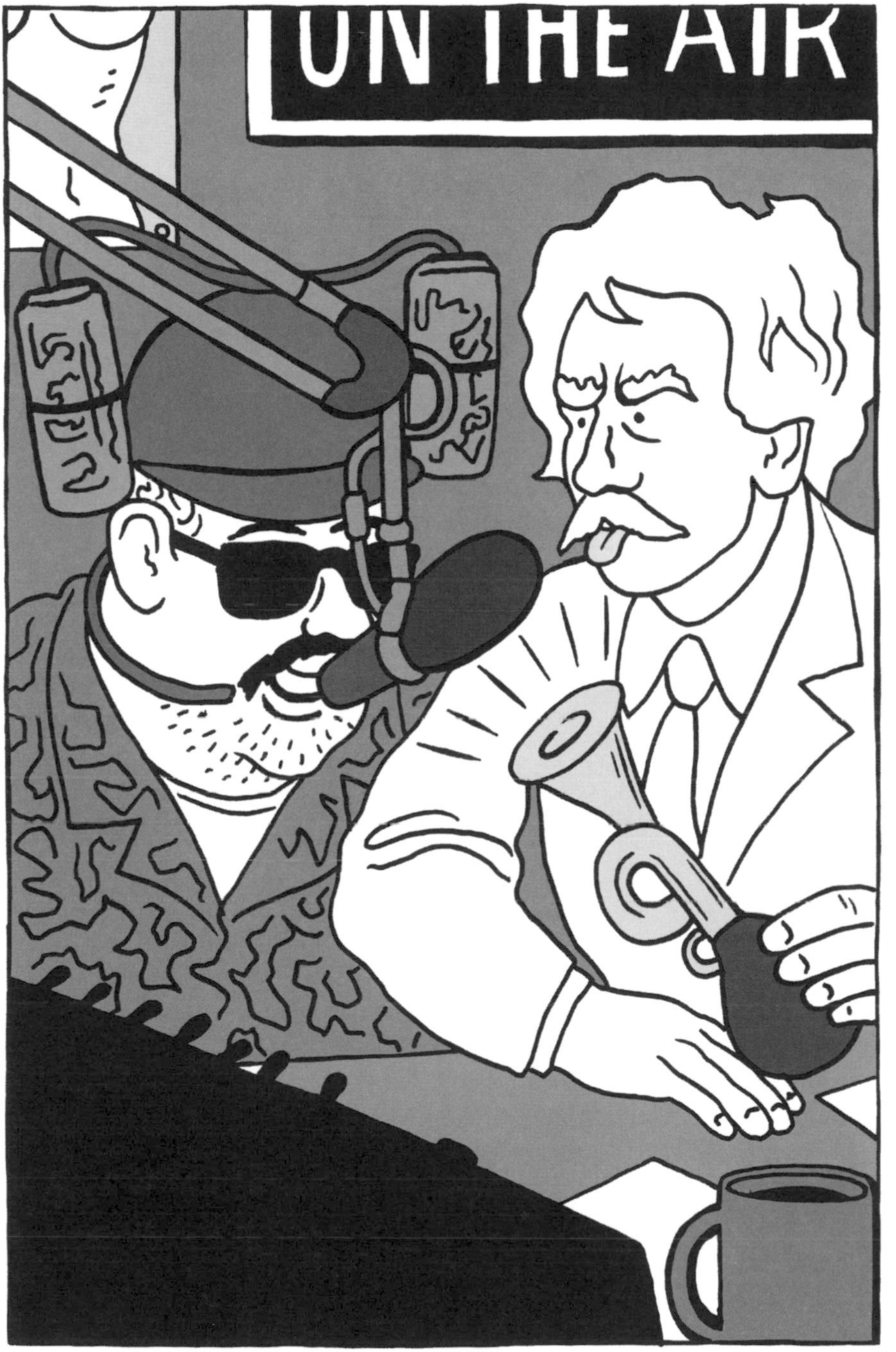
ON THE AIR

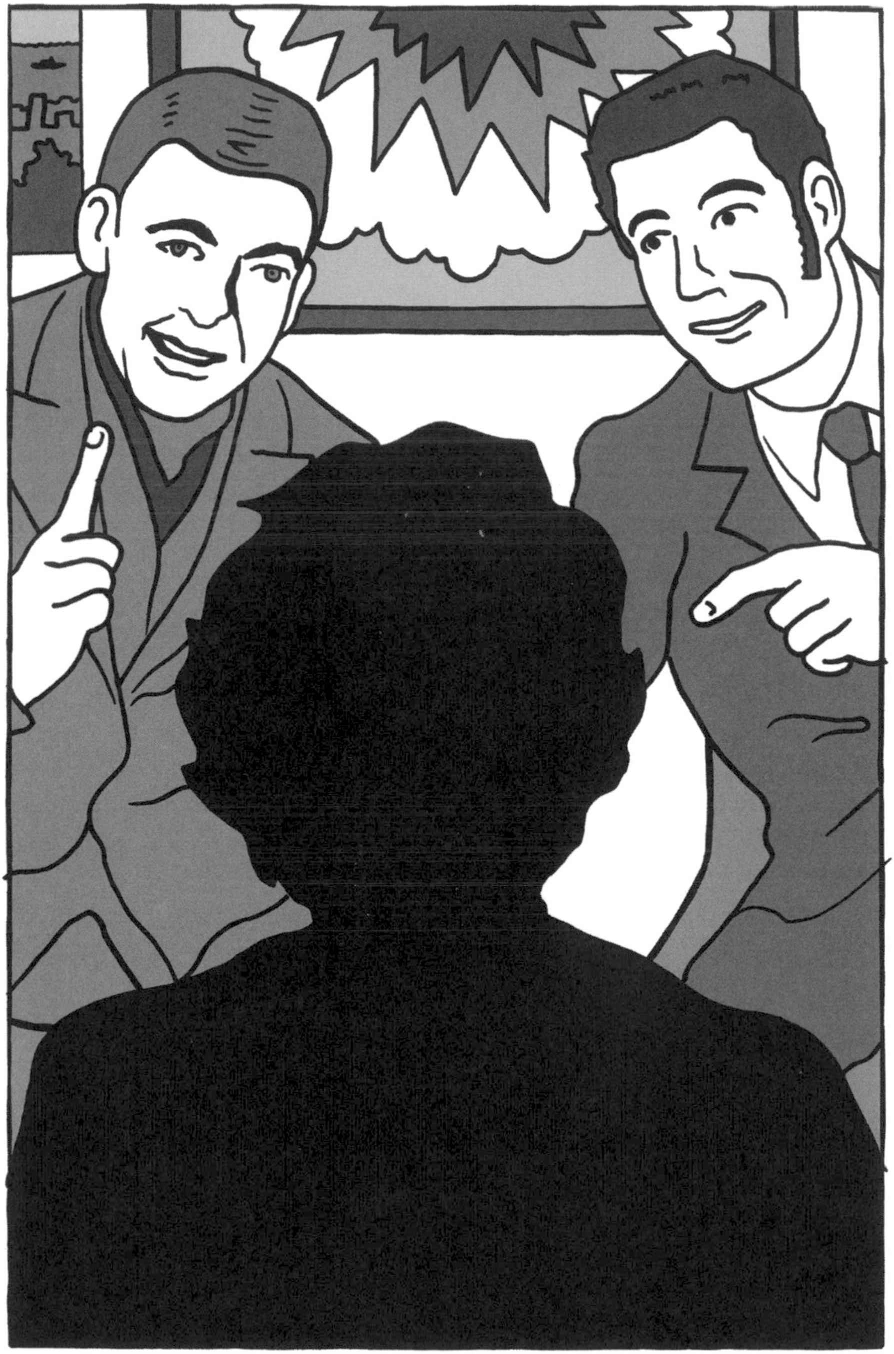

CHAPTER THIRTY-FIVE:

A TRIP TO TINSELTOWN

I was present at the birth of cinema. I saw the very first film, *Man Falls Off Chair*, when it premiered at the Super-Luxury Nickelodeonatron over a hundred years ago. In those days no-one dreamed that motion pictures would be in full color, 3D, stereophonic sound, CGI, and all the rest of it. And the quality of the actors falling off chairs these days—incredible! So I was incredibly excited when I got word that Taxco Pictures had signed a multi-million dollar deal to film a big-budget Tom and Huck Movie. Tom and Huck, of course, are my most popular characters, and their stories are the standard by which American literature may be judged, if I do say so myself.

I immediately got myself hired as story consultant and executive producer, then flew out to do a meeting with the producers, Ira Green and Bob Conners. I was driven directly from the airport to their offices, a huge impressive confection of steel, glass and cardboard. After a brief wait in the foyer I was escorted in to see them in their office/gym. They stopped pumping iron and led me over to an arrangement of chairs next to the treading machine. After some brief flattery on their part, they started telling me their ideas.

"Okay, first we have the scene with him painting the fence." "But this is a movie. We have to go larger." "So maybe instead of painting a fence, he's surfing on a shark." "Then he blows up the shark, and lands on the raft with Huck." "Then maybe the raft explodes." "Rivers are part explosive, aren't they?" "Instead of riding the water they could be riding explosions." "Maybe Huck can be part explosion himself." "Could we possibly change his name to Nuck? It scans better." "Mark, you're looking pensive. Thoughts?" "I—" "Of course Nuck could be in love with Dom, if she's a chick." "Maybe the sex gets out of hand. Maybe he pushes it too far." "He's addicted to rough sex and he's drinking so much, he doesn't know if he's actually doing these murders—" "But it's actually his mistress, she's secretly the Ice Pick Killer." "Now she's in jail and he has to prove his evidence." "And the black guy— what's his name, Black Guy Jim?—gets crushed in an unlikely accident." "Who did it? Maybe— the government." "And this other dude is like 'You have no idea how far this goes.'" "Hackers in a control room are looking at his credit card statements from a satellite, they can track him everywhere every time he orders a pizza." "And his kid's all like, Where's my mommy? Boohoo." "He needs a friend. Enter, this robot, or maybe he's some kind of toy, he's all magical and shit." "And the kid is amazed, everything's fun, but then it turns out, the toy's got a plan… to invade Earth, really take a dump on the human race." "Nuck don't like that— we'll come up with a catchphrase." "He's gotta go to war." "Strapping on big guns, 'Bad to the Bone' on the soundtrack, grenades, maybe an automated pogo stick with a bayonet on it." "When he kills them, they stay dead." "His ex-wife can be played by my ex-wife." "He rescues her and they ride an enormous explosion around Central Park." "You look pensive, Mark. Thoughts?"

Nuck the Rough-Sex Explosion was released ten months later, and was one of the most financially disastrous movies of the decade. I never saw it. But the money I made enabled me to finally buy a small island to live on… if only the one I chose hadn't turned out to be actively volcanic. The dishonesty of real estate agents never fails to sicken me.

CHAPTER THIRTY-SIX:

ANOTHER CENTURY

A new century dawned—my third—and a whole new millennium. I marveled at the advances in sandwiches, and there are even more kids to inspire than I have ever seen before. Unfortunately, there are also new challenges to the human race, and one of the biggest is fear. Now we have seen what terror can do, ghosts can no longer be tolerated in the same way.

Because of my experiences with ghosts in the Princeton nuclear lab in 1951, Homeland Security paid me a visit and asked me to be a consultant to their new supernatural division. "There's no such thing as terror, there's only terrorism," is one of the things they're fond of saying. As they see it, if some guy from the 17th century with his head under his armpit thinks he can threaten the soil of America, then he's getting taken down hard. And if some old man with a screw loose wants to impersonate a headless horseman so that he can scare kids away from his abandoned amusement park, he risks taking a trip to Ghoultanamo (the supernatural version of Guantanamo). There was a very real plot several years ago where a ghost was going to moon the President during an important speech. Imagine ghostly glutes distracting the Chief Executive as he spoke in front of the world! Luckily we foiled the loiny spectre, but there are always other threats, and the stakes are too important now for us to tolerate supernatural hijinks.

Recently young men, all bankers, were going missing from the city's streets. No-one could figure it out, but I found some ectoplasm leading to the harbor and figured out it was naval ghosts. Sure enough, we found the legendary pirate Boo-beard was behind it all. He had returned from death because of a prophecy and forcibly recruited men who "did no useful work" to toil as his crew in order to fight terrorism. I could appreciate his zeal in wanting to fight terrorism, but as I pointed out, this was not the way to do something constructive. Only bankers had been harmed, so I let him off with a warning.

As usual I've tried to balance my right-wing activities with some left-wing ones, and have joined with comedian Dan Aykroyd to sponsor Casper's House, a string of rehab houses for down-at-heel ghosts. Most of them are not bad spirits, they've just lost their way and need help to get their afterlife together. Many of these ghosts then find work in our "Scared Straight" program, which has helped to keep numerous teens on the straight and narrow. Nothing scares a kid more than finding out he could become a ghost bum.

I've also been involved in ecological causes, such as my efforts to save the Golden Throat-Winged Wobbler from extinction. Imagine my embarrassment when I found out that this beautiful creature had never existed at all. It's crazy when a creature becomes not only extinct but fictional, and it breaks my heart.

The other thing that has taken up much of my time lately is the promulgation and encouragement of various scams. America has lately shifted onto being a nearly completely scam-driven economy, and I sincerely believe it's every patriotic American's duty to work at least some form of grift or flimflam. So it may be me behind those scrambled emails hawking low interest rate loans, or behind those automated calls telling you that there's a lien on your house. Don't like it? Well, why aren't you doing your part? Get out there and start scamming others! Involve your neighbors in a pyramid scheme, or if you're good with computers you can develop some new cyberswindles. There's a world of suckers out there—go get 'em!

Well, that's my story for the last century. To make for smoother reading I've left out lots of stuff, such as my marriage to Eva Braun, my career in rap music, and the time that Al gave me a youth pill that turned me into a hot TV chef. Hopefully, in another 100 years I'll have a fresh set of outrageous adventures to spread out in front of you. Until then, I'll just leave you with this parting thought:

insert thought here

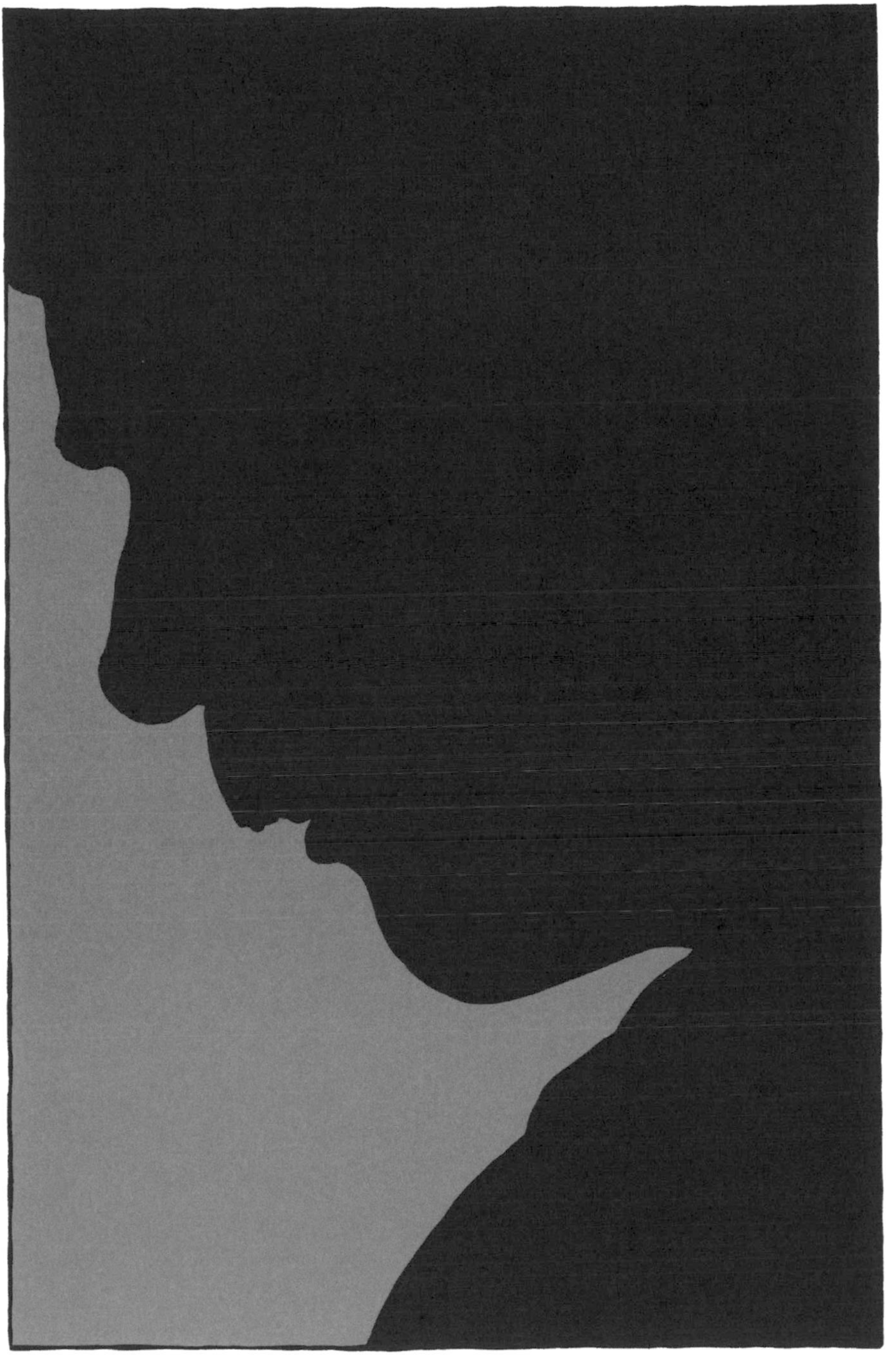

FANTAGRAPHICS BOOKS
7563 Lake City Way NE. Seattle WA 98115 USA

Written and illustrated by Michael Kupperman
Edited by Kim Thompson
Editorial assistance by Muire Dougherty, Joe Randazzo and Eric Reynolds
Production by Paul Baresh & Tony Ong
Design by Michael Kupperman
Associate Publisher: Eric Reynolds
Published by Gary Groth & Kim Thompson

To receive a free catalog from Fantagraphics, call 1-800-657-1100 in North
America or write to us at 7563 Lake City Way NE, Seattle, WA 98115 USA. Or visit
us at www.fantagraphics.com.

Distributed in the U.S. by W.W. Norton & Co. (800-233-4830)
Distributed in Canada by Canadian Manda Group (416-516-0911)
Distributed in the United Kingdom by Turnaround Services (44 (0)20 8829-3002)
Distributed to the comics market by Diamond Comic Distributors (800-452-6642)

First printing: September 2011

ISBN 978-1-60699-491-7

Printed in Singapore

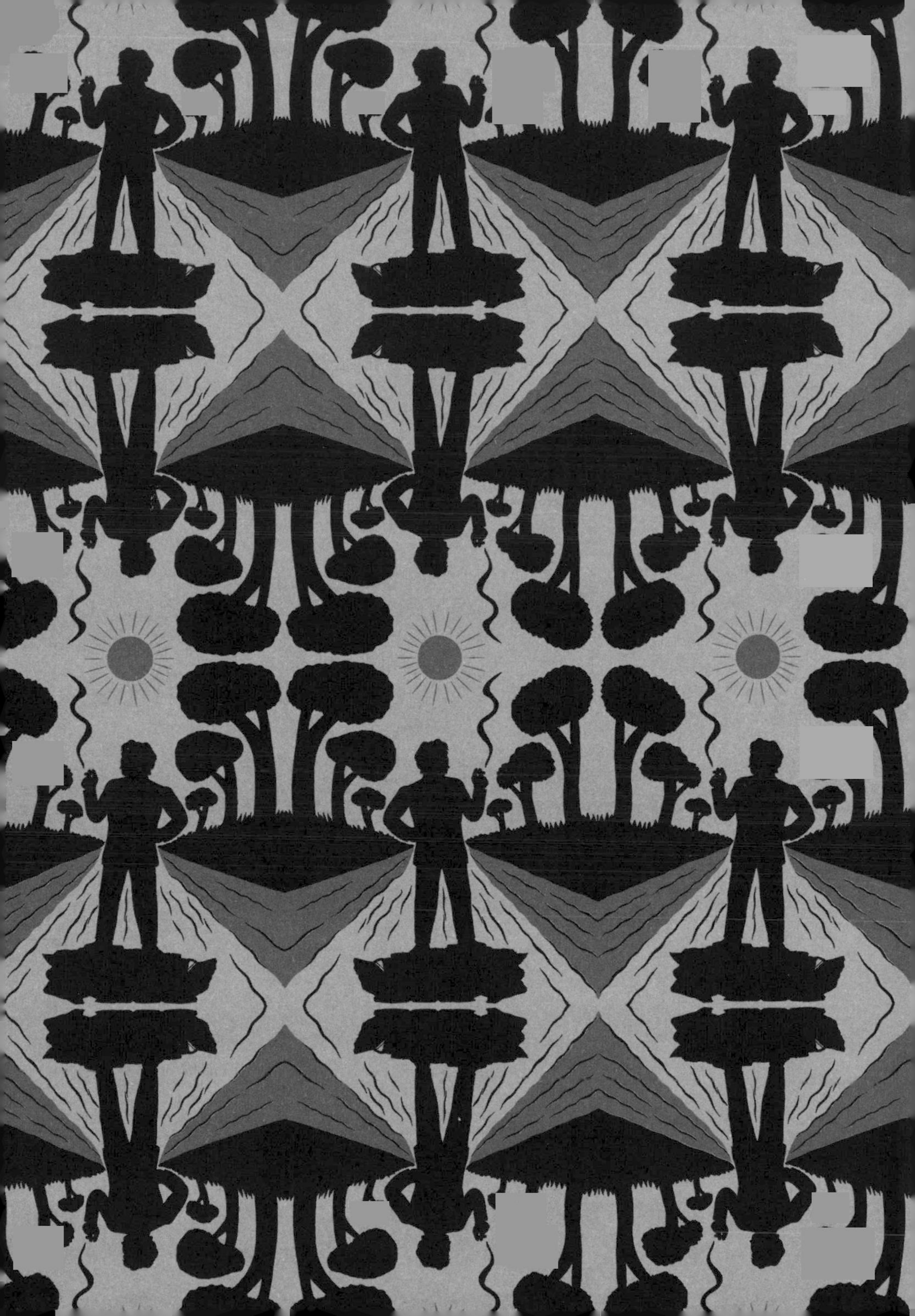